Customer-Centered Design

A New Approach to Web Usability

ISBN 013047962-4

9 780130 479624

90000

Hewlett-Packard® Professional Books

OPERATING SYSTEMS

Diercks	MPE/iX System Administration Handbook
Fernandez	Configuring CDE: The Common Desktop Environment
Lund	Integrating UNIX and PC Network Operating Systems
Madell	Disk and File Management Tasks on HP-UX
Mosberger, Eranian	IA-64 Linux Kernel: Design and Implementation
Poniatowski	HP-UX Virtual Partitions
Poniatowski	HP-UX 11i System Administration Handbook and Toolkit
Poniatowski	HP-UX 11.x System Administration Handbook and Toolkit
Poniatowski	HP-UX 11.x System Administration "How To" Book
Poniatowski	HP-UX System Administration Handbook and Toolkit
Poniatowski	Learning the HP-UX Operating System
Poniatowski	UNIX User's Handbook, Second Edition
Rehman	HP Certified, HP-UX System Administration
Roberts	UNIX and Windows 2000 Interoperability Guide
Sauers, Weygant	HP-UX Tuning and Performance
Stone, Symons	UNIX Fault Management
Weygant	Clusters for High Availability: A Primer of HP Solutions, Second Edition
Wong	HP-UX 11i Security

ONLINE/INTERNET

Amor	The E-business (R)evolution: Living and Working in an Interconnected World, Second Edition
Caldwell	The Fast Track to Profit: An Insider's Guide to Exploiting the World's Best Internet Technologies
Chandler , Hyatt	Customer-Centered Design: A New Approach to Web Usability
Greenberg, Lakeland	A Methodology for Developing and Deploying Internet and Intranet Solutions
Greenberg, Lakeland	Building Professional Web Sites with the Right Tools
Klein	Building Enhanced HTML Help with DHTML and CSS
Werry, Mowbray	Online Communities: Commerce, Community Action, and the Virtual University

NETWORKING/COMMUNICATIONS

Blommers	OpenView Network Node Manager: Designing and Implementing an Enterprise Solution
Blommers	Practical Planning for Network Growth
Bruce, Dempsey	Security in Distributed Computing: Did You Lock the Door?
Lucke	Designing and Implementing Computer Workgroups

Customer-Centered Design

A New Approach to Web Usability

Kreta Chandler

Karen Hyatt

Hewlett-Packard Company

www.hp.com/hpbooks

Prentice Hall PTR
Upper Saddle River, New Jersey 07458
www.phptr.com

Library of Congress Cataloging-in-Publication Data

A CIP catalog record for this book can be obtained from the Library of Congress.

Editorial/production supervision: *Mary Sudul*
Cover design director: *Jerry Votta*
Cover design: *DesignSource*
Manufacturing manager: *Maura Zaldivar*
Acquisitions editor: *Jill Harry*
Editorial assistant: *Jeanie Joe*
Marketing manager: *Dan DePasquale*

Publisher, Hewlett-Packard Books: *Patricia Pekary*

Published by Prentice Hall PTR
Prentice-Hall, Inc.
Upper Saddle River, New Jersey 07458

Prentice Hall books are widely used by corporations and government agencies for training, marketing, and resale.
The publisher offers discounts on this book when ordered in bulk quantities. For more information, contact Corporate Sales Department, Phone: 800-382-3419; FAX: 201-236-7141;
E-mail: corpsales@prenhall.com
Or write: Prentice Hall PTR, Corporate Sales Dept., One Lake Street, Upper Saddle River, NJ 07458.

(trademark info)
Other product or company names mentioned herein are the trademarks or registered trademarks of their respective owners.

Printed in the United States of America
10 9 8 7 6 5 4 3 2 1

ISBN 0-13-047962-4

Pearson Education LTD.
Pearson Education Australia PTY, Limited
Pearson Education Singapore, Pte. Ltd.
Pearson Education North Asia Ltd.
Pearson Education Canada, Ltd.
Pearson Educación de Mexico, S.A. de C.V.
Pearson Education — Japan
Pearson Education Malaysia, Pte. Ltd.

CONTENTS

Part 3   Tools and Rules for Winning Websites 169

Chapter 6 Designing Intuitive Online Customer Shopping Models 171

Part 4   Case Studies and The Future 227

Chapter 8 Case Studies 229

FOREWORD

At the time of this writing (2002), e-commerce has a bad name. Many investors stay far away from anything that has "e" in its name and even farther away from pure-play e-commerce. This is understandable because we have just come out of a period where many e-commerce sites went under. A great many of these closed sites seemed to be based on a business model of losing money on every shipment but assuming that this would be OK because they were Internet companies. Many of these same sites also went overboard with expensive, but useless, web design that made it hard to find anything and prevented many users from shopping. I can only cry dry tears over the death of these many clueless e-commerce sites. Good riddance.

There were also some good sites that closed in 2000 and 2001 and I do miss these sites.

Investors sometimes go overboard—one way or the other. E-commerce may not be a diamond-studded goldmine, but nor is it a black hole that sucks money in and never generates a return.

I am a firm believer in the potential of e-commerce. Anything that can be sold by mail order can be sold better on the web, where you can provide much better information than is possible in a print catalog. Multimedia, if used correctly, can add a dimension we will never get in print. Personalization and search tools can allow fast access to a vastly larger set of products and variations than would fit in even the fattest catalog. And instantaneous split-testing of offers, promotions, and wordings is a dream for any marketer who wants to adjust a campaign to the realities of the market in real time instead of shooting off 100,000 mailings before collecting the data.

E-commerce is great for B2C, B2B, C2C, and any of the other weird combinations of letters so beloved by analysts. For many of the more complex B2B products, it is important to realize that people may not add, say, a Gulfstream executive jet to an online shopping cart, but they may still research the purchase (or leasing options) on the vendor's website. Online merchandising and presentation of the complex buying options that are common for big B2B orders can be a major way of reaching customers, even when the final sale is closed through traditional channels.

In a recent usability study, my team and I watched users make 496 attempts at performing tasks on e-commerce sites. The test spanned 20 sites based in the U.S., focusing on large sites but including a few smaller ones as well. On average, the user success rate was 56%.

E-commerce sites lose almost half of their potential sales because users cannot use the site. In other words, with better usability, the average site could increase its current sales by 79% (calculated as the 44% of potential sales relative to the 56% of cases in which users currently succeed).

International usability is even worse. Based on our study of overseas users shopping at the same 20 sites, I estimate that the sites could increase their overseas sales by 49% if they provided those users with the same quality of user experience that they offer domestic users.

Clearly, e-commerce sites have great potential for improving usability and, thus, increasing sales. My twenty-site usability study resulted in a list of 207 guidelines for improving the e-commerce user experience (the study can be downloaded from www.nngroup.com/reports/ecommerce). After reviewing several mid-sized e-commerce sites, I found that, on average, they complied with only 37% of the 207 usability guidelines. Compliance was particularly egregious in international usability, where the sites followed only 15% of the guidelines.

Best-selling sites are better at following the e-commerce usability guidelines: across 10 big e-commerce sites, I found an average compliance rate of 53% with the 207 guidelines (i.e., 110 guidelines followed; 97 violated).

These simple numbers tell a deep story: e-commerce sites can do so much better than they do today if only they would design more for the special characteristics of the online medium. That's the main reason I am bullish on the future of e-commerce. I haven't even talked about the potential of new technology or the fact that the number of Internet users worldwide is expected to double from about half a billion in 2002 to a full billion in a fairly small number of years. Yes, both of these changes will happen, and they will both add substantially to e-commerce sales. But even today, with no need for anything else to change, most e-commerce sites could double their sales if they would improve their websites to comply with well-documented best practices.

I highly recommend the expert guidance provided by Chandler and Hyatt. This book provides readers what they need to know to greatly enhance the customer online shopping experience and webstore usability – and, therefore increase sales.

Jakob Nielsen, Ph.D.
Nielsen Norman Group

PREFACE

Nothing would be more disturbing than discovering that customers find shopping on your website frustrating and confusing. Worse yet, what if most of them said they would not purchase from you based on that experience? It would not only be disturbing, it would mean disaster for your business.

Online shopping research we've conducted over the past several years confirms that people will purchase on websites that are easy to use. And, they *won't* purchase on websites that are confusing or take too long to find what they want. Confusing websites lack customer focus.

Creating a customer-focused superior online shopping experience is the key to consumer-centered design. By adopting the techniques in this book, you will improve the success rates and satisfaction levels of your customers, thereby increasing sales.

Confusing website navigation, minimal assistance during the shopping process, and information overload all cause the consumer to change the "currency" from "money" to "time" as they measure their experience online. Customers will look for ways to reduce the amount and increase the quality of time they spend on the process.

To the customer, quality means education—not a sales job. It also means relevant information and communication, control of when, where, and how to get information, and the ability to ask questions and get answers.

Does your website do all of those things? This book tells you how the customer shops, how to develop and manage your website to respond to customer needs, and provides the methodologies and techniques to employ. You'll also learn about the various disciplines of retailing, cataloging, e-tailing, and usability engineering. It will take integrated knowledge of each to compete in the online shopping environment of the future.

Customer-centered design must start with the customer and grow from there. Knowledge and insight of current shopping behaviors—at retail, in catalogs, and online—are blended with product category information and user-centered design methodologies to develop intuitive website navigation. As a result, customers are interested in your website and can easily find and purchase your products.

The most common form of e-commerce website today is the product-database approach. This type of website is usually designed around the products the online merchant has for sale. The website and category structures are constructed on database software code efficiencies and ease-of-maintenance goals rather than on customer needs, ease of use, or the entertainment value of shopping.

Merchants are usually concerned with abandoned shopping carts. But there are silent customers who get away because they can't find products to place into the cart. And, when the searching gets tough, the shoppers get going and won't hesitate to click to another store. They just don't have the time to spend on confusing or hard-to-use websites.

Although it is unpleasant to hear that customers don't like your store, it is important to listen to their concerns, observe how they interact with your website, probe why they click on selected links, and understand what they expect. You can't tell by merely measuring clicks and hits to pages. You have to know their purpose for shopping and other factors they consider as they shop. If you don't know why they found your website confusing or difficult, you can't improve their experience.

We've found that commerce, whether on the web, in a store, or through a catalog, involves market development, channel development, advertising, usability engineering, retailing, direct marketing, cataloging, and customer research—all disciplines we have worked in at one time or another.

We've discovered that it is not one element that is responsible for successful e-commerce website design, but it is the combination of many elements. The integration of all of the various disciplines provides a holistic view of the online marketplace that creates this novel approach to a customer-centric online store design. It's a blend of new and old rules with a redirected focus that will enable success for the future.

Today's marketplace has grown rapidly and is constantly evolving. We must anticipate and respond to these changes in business, technology, products, competition, and customer dynamics. In today's marketplace, consumers are driving this change.

We're now in a period of merging companies and channels—brick and mortar with web properties, web properties with other web properties—and resurgence of public confidence in online shopping. To win back the online customer, a re-balancing of strategies is required with more emphasis on the customer and more weight on the customer experience. The past was about attracting buyers not customers. The future will be about developing and keeping loyal customer advocates.

Do You Know What You Don't Know?

For the first time, valuable customer insight, usability engineering methodologies, successful retail business drivers, and new concepts of integrated shelf management, are brought together and disclosed in one book. This book is a practical and actionable guide for the new e-commerce marketplace with the customer at its center.

While consulting with many retailers, catalogers, and e-tailers throughout the past several years, we discovered that each of them has had successful business practices that—up until now—have only been applied to one specific selling motion. Also, because the Internet is a tool of *human computer interaction*, fundamental principles and methodologies of usability engineering were not being applied to the design of most stores.

The conscious integration and balancing of these traditionally distinct functions and applications is the foundation of customer-centered design. We have blended together many proven principles from disparate occupational fields to offer a new approach. It is the unique blending of all of these considerations that makes the website greater than the sum of the individual influences.

Although you may work in only one specialized occupation, such as merchandising or web design, it is critical to know how each of the other elements can make or break a customer's experience. Otherwise, you may be surprised to find your customer may not be able to complete even a simple purchasing task.

Is This Book for You?

If you are an online merchant, you will learn to align business drivers and customer insight with overall e-commerce strategy from which the online store will be created. This book does not tell you how to create a business plan, but it will give new and innovative perspectives that will drive incremental sales, maximize profitability from electronic shelf pages, and attract and retain customers.

You'll also learn why the customer experience and satisfaction with your website is critical to the store's success. In addition, you'll learn about the necessary usability engineering principles and customer navigation models to enable you to better support your design team's efforts.

If you are a buyer or merchandiser, you'll learn successful techniques from retailing and cataloging and learn about appropriately weighting categories and products. You'll also learn how you can help balance your organization's short-term profitability needs with long-term business needs based on fulfilling customer expectations.

If you are a web-page developer, usability engineer, or other IT professional, you will learn to integrate online business strategy with consumer needs to create profitable, customer-centered web pages and sites. You will also learn which business drivers are important for you to consider and how they can be applied to navigation models, page content, and product page layouts. You'll also learn how customer shopping behaviors and preferences in a retail store environment can be applied to the online shopping experience to minimize abandoned shopping carts.

If you are a business or web design student, this book is a fundamental textbook incorporating all the disciplines you will need to understand to be successful. It is also for anyone who will be involved in e-commerce in the future.

The following questions highlight answers that are revealed in this book. Do you know...

- How knowledge of a retail or catalog customer shopping experience can improve an e-tail customer shopping experience and minimize the potential for an abandoned shopping cart?
- What usability engineering has to do with shopping?
- What are destination categories and which products on your website draw customers in for repeat, routine purchases? Or, why the value of a product to the business determines web page layout?
- Which common mistakes online stores make that ruin the customer's shopping experience and how you can avoid them?
- Who your best customers are today? Or, who your future customers will be and what affect that will have on future website redesigns?
- Why it's critical for online merchants to know how task analysis and other usability engineering measurement methodologies affect product sales and customer satisfaction?
- The new rules for online merchandising, customer experience, and web design?

Here, we combine new and old rules that result in a virtual shelf that is business focused, friendly to the consumer, and profitable for the online merchant, resulting in more bang for the byte.

Book Organization

In the nine chapters of this book, you will find answers to the questions above and learn how to create a conceptual framework targeted to the individual consumer. In addition, you'll discover the secrets behind successful merchandising specifically designed for the web environment.

- **Chapter 1: New Rules of Engagement** Looks at the morphing business landscape and the elevation of the customer's power in the selling mix and how this might affect your store in the future.
- **Chapter 2: Walking a Mile in the Customer's Shoes** Gives you insight from the customer's perspective. While current Internet tools track *where* they go and *what* routes they take, this chapter identifies *why*. You'll discover what customer knowledge is imperative and how to apply it to web store design.
- **Chapter 3: Retailing Secrets: Tips from the Pros** Shows what retailers have learned over the past 30 years as they concentrated on perfecting the customer in-store shopping experience. This chapter reveals business strategies and tools that have belonged exclusively to the retailing industry and how you can apply them to your online store.

- **Chapter 4: Catalog Marketing: Taking the Best and Leaving the Rest** Looks at traditional catalog marketing best practices that transfer successfully to the online store. You'll learn which techniques to adopt and how to adopt them.
- **Chapter 5: Anatomy of the e-Shelf** Identifies key web pages, navigation paths, and page content. Integrates these pages with other "e-tools" that guide customers through the e-store and help them make purchasing decisions.
- **Chapter 6: Designing Intuitive Online Customer Shopping Models** Takes methodologies from software product design and shows you how to apply them to website design. Provides insight on benchmarking and measuring current shopping models.
- **Chapter 7: Winning Webstores** Gives top critical success factors for online stores, provided by Dr. Jakob Nielsen, world renowned web usability expert. Dr. Nielsen provides a practical listing of "do's and don'ts" for web design for you to apply – starting with when your customer enters the online store and ending at the checkout counter. This chapter also includes a simple testing model you can deploy immediately to evaluate your own website.
- **Chapter 8: Case Studies** This chapter provides four case studies that apply various combinations of the techniques disclosed in this book.
- **Chapter 9: The Future: The Not-So-Final Frontier** This chapter presents viewpoints from various industry leaders representing a variety of disciplines from retailing to research to Internet usability.

Customer-Centered Design: A New Approach to Web Usability is a practical guide to understanding the e-Shelf. Designing and structuring information correctly enhances navigation through your site as well as delivering your customers a satisfying shopping experience.

ACKNOWLEDGEMENTS

This book is only possible from the contributions, e-commerce relationships, and support of many people whom we'd like to thank:

Jakob Nielsen, Pradeep Jotwani, Pat Pekary, Jill Harry, Mary Sudul, Luice Hwang, Sarah Alter, Susan Boyce, Patricia Graca, Amanda Gooding, Bruce Martin, Paco Underhill, Steve J. Brown, Ken Bronstein, Dex Smith, Lucy Honig, Charlie Fernandez, Greg Linder, Bill Delacy, Bill Cooper, Stan Lehman, Dana Greer, Ron Wilbur, Judith Herman, Phil Lauria, Leigh Greenberg, Larry Hays, Steve Shields, Howard Markman, Steve Hassall, and Steve Powell.

Special acknowledgement for the support from our families: Ally, Charlotte, and Michael Espeland and Renée, Daniel, Kerry and Mavis Hyatt.

We're pleased to bring a new perspective to not only online merchandising and sales, but also to business in general. The customer must reside at the center of every business decision. By focusing on the customer first, profitability will result. By focusing on profitability first, the customer may go away. We hope we can influence online businesses to take the first step into this new world of design.

Kreta Chandler
Karen Hyatt

ABOUT THE AUTHORS

The two authors have extensive experience in many fields:

Kreta Chandler: A former learning products engineer and award-winning author of UNIX user manuals and online help, Ms. Chandler has spent the past 21 years with Hewlett-Packard Company consulting with major online retailers, managing customer online shopping research, and leading the development of online shopping tools that are revolutionizing the way customers shop online. She has also managed direct marketing catalog programs and developed user interface navigation models for the first interactive printing supplies vending machine. She was part of the engineering team that pioneered HP-VUE, the first graphical user interface for UNIX.

Karen Hyatt: A former editor and columnist, Ms. Hyatt has spent the past 20 years with Hewlett-Packard Company managing competitive intelligence, category management strategy, advertising, press relations, and merchandising. In demand for her expertise in retail theft prevention, she has served as a consultant for major retailers and industry associations. At HP she developed retail strategies that pioneered consumer-centric marketing including innovative category management plans and consumer shopping behavior research. She currently manages legal strategy for HP's largest business.

Customer-Centered Design

This section of the book looks at new concepts, new rules, and customer insights that are requirements for the new e-commerce marketplace. It consists of the following two chapters:

Chapter 1 explains the issues and circumstances surrounding the morphing online marketplace and customer experience.

Chapter 2 describes the customer and the shopping experience.

New Rules of Engagement

What am I doing wrong? I guess they don't have it," Charlotte muttered to herself while she attempted to hide her frustration. The fact is the major retail website Charlotte was exploring did have the product she was looking for; she just couldn't find it.

Charlotte is representative of hundreds of shoppers who participated in major task-analysis research conducted by Hewlett-Packard Company over the years to understand the customer challenges of online shopping. The scenario for her task was simple: "Your printer is out of ink. Go to this website, and find and purchase what you need to get it going again."

Charlotte knew exactly what she was looking for. The product was a popular item in its category, and the online merchant had it on the website. But she still got lost several times during her search and needed to start over from the home page. She spent nearly 15 minutes searching just to come up empty-handed before aborting the task. She was visibly agitated with the experience, and, at the end of the allotted time, she said she would never shop at that online store again.

In an actual situation while shopping from her home computer, she would most likely be surrounded by normal, everyday distractions that would cause the task to take even longer. She would have spent only a fraction of the time on the original website before clicking to another for a more satisfying shopping experience.

You must realize that customers won't shop on websites that are difficult or that take too long to use. Can you blame them?

After analyzing the results at hand, we identified two key problems with the website in the example:

- Charlotte did not use the website the way the developers intended.
- The top-selling, routinely needed item for which she was searching was buried too deep within the website.

On the surface, these two problems seem simple. But after diving down into their root causes, observing customers and analyzing research, this example is symptomatic of a widespread e-commerce problem: applying old design rules to a new medium.

> **"If customers can't find it, they can't buy it."**
> —*Dr. Jakob Nielsen, Web Usability Expert*

You must also realize that customers in research settings represent only a fraction of real shopping customers and the trouble they have finding and selecting products in online stores.

The Trouble with Websites

Many websites have products that people can't find. It is clear that a big gap exists between how online stores are organized and how customers want to shop for products. This results in unsuccessful searches and abandoned shopping carts. Shoppers give up when they can't find what they are looking for easily and quickly.

Most websites lack a customer-focused approach. Web developers often design e-commerce websites that are database driven rather than customer driven. Database-driven websites are organized around products that an online store has for sale and are designed for efficiencies of code. Customer-driven websites are based on how a customer shops for the products on the website and are designed after understanding customer needs.

Fundamentally, e-commerce and online shopping are new paradigms, while traditional methodologies and principles—the old rules—are applied. These old rules and techniques haven't translated well to this new type of store and have not provided shoppers with an intuitive shopping model. As a result, customers can't accomplish simple tasks such as finding popular products on major websites.

Online stores were historically developed by taking existing information and importing it into a website. Most websites are designed to allow shopping for one product with little consideration for multiple product purchases. This approach does not work successfully and customers expect more from this new technology. Information should be specially developed and tailored to online shopping and must be kept current.

Costs of Poor Usability

Do you know how much poor usability costs? Most online stores know how much it costs to run the business. They even know how much money they save by creating more efficient, database-driven stores. But few recognize how much they lose in the long run if a website does not meet basic customer usability needs.

Poor Usability Cost Factor

What does poor usability cost the customer in time and frustration? Let's look at a couple of examples.

In the opening example, Charlotte attempted to find a common product on a website and spent 15 minutes before aborting the task. The same task on another website took her less than 60 seconds. The second site had been developed by applying customer-centered design principles and techniques revealed throughout this book.

Charlotte and other shoppers tested that day spent an average of 9.5 minutes on the same task on the first website and an average of 1.1 minutes on the second website. Multiply eight shoppers times 9.5 minutes, and you get a total of 76 minutes. Compare 76 minutes with 8.8 minutes total on the second website. Imagine the amount of time spent by 1,000 new customers shopping for the same item on the first website. Which site would you choose to shop?

But wait, there's more. When the shoppers were asked if they would be inclined to purchase from the first website, all said that they would not because of their unsuccessful experiences. They would, however, purchase from the second website—because it was easier.

The cost of poor usability is the total number of customers who attempt—and fail—to find a product on a website. It's also the cost of the item they failed to find and purchase, the missed opportunity for additional sales, and the lifetime value of the customer, which is discussed in Chapter 2.

Compounding Navigational Mistakes

Consider another example that illustrates how navigation mistakes compound. Web store navigation is a sequential process. Usually, there is only one correct way to successfully navigate— by clicking links—from the home page to the destination product page when searching for a known product. Each new page displayed in the process requires the shopper to make a correct choice and click to the next page in the sequence. Each page in the sequence invites a chance for an incorrect choice. The more pages in the sequence, the more chances there are for a shopper to make an incorrect click.

The problem compounds each step of the way, especially when shoppers unknowingly make several incorrect choices. This causes them to use trial and error methods until they are successful, are forced to start over at the home page, or just click to another store.

Take, for example, a navigation consisting of six sequential pages, starting at the home page with 24 links, page 2 with 17 links, page 3 with 12 links, page 4 with 17 links, page 5 with 36 links, and page 6, the destination product detail page. The total number of clicks is 106. If you compound that by three—the incorrect click, back-up click, then choose another click— there is a potential of 318 incorrect choices.

How many clicks do you think the shopper is willing to make before abandoning the shopping cart?

Customer Opportunity Costs

When a customer spends time searching a website for a known product, it takes up time he could spend doing something else. That "something else" is the opportunity cost. Time spent searching adds up. Collectively, unacceptable shopping experiences give online shopping a bad reputation.

A word of mouth endorsement is a powerful tool. A friend's opinion or recommendation carries more weight than traditional advertising. It can also be a detriment to your company when people have unsatisfying experiences with your website. They won't hesitate to let their friends or business acquaintances know when asked about good shopping websites.

Customer-Centric Vision

Customer-centered design draws from successful usability engineering methodologies typically applied to software product design. At its foundation, usability engineering employs user-centered design principles. Successful software product design starts with user insight and needs. These needs determine the product design so that software products are easy and intuitive to "operate."

Customer-centered design starts with the user-centered design approach and then carefully balances and blends relevant customer behavior data from shopping research and behavioral studies. It integrates the value of the shopped product, business factors that drive profitability, customer needs, the uniqueness of the shelf, and other business factors.

Applying this approach optimizes web store design and benefits the business, the customer, and the manufacturer. The customer enjoys a superior shopping experience that enables him to easily find, select, and purchase products and services. The merchant maximizes the online shelf for profitability and attracts and retains "customers" instead of "buyers." Buyers typically "price-shop," but customers are willing to potentially pay more in return for customer service and trust in the merchant. The manufacturers' products and brands are represented in the best possible manner.

The motto in retailing used to be "the customer is always right." Stiff competition and intense focus on profitability required a shift to shorter-term, sales-oriented store goals. While profitability is essential to the survival of a business, customers have been lost in the process. Consumers are now required to take more responsibility for shopping services that were routinely provided by the store. Depending on the outlet, these include unloading carts at the checkout counter, marking prices on products, and even scanning their own purchases into the cash register. Customers prefer to shop where they can find their selections quickly, where they enjoy shopping, where they receive added service, and where they perceive value.

Customer-centered design not only integrates and balances customer shopping goals with store business goals, it also places the emphasis on the customer experience. Customers want to be able to find what they need but they also want to be entertained and enjoy the shopping experience. The merchant's goals are satisfied as well: attract and retain customers and sell products profitably. It's important to make sure that the merchant's goals don't unintentionally interfere with the customer's goals.

The online merchant must provide a value proposition, the right product mix, and the right experience to increase sales and achieve customer loyalty and return visits. To stay in business, stores must focus on profitability, product, category margins, and overall sales as economic success factors. They must also achieve operational excellence in managing the technology infrastructures and supply chain efficiencies. These metrics will be achieved by securing a strong customer base.

Online customers' needs are not different from traditional retail customers' needs. They are focused on time, convenience, getting the most value for their money, and ease of purchasing a product. They are similarly interested in the availability of quality products. Balancing the needs of the business with the needs of the customer requires intimate knowledge of both groups. Understanding customer segments is discussed in Chapter 2.

So What's New?

The world changed with Internet adoption. Online stores emerged as an entirely new marketplace. Shoppers changed their shopping habits as new choices and an abundance of information became available. Marketplaces morphed and traditional channels of distribution blurred as new entrants came onto the scene creating a new competitive environment. With the adoption of the Internet came the following new factors influencing shopping:

- Online stores displayed products on a new kind of "shelf."
- Hybrid online stores emerged from traditional organizations and skill sets.
- The marketplace focused increasingly on alternative channels.
- The Internet reinforced the importance of a global marketplace.
- The online renaissance created a new awareness of information as a shopping driver.

Given this new environment, it's important to take a fresh look at the features the online store offers and the factors that influence it. These new shopping methods require the merchant to play by new rules.

A New Kind of "Shelf"

The online store is a hybrid with traditional influences. An online store is neither a typical catalog nor a retail store. It's a combination of both—plus added technology brings the capability to present products in brand new ways. The online store has evolved into its own organism and the following five factors are part of its inherent nature:

- The online store is a software product.
- The online store is a product catalog.

- The online store is a retail shopping experience.
- The online store is a communications vehicle.
- The online store is virtual sales representative.

Some of these factors have influenced online shopping as e-merchants have tapped their value. The next few chapters explore these influences in depth so you can understand how to apply each to add value and determine what to leave behind.

The Online Store Is a Software Product

Many of the early online stores were designed by advertising agencies. In reality, the online store is a software product and requires the same rigor that is employed by software product development processes and methodologies. This is now being recognized as development is beginning to transfer to IT professionals who have the required skill set and now develop the infrastructure and make technology decisions. Many online stores have proprietary architectures because few off-the-shelf applications can handle the specific needs of the larger businesses and customer bases. At the core of software product development is the lifecycle that includes usability engineering throughout the process, as shown in Figure 1-1.

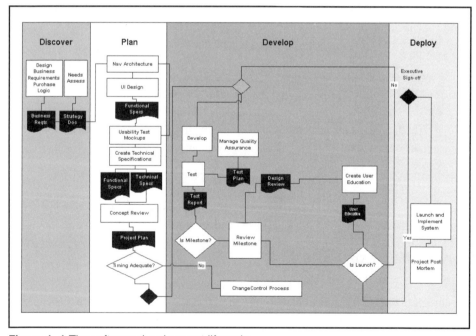

Figure 1–1 The software development lifecycle.

Chart used with permission courtesy of Luminor

The typical software development cycle is a rigorous process that begins with investigation, moves through design and development, and continues into implementation. Three essential components of the online store are the database, the user interface, and the server architecture and machines on which the first two reside and run. The development team looks at the most efficient methods of managing these components. The product and content database is always in flux as new products are added, old ones are taken out, prices change, and promotions are added to stimulate sales.

Customer needs influence the operational elements of the user interface and determine the intuitiveness of the navigational models. It is critical to the usability of an online store for the designers and developers to know and understand customer needs, current behaviors, and how consumers shop the virtual "aisles." Chapter 2 discusses what you need to know about your customers, including behaviors and shopping preferences.

Managing the complexities of the database and the need to keep current with customer preferences in the user interface should result in continual pulsing of the website. Usability measurements that will help monitor the pulse are discussed in Chapter 6.

The Online Store Is a Product Catalog

E-commerce websites have deep roots in the direct marketing catalog business. Web store organization reflects the "table-of-contents" model from this industry, one that is based on product categories and sub-categories. Even though e-commerce is identified as a new channel, it's very similar to the older, traditional mail order and catalog channels. It borrows from these established industries while adding a brand new interface. While the "shelf" is different, the system that shoppers employ to select their products is very much the same. Unfortunately, many of the more attractive attributes of catalogs have not been incorporated into web shopping. Effective and leverageable principles and techniques from the direct marketing catalog business are provided in Chapter 4.

Many e-commerce sites today are an extension of company internal electronic product catalogs. These catalog databases are often transferred "as is" to a website without adjusting to the medium. Although this may be the most expedient way to get a list of products online, customer research indicates that online shoppers are confused by the catalog-type organization and frustrated with the shopping experience. These catalogs also often include internal industry jargon and internal product part numbers that are not recognizable by consumers.

The Online Store Is a Retail Shopping Experience

Customers are more familiar with a retail shopping experience than with a catalog or online purchase transaction. Because most websites are electronic versions of traditional printed product catalogs, it is necessary to apply the cataloger's best techniques. But it is just as important—and possibly even more important—to understand and apply retail shopping expertise because the customer is most familiar with shopping in traditional retail stores. The best practices in retail will be discussed in depth in Chapter 3.

Customers struggle with knowing which routes to take when they enter an online store. Retail shopping behaviors give clues to how customers shop for products, thus enabling a more intuitive store navigation model that easily guides them from the home page to their destination product detail page.

The Online Store Is a Communications Vehicle

The online store started out subsidizing its business through advertisements and eventually became an electronic billboard. In practicality, the ad space interferes with customers' shopping tasks. Customer research reveals that customers learn to ignore these ads and attempt to stay focused. Customers won't continue using a website if the ads become too prevalent and—to many customers—annoying.

Online stores have unique advantages over traditional retail and direct marketing channels for advertising a broad range of categories that reach more targeted customers inexpensively. Balancing ads with navigational elements that help customers complete tasks is a skill. New techniques and unique capabilities of the online store are discussed in Chapter 5. Overused ad and promotional boxes create obstacles for customers to overcome before completing the next step in their shopping process.

It's important to recognize that the main communications influence online is information. The web is used as a resource for virtually every subject. Manufacturers and e-merchants should provide customers with their brand promise and differentiate their products and services. Shoppers will make purchase decisions based on product attributes and services, but also on the strength of the brand.

The Online Store Is a Virtual Sales Representative

What if you could control everything that was said and presented by your sales staff? An online store makes this possible. It acts as a floor sales rep and as an inbound/outbound sales force. It has the ability to combine information and sales.

Around the world, the most influential retail in-store customer touch point is a retail sales associate's recommendations. Store sales personnel cannot reliably provide customers with all key product features and benefits due to a number of factors. Most are inexperienced and do not receive the appropriate training. These employees usually receive low salaries, and employee turnover rates are high.

Many sales reps must cover a broad range of categories and products, frequently with short lifecycles, and products are replaced consistently with new versions or new styles. Also, only brief encounters with customers are permitted because there are typically others waiting to ask questions.

The web store can also act as an inbound and outbound sales force. The web's ability to provide consistent and accurate information is a benefit over traditional retailing. Accurate content also shortens the purchase decision process by providing detailed information and recommendations. But how many stores provide recommended choices instead of simply listing everything they have for sale? This places the entire burden of choice on the customer. For some products, that is acceptable, but for more complicated technology products, customers rely on experts to make recommendations. A customer-focused viewpoint revolves around understanding products and services to help customers make decisions and provides them with sales assistance online through effective content. Chapter 5 discusses new techniques for facilitating sales.

A New Kind of Shopper

Shoppers are more knowledgeable than ever before. The Internet allows access to information that was previously unavailable to them. They also have more places to shop—retail stores, online stores, catalogs, and TV shopping networks.

To customers, shopping is shopping. They have ingrained knowledge that doesn't often transfer easily between the kinds of stores they shop, unless these stores are designed to be familiar. Each store has a unique format, yet customers seek consistency from format to format. Intuitive store design is based on how people shop for products and applies that knowledge to the store plan.

People shop on the web because they seek information about products to purchase and because it's convenient. Sometimes they will then purchase from an online store and become a customer instead of a shopper. Or they may purchase at retail or from a catalog. Regardless of where they actually make the purchase, their experience with an online store in seeking information determines whether or not they would purchase from that store either now or in the future.

A company that sells through multiple channels, for example, online stores, catalogs, and retail store outlets, is particularly affected. These days, customers can do their "shopping homework" online, and then go to the retail store just to pick up the item.

Integrated Shopping Behaviors

This new online shelf integrates historical shelves, the customer, and the new frontier. Now with more options, customers decide where and when to purchase a product—and the choices continue to grow. Today's customers have many shopping alternatives. Their experience extends from retail, TV, and catalog to online shopping. Traditional retail, however, is still by far the most dominant influence.

Customers don't think about the type of shelf they buy from or the process they use. Even within the retail channel, consumers don't necessarily focus on the type of store they visit. If they have a particular need, they will go to Costco, for example, to find it. They don't consciously think about visiting a club store. It's natural for customers to think of purchasing a toaster at Wal-Mart. But it's rare for a consumer, in her search for a toaster, to identify "a mass merchandiser" as her target retailer.

That's why shelf integration must be transparent to customers. Their only concern is finding their product, getting a good value, and obtaining good service.

The Role of Product

Product plays a critical role in the online business's value proposition, in effective web store merchandising, and in the customer's ability to find and select specific items. But not all products are created equal. Most web stores, however, treat them the same when they list the products with only one-line descriptions.

The customer's relationship to the product is also important. As more customers become more experienced with shopping for a product, they will choose stores where the shopping process is the easiest. The Internet opened doors to scarce, unique, and hard-to-find items. It also changed the marketplace and added auction websites, allowing anyone to have an online "garage sale" of used items or to shop a worldwide "flea market."

Store product mix complicates online merchandising and influences the web design and navigation models that ultimately lead customers to the products they seek. Knowing the product and category value determines appropriate placement levels in the web store category hierarchies. Product knowledge as it relates to the total store performance, to other product performance, or to other category performance requires analysis to regulate profitability.

Other factors influencing web store design are product complexities, characteristics, and lifecycles. Many people research complex products online where the information is more in depth than retail sales help can provide, but they ultimately purchase at retail. Some products are shopped for frequently and routinely, while others are a one-time purchase. Still others are planned or impulse purchases.

Intimate product knowledge and customer insight determines the appropriate product mix for an online store. Product knowledge also brings organization to the category and online store and will better reflect customer-driven needs. Product brand, category value, and even product usage influence how products should be merchandised. Product information must be blended with target customer information relative to how people shop. Only then can successful navigation models be designed. Products, category market structures, and valuation are discussed in depth in Chapter 3.

The Morphing Marketplace

Markets and customers affect website organization, design, and navigation models. The blurring of channels and complexity of choices makes it a science to match up the right sales channel with the right market for the right customer. Channels are still evolving, but niche websites make it possible to target customers with specific products.

The marketplace and channels of distribution have experienced rapid change over the past few years. Not too long ago, traditional major channels were simple and had distinct customer bases and value propositions. The following is a list and description of major traditional channels:

Retail: Retail stores are shopped primarily by home, home office, and small-business consumers. These are physical "brick and mortar" buildings with broad or specific category and product assortments. There are also variations, such as "big box" super stores, department stores, consumer electronics stores, mass merchants, convenience stores, grocery stores, "mom and pop" sole proprietorships, specialty stores, club or membership stores, and discount or outlet stores. Their value is in their proximity to the customer, convenience, entertainment value, and ability to offer immediate gratification. They have a steady product mix and seasonal product offerings, and they offer special promotions.

Business Direct: These companies provide both products and services and operate predominately on a contract basis with businesses. They often provide a printed catalog containing a broad range of products and cater to calendar-budgeted purchases.

Direct Mail: Direct mail companies provide targeted printed catalogs, letters, and brochures to home and small-office consumers. These "retail in the mail" catalogs and mailings cover a wide variety of products such as clothing and jewelry, food, furniture, home furnishings, and computers and peripherals, and they generate both planned and impulse purchases.

Wholesale/Distribution: These businesses act as a "middle man" and serve as a hub for small to large business customers. They buy products from manufacturers and resell them through printed catalogs or showrooms with true wholesale prices. They receive truckloads and pallets of products from the manufacturer but ship smaller boxes, pallets, and truckloads to retailers and other channels of distribution.

Brokers: These companies are the intermediaries to business customers and provide services and sales to grocers and other industries. Some of their primary products are perishable goods, which they move through the channels quickly.

Pure-play Internet: These companies have only one selling motion—online. They provide public websites to home and small-office consumers (B2C) and to businesses, corporations, and enterprises (B2B). In some cases, they provide non-public websites, extranets, to larger companies. Internet companies can carry all products and are "perceived" to have low cost structures and prices. They have an additional value proposition in providing a broader product offering than retail or catalogs due to their virtually unlimited shelf space. They also can economically carry hard-to-find items.

Manufacturer-Direct: Many manufacturers have branded retail outlets for home consumers. These stores offer products such as clothing and housewares. They typically carry quality products and feature a trusted brand name.

Historically, reseller transactions were based on one-to-one mapping to the customer. Mail order companies sent out catalogs to customer's homes, people shopped in retail stores for products, and business-direct companies sold to big corporations under contracts.

In the past few years, some retail businesses sought to increase their reach to customers by adding an additional selling motion to their channel mix, such as a catalog. Now, with expanded technology capabilities and public and commercial adoption of the Internet, most businesses are adding e-commerce to their mix. Current marketplace trends are for single-channel businesses to become multi-channel businesses. These new hybrid models cause traditionally distinct channel models to blur and new combinations such as "clicks and mortar," a combination of retail and online sales, to develop. These new models are shown in Figure 1-2.

Although the percentage of the overall business is still small, sales are shifting online from other selling motions as businesses find efficiencies and transactional cost savings over traditional selling venues. It is also now possible to have multiple web properties in the selling mix. These properties target niche or specific markets. There is also a downward trend in the number of pure-play e-tailers as they merge and form alliances with other businesses to survive.

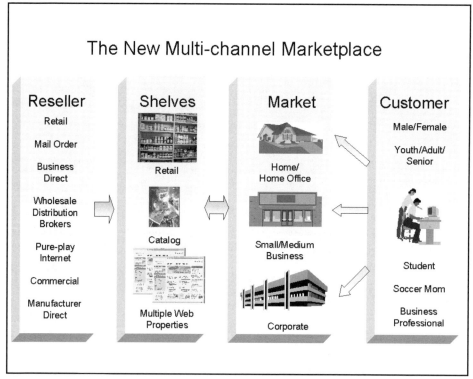

Figure 1–2 Traditional channels, selling motions, markets, and customer models blur.

Each customer can represent multiple customer segments. Not only do multiple selling motions complicate business models for the merchant, but the customer segment models are also complicated because many of the sales channels were created based on shopping needs for the home, home-office, micro-business, medium-sized-business, corporate, and enterprise markets. Unfortunately for stores, customers don't necessarily segment themselves the same way retailers might want them to as they work through their business plans.

As customers and their needs change, the channels and shopping experiences also change. For example, with the adoption of business purchasing via the web, home consumers are influenced—because all business customers are also home consumers. When a business customer shops online for office needs, she can also shop for personal items. Every point of contact that a customer makes with a "shelf" is an opportunity for the reseller to gain a loyal, multi-segmented, and multi-channel purchasing customer.

Managing Multiple Stores and Shelves

In the process of selling through one channel, it's important to consider all the other selling motions. At any given time, customers can have access to any one of the stores—whether they are physical, virtual, or in print. Multiple channels spawn additional stores, and the proliferation creates a variety of ways to purchase a product. To the customer, each of these is just another shelf on which a product is displayed. It doesn't matter if it is a retail shelf, a catalog shelf, an e-shelf, or a TV broadcast (shopping network) shelf.

Most consumers will shop through multiple stores to buy products and services. It is evident that online shopping directly influences offline purchases. Online activities shorten the purchase process by providing to the shopper decision-making information that may not be found on the store floor. The shopper then decides from which store to purchase.

Many businesses are moving toward balance and integration to maximize sales, product mix, and customer experience across all of the individual offerings. At the same time, many businesses are not. The value of a multi-channel shopper appears to be greater than that of single-channel shoppers. Shopping research indicates that consumers shopping multiple channels are more likely to be loyal and spend more. On the flip side, a disappointing online experience can taint the entire store brand in the customer's mind and may affect future purchases at the retail store.

Practicing "integrated shelf management" is a critical business practice for today's marketplace. This technique presents each shelf or store in the same way regardless of the channel. The benefit is to present a company as a unified entity to the consumer, regardless of the type of store in which the customer shops. Figure 1-3 shows the similarities of the different types of "stores" from a customer's viewpoint.

Customers become uncomfortable when shopping experiences stray too far from the familiar—and the most familiar experience is the traditional retail store. For example, web stores have random, multiple entry points through links. Customers "get lost" by dropping into the middle of a web store via some of those links. For years, retail stores have studied and designed

Retail	Catalog	Online
Physical building, mall	Printed paper	Systems, content databases, and graphical user interfaces
Access by car, on foot, public transportation	Access anywhere; phone, fax, or mail is available	Access by PC and other devices
Store front	Cover	Home page
Store entrances, fixed	Multiple, random	Multiple, random
Store map	Table of contents/index	Site map
Aisles	Catalog sections	Category links
Shelf	Catalog page	Web page (category page)
Product (package or SKU)	Image and description	Web page (product detail page)
Planograms	Category product page layouts	Web page organization
Fixtures	Pictures and type	Images and presentation
End cap	Front and back covers, prime positions, boxed features	Featured positions, brand and specialty stores
Traffic flow patterns	Reading and catalog access patterns	Sequential navigation models/direct search
Merchandising	Graphic design elements	Graphic design elements
Check out counter	Order form/fax/telephone	e-check out/telephone
Shopping basket	Order form	e-shopping cart/order list
Stockrooms, warehouses, distribution centers	Virtual warehouses, distribution centers	Virtual warehouses, distribution centers
Pick up in store	Receive in mail/delivery	Receive in mail/delivery
Point of sale data	Order data	Real-time point of sale data
Conversion rates	Conversion rates	Conversion rates/hits

Figure 1–3 Different kinds of "stores" have similar components.

traffic flow patterns to help customers navigate through their stores. Not all retail stores are successful in guiding customers, yet studying these elements will give you assistance as you create familiar online traffic flow patterns—navigation models—that can help customers find products. Customer retail experiences are discussed in Chapter 4.

A New Kind of Business

As retail stores added catalogs and/or the Internet to their channel mix, they initially feared cannibalization of customers and sales by the new organizations within their own companies. Also, most corporate structures created profit and loss silos within the organization, intending to effectively measure each type of store. In actuality, it set up the sister channels and stores to compete against each other for customer sales, internal resources, and power. There was no top-level support for integration.

What results from this model is *dis*integration, when individual stores have no incentive to share their best practices and information or leverage promotions to their sister stores. A few businesses now recognize the importance of integration across all of their stores to maximize sales, marketing activities, customer experiences, infrastructure and supply chain efficiencies, and overall corporate profits. They are creating and applying new business models that recognize integration to create a whole that is greater than the sum of the individual parts.

A fundamental integrated marketing principle determines that every point of contact with a customer is a chance to communicate coordinated, consistent messages. Multiple *impressions* result in a higher chance of action including product purchase. Common representation across a business's multiple-channel shelves also maximizes its brand and marketing programs or activities.

Integrating models can solve home or business delivery obstacles. For example, some retailers allow customers to find, select, and purchase online and then go into the retail store to pick up the products. Other businesses enable customers to return a web-purchased product to a retail outlet or make it easy to return the item. Nordstrom's provides a postage-paid, return envelope and clear return instructions with each new order. Returned items can be simply put into the envelope and conveniently placed in any U.S. mailbox, even from home.

In some major metropolitan areas, store trucks deliver the merchandise to a business customer's location. In New York City and other densely populated locales, Mercanti Systems offers a retail/Internet model in which the customer can shop online and then pick up paid-for merchandise at a special no-wait window at the store—even while walking home from work. This capability works just as conveniently in less urban environments—for example, while driving home from work or running family errands.

Integrating Multiple Web Properties

With channel alliances and mergers, some businesses ended up with multiple web properties. These properties can consist of a variety of public Internet e-commerce websites catering to consumer, business, community, or niche markets. They can also be *intranets*—providing information and content to internal "customers" in an organization, users of the information—or *extranets*—providing private access to another business for commerce, content, information, or service.

Integrating and centralizing systems optimizes resources, minimizes redundancies, and provides consistent information and common deployment of information. One data source can serve the variety of websites in a company's domain. This saves resources and provides consistency of information that is "served up" from one source to many websites. Commerce, community, product information and training, and technical support websites can be served by one web server farm. This is the future of the Internet.

Who's Minding the Store?

Which department in your organization is responsible for the customer experience? Along with a new business must come a new dynamic within the organization itself. There are many people and many departments that make up an online store and most are organized in functional areas. Yet, in most companies, no central group is responsible for the customer experience.

Even though there is no official responsibility, everyone has an influence on the customer. Each department—buyers, merchandisers, marketing departments, and IT departments—impact the online store. However, internal measurements can conflict with successful customer navigation requirements. For example, buyers may be measured on product margins, IT departments may be measured on efficiencies of code and ease of database maintenance, and marketing departments on how much advertising space is sold and revenue brought in. Translated online, buyers would promote higher margin products, IT might develop practical yet non-intuitive navigation models, and marketing would create advertising and promotional boxes on the web. These all could directly conflict with customer navigation and purchasing tasks.

Not only do the goals conflict with the customer experience, but they also conflict with each other. Collapsing department boundaries and integrating teams across the traditional boundaries will foster a website that more easily creates the right balance of influencing factors for the store. It takes all people and departments in an online store to make a good online organization that recognizes the value of the customer experience. The organization needs support from the top to achieve a website that is a balance of customer focus and store business drivers.

Competing in the New Marketplace

Your competition is not just another online store—nor is it just retail, nor just catalog. Today, it's every store, and tomorrow it will increase even more. The more you know about your competition, the more you'll know about how to acquire and retain customers.

Understanding your competition will help you position yourself in the marketplace. You'll need to know their financial positions, their customer value propositions, and how target customers view them. Are their suppliers reliable? What solutions do they offer the customer? How big is an online competitor? The Internet hides the size of businesses, unlike a physical retail store. It is difficult to know whether a given company is a large enterprise or a home-based company.

Customers have a basic level of online shopping expectation, which sets the bar. The most successful and popular online stores today are raising that bar as they integrate emerging technologies and refine website design to accommodate shopper preferences. Every day, expectations grow higher and the bar continues to move. There is no room for complacency in today's business environment. The competition is only a click away.

The online store must differentiate itself from all channels and all competitors. The most difficult task is to create a truly unique website. Retail stores that are the most memorable provide something that other retailers do not. Wal-Mart's success is attributable, in part, to the company's strategy to build stores in smaller towns and cities. Consumers found the stores to be accessible and convenient.

Nordstrom differentiates through its special service and store ambience. Online, Amazon.com doesn't just list titles of books. It gives customers access to excerpts of books and even allows individual consumer comments and reviews. Online merchants each need a unique position in the marketplace.

Integrating into Global Markets

Many e-commerce businesses selling to international audiences have recognized the need for country-specific websites that are based on products, customs, languages, and cultural influences. In many cases, countries will have unique retail shopping experiences that are part of the makeup of the people in that country. These considerations need to be factored into website design and development. As a rule, one global e-commerce website does not fit all.

While some consumer online shopping trends are global, it is good practice not to rely on those trends but to heavily consider each country's specific insights. For example, although mostly men purchase online worldwide, in the U.S. more women are shopping and purchasing online. This has changed over the past few years and demands a demographic refresher for many U.S. e-commerce websites designed in the years when men were the dominant online shoppers. While this trend is true for the U.S., other countries may not yet be ready for women-focused shopping websites. In new business channels, there will be early evolutionary behavioral changes until the model becomes more mature and becomes integrated into the culture.

A country's economic environment and culture affect online shopping adoption cycles. Each culture and each industry fosters different adoption cycles. Technology's early adopters, for instance, were predominantly male. In some countries, students lead Internet adoption. Determining the adoption cycle for each environment must precede Internet design.

Similarly, global issues such as currency conversion, taxation, and privacy laws need to be researched before launching a website. Internet-related laws and regulations, as well as commerce in general, tend to change rapidly.

Specific country trends in online shopping, products, and demographics of the target customers must be monitored to ensure the website design keeps up with changes in the country and in the marketplace.

Finding the Niche

Web merchants, bricks-and-mortar retailers, and catalogers are all vying for the same customer. In order to succeed, each will need to establish a channel value proposition. The customer is at the center of the decision.

What attribute will be the most important? Will it be price, convenience, experiential shopping, entertainment, service, or something else? Because each channel is superior in at least one of these, the customer will not believe that a single channel can provide everything. Providing a singular focus, however, doesn't mean that the other issues don't matter. Delivering as many as possible will be key.

Because customers shop in more than one channel, resellers will have to share sales. But they don't want to lose customers from their channels due to mistakes they make. The game is theirs to win or lose.

The New Rules of the Online Renaissance

E-commerce is moving into a new era, a renewal of consumer faith in this evolving channel. This channel is also moving into a reawakening of the need for customer-focused practices and considerations to survive and thrive in the new marketplace.

Fulfilling customer expectations, providing product value, and applying excellent usability engineering factors all contribute to a successful online shopping experience for customers. Unfortunately, most online shopping experiences do not yet meet the basic retail customer's shopping expectations. For people to shop online, the experience has to be on par or better than at retail. An improved and intuitive website is dependent on holistic integration of the following actions:

- Begin with the end in mind. Thoroughly understand your customers: who they are, what they expect, what they fear, and other psychographic considerations. Also understand what their pleasant—and unpleasant—shopping experiences are at retail, via catalog, at other online stores, and wherever else your web store's products are sold. Understand the roadblocks to purchasing. It's not just about how shoppers navigate the page today. It's also about how they shopped last year for the item and the year before that. Customer knowledge will be discussed in Chapter 2.
- Bridge the gap between web store design and customer expectations. Most online stores start with the products they currently have, not with how the customer expects to shop for them. Just because you have a good process does not mean that you are meeting customer requirements. While online stores are streamlined in hierarchies and schematics, you cannot anticipate the way the customer wants to navigate unless you ask. Apply customer-centered design principles and methodologies to your web store modifications or design. These will be discussed in Chapters 6 and 7.
- Factor in the value of products both to your customers and to your business profitability. Some products represent destination categories, and some are impulse purchases. Understand how each category operates and which creates the highest value.
- Integrate and balance knowledge of customers, channels, and products. There is no magic elixir. The solution lies in the ability to unify these factors and to create improved websites.
- Proliferate and cross-pollinate this integrated knowledge throughout your entire organization: marketing, IT departments, web design, and purchasing. Web developers should step into the shoes—and functions—of the buyers and merchandisers. Buyers and merchandisers should understand usability engineering methodologies and be ready to apply customer-centered design principles along with their recommendations on product mix. Understand the challenges facing everyone in the organization.

Each person in an e-commerce organization must be conscious of the multiple roles required to make an e-business work. You must be a marketer, a businessperson, a web designer, a shopper, and much more. Chances for success increase by taking a three-dimensional look at everyone's role in the organization and unlocking the secrets of traditional retail and catalog merchandising and human factors engineering. It requires an optimal balance of customer needs, store business drivers, and product knowledge, as shown in Figure 1-4.

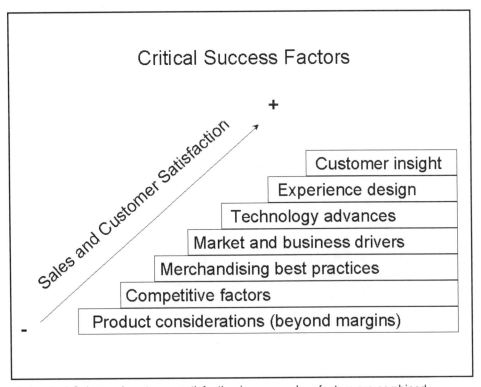

Figure 1–4 Sales and customer satisfaction increase when factors are combined.

As e-commerce enters this new era, short-term business models move from being product-centric to long-term category marketing solutions and from being store-centric to being customer-centric. There is a revitalized focus on cultivating long-term customer relationships. This book presents new rules that replace old methods. It's about intuitive navigation for the customer, relevant content, and effective merchandising techniques that are uniquely tailored for the electronic world. It's also about managing the delicate balance between the needs of the customer and the needs of the online merchant.

With the dawn of a new era, this online renaissance requires fresh perspectives and thinking. But, you have to do more than just have new rules; they must be applied.

- Understand your customers…*intimately.*
- Tap into best practices and successful methodologies and techniques from retailing, cataloging, and e-tailing…and *integrate them.*
- Apply customer-centered design usability engineering methodologies to your new or improved web store…and *keep doing it—it's not a one-time event.*
- Understand that sales are a result of everything else you do…*and sales are a measure of how well you've done it.*

As Mark Twain said, "Even if you're on the right track, you'll get run over if you just sit there."

Today, the only way to win is to focus on the customer. The days of cutting corners, sacrificing the consumer for increased profitability, and providing minimal service are over if companies want to succeed. The new era is all about providing the quality products the customer wants, where and when he wants them, along with superior service and convenience. Even if the investment is a little higher, profitability will increase with improved customer loyalty and higher revenue. The next chapter will give you an in-depth view of the customer.

Walking a Mile in the Customer's Shoes

How many customers can you afford not to attract, and how many current customers can you afford to lose to a competitor? Websites that are designed with a consumer-centric focus attract and retain customers better than those that are database driven. Business profitability depends on customer attraction and loyalty. Marketing experts express it in terms of satisfaction and delight. It's neither. Customers don't want to be merely satisfied. They *expect* you to meet their needs. They want you to recognize them as individuals and provide convenience, purchasing information, customer service, security, and speedy transactions.

Online shoppers have more power than any other type of shopper. The competition is only a click away. They are more in control of where they shop, when they shop, and how they shop than ever before. If they don't like a particular website, there are several others to take its place—instantly. Comparison shopping is simple. There's no need to get into a car and drive several miles to find another store. The customer never has to leave his chair.

Designing a successful website is not only about the process of shopping and the efficiency of moving from one web page to another. It's all about understanding those people who enter the site, why they're there, what they like, and what bothers them. Helping customers move from one domain to another is meaningless if they can't relate to the overall environment.

Every day, real estate agents attempt to find home-seekers the most suitable house for their needs. If all customers were the same, architects would need to create only one building design to satisfy everyone. But in the real world, each person wants and needs different features in her home. Customers purchasing pre-built houses know that they will not get a residence built to their specifications. They usually have to compromise and accept one that, from their perspective, has some flaws. The only way to provide a structure that fills all their needs is to construct a custom-built home.

There are two approaches to designing a house. The first analyzes the space and utilizes it efficiently. The builder might decide to position appliances in the kitchen based on their proximity to the appropriate wiring or plumbing. He could locate the laundry in the garage because it would be logical to put it next to the hot water heater. It would also be appropriate to design the home with small windows to help the structure retain heat. All these elements might be cost-saving procedures as well.

The second approach focuses on the needs and desires of the future occupants. Will the refrigerator be close enough to the stove for daily cooking? Is the counter space next to it sufficient to hold groceries? Each daily activity is analyzed to understand how this particular family functions. This method seeks to deliver efficiency and comfort of movement, which is reflected in the *usability* of the home.

The most important attribute, however, is how the family members *feel* in the home. They will want it to be comfortable and attractive and to fit a very individual lifestyle. Locating the laundry in the garage might be logical, but these folks may not want to go into a cold garage during the winter to wash their clothes. They may also prefer large, expansive windows to let in light and take advantage of their view. This approach will address the ambience of the home and provide the family members with the warmth and beauty they desire.

The home also needs to relate to its external environment. How it will be used should be evaluated within the broader context of its proximity to local businesses, schools, and health care. In real estate, primary success is measured by location, location, location. Online, it's convenience, convenience, convenience. To create convenience, you need to know your customers intimately.

Understanding Customers

Truly understanding your customers means determining their preferences and capturing, at a moment in time, their emotional responses to any given number of stimuli. Even though some customers believe they shop analytically, every shopper is influenced by the shopping environment. In fact, many decisions the customer makes are emotional. Preferences and opinions are the result of experiences as well as beliefs. Customers' opinions are not static and can change with time.

After customer information is collected, the process needs to be repeated to reflect the continuum of behavior that can ultimately be incorporated into a profile.

Excellent website development depends on understanding individual customer's wants, needs, opinions, and reactions. Becoming the customer is different than merely conducting surveys or watching clicks around a website. Becoming the customer involves stepping into his shoes to determine actual experiences both current and anticipated for the future. Shopping is usually triggered by a need.

The only way to understand your customers' needs is to create a dialog with them. The web, fax machines, and phones make it possible to transact business without ever dealing with an actual person. Developing assumptions about a consumer based on a logical process will only lead you astray. You must talk to them and discover how they relate to your site, your products, and your company. The voice of the customer is getting louder. More people are becoming vocal about what they like or dislike about stores.

Customers will tolerate an average product, store, or website only if they have no alternative. But they will not hesitate to switch as new and better choices become available. We found this to be true time and again while conducting customer task analysis research. Customers define the worth of a company in relation to other companies offering similar products and services, with preference given to those that offer a more intuitive and easy-to-navigate website.

Five Common Customer Myths

Over the past several years, we have listened to online retailers and especially to customers who shop online. As a result, we've been able to identify five common misperceptions held by merchants and manufacturers.

Myth 1: We Can Educate Them

The most popular common myth is that customers will take time to learn to operate your website. Modifying a person's behavior may be possible over time in situations that can be controlled and repeated. However, each time a person comes online is a unique experience. In addition to shopping your site, the customer most likely has surfed or shopped other sites that behave or are operated differently.

Customers want intuitive, easy, and similar experiences that transfer from one site to another. This can be the opposite from merchants' desires to differentiate their websites. An e-store's implementation may stray too far from customer familiarity and acceptable comfort levels.

Software application programming standards were created to provide consistency in software product development. Sometimes, resellers know that a site is not optimized for a customer, but because of resource or technology limitations, it's easier to put the responsibility on the consumer. Shoppers don't want to visit online stores that require them to learn new techniques to accomplish simple tasks.

Requiring customers to adapt to your site's navigation or unique graphical elements requires an extra step on the customer's part that negates the benefit of convenience. Your store must accommodate the customer. Just as you can't teach an old dog new tricks, you can't teach an online shopper new ways to operate a website.

Myth 2: It's the Customer's Fault

Some online merchants tend to blame the customer for not reading the instructions they have carefully crafted and provided. Time and again during user testing of websites, shoppers questioned what they were doing wrong and many commented about how stupid they must be. They tended to blame themselves for the poor design of the website. People will not shop on websites that make them feel stupid. If they aren't successful in their shopping attempts, they won't be back.

Perhaps customers don't operate websites the way the web designers intended. Websites—especially home pages—bombard customers with information, and most customers won't take the time to read instructions. Customers migrate to websites that help them complete their shopping tasks successfully. The true art of web design creates an experience of success and accomplishment for the customer.

Myth 3: One Size Fits All

Customers are not all the same. That's why leading marketing experts have developed programs that focus on the individual. Whether they're called one-to-one marketing or customer relationship management (CRM), they all have one principle in common—you must customize a relationship with each customer. You must also ensure that your design caters to your most valuable customers today and to your most valuable predicted customers in the future.

One-size-fits-all websites were fine in the early days to get stores online and products out of boxes and on the virtual shelf. Today, however, customers have more choices and will exercise their options readily. The customer base determines the appropriate composition of an online store. The store must cater to those customer segments that will do the most shopping and purchasing.

Myth 4: Fewer Navigation Clicks Are Better

In some cases, this might be true, but only as long as the customer glides through each click easily without having to use too much effort. This is rarely the case, however. The right number of clicks from start to finish depends on how long it takes for the customer to study the page to understand its relevance and to make an additional choice.

During our research, we timed shopping tasks to better understand navigation issues. We found customers experienced difficulty with simple tasks even when the target page was designed to be only three screen clicks from the home page. While this navigation looks great in a site schematic, the true test is ultimately with the customers. Each page was packed with choices that the customer had to evaluate before making a decision. Each time a shopper pauses to study a page is a chance for them to decide they've spent enough time on the task and to abort. Customers won't hesitate to do so. In fact, in real-life online shopping, they would do it well before the allotted time was up.

Myth 5: Build It and They Will Come

It's a fallacy to believe that if you build a website, the customers will come flocking. You must first do your homework to understand the consumers, what they want, and how they interact with your proposed site and then get the word out.

Promoting pervasively and consistently in the right places is imperative to attract your target customer segments. Where you advertise your site depends on your customer base and understanding the various points of contact they can have with your store:

- What portals or Internet Service Providers (ISPs) are they likely to use most frequently?
- What magazines and newspapers are they predisposed to subscribe to or read?
- Are there community groups that would be likely to refer to your site for its relevance?

Answers to these questions will help you target your store's advertising and marketing tactics to the right people. Traditional direct marketers are experienced in using promotion to their advantage. Chapter 4 reveals their successful tactics.

Avoid falling into the trap that these myths perpetuate, and you will be on the path to consumer-centered design. Treating customers as individuals and understanding their issues—even if it means redesigning your site—is the first step.

Customer Profiling

Customer intelligence is not about the customer's IQ; it is about intimately understanding the customer. Customer intelligence is the body of knowledge—everything you need to know about the consumer—captured and analyzed. But how do you relate to someone you've never met? A body of customer intelligence integrates many types of research data to gain a 360-degree perspective of the "whole customer."

There are several methodologies you can use to discover your customers' needs. We'll examine how customers may be grouped by their demographic and psychographic attributes. Then we'll explore ways in which you can identify and relate to them individually. Creating an ongoing dialog with your customers will gain you long-term loyalty.

Today's customers suffer from information overload. It's difficult to keep up with all the technological changes in both product and system complexities. There are more choices in the marketplace as well. These factors contribute to complicated decisions for the consumer.

Defining who your customers are and the issues they face helps determine their expectations and purchase motivations. It also helps to decide how the website can be constructed to minimize confusion.

Four Investigative Factors

The following four key factors merit investigation:

- What motivates people to purchase?
- How are their attitudes different from their behaviors?
- How do you make a customer feel like she is your *only* customer?
- What is the value of a customer segment to your business?

Not all customers are of the same value to your business. You must not only know who your customers are, but what they purchase or will likely purchase in the future. You should focus your efforts on the right customers in the right segments. Customer insight is determined through understanding current life stages, demographics (statistical depiction of social and economic characteristics), and psychographics (variable complex behavior patterns). This investigation is not just a one-time analysis, but rather an ongoing discovery to keep current with changes in your customer base.

Consumer Demographics

Learning about your most valued customers depends on determining the size and distribution of each identified segment. Groupings may be established on a variety of attributes:

- Age
- Gender
- Income
- Education
- Lifestyle
- Life Stage
- Household Size
- Ethnic and Cultural Background
- Geography

These are traditional groupings and must be used in the context of your more targeted segmentation. They should be incorporated as directional to help give you more insight about your customers. It's dangerous, however, to make too many assumptions based on these demographic designations without actually profiling your high-value consumers through primary research. Those studies will identify your key target segments more succinctly.

Age

Determining the age of the customer will help you make the following decisions:

- Information flow needs
- Font size
- Image content necessities
- Help functionality features
- Data presentation

Age is an indicator of varying experiences. Because educational styles have evolved over the years, learning patterns have changed. Teaching techniques used to be more formal and structured, so older people may desire more written and visual explanation. Younger customers may have been taught through more experiential methods.

Age is also an indicator of biological differences. Eyesight changes as individuals age, and smaller type and images are more difficult to discern. Easy-to-read fonts and larger type will help older people navigate with ease. Many people in our user tests—even those in their 20s—brought up concerns about the difficulty of reading font sizes that were too small. This affects the feel and comfort of the site for the customer. If they have to strain to see information, it may skew them toward an undesirable experience.

Surveys normally identify clusters of customers according to advertising demographics. These may work well for promotional purposes, but you may want to establish your own criteria based on your products, expected usage, and your customer targets. Establishing broad categories could result in lumping everyone into arbitrary segments—for example, those between 25 and 40 years of age or 55 and over. There are very real differences between a 25-year-old and someone who is 40. Similarly, one category could include customers both 55 and 75 years of age. Smaller variances provide tighter and more illustrative personal descriptions. The number of segments is dependent on products and markets.

Generational differences influence how people relate to the content in images. Pictures are more effective when they create associations easily drawn from experience. Images that don't apply to selected age groups will miss their intended target.

Older people are adopting the Internet with unprecedented speed. They have money to spend, and their sheer numbers will make them extremely important as customers for any business. The baby boomer and elderly markets are growing in size and importance. The 65-and-over market is quite affluent with a high level of discretionary purchasing power.

Younger consumers are comfortable with technology because many grew up with the web. They use the Internet for communication and entertainment as well as a source of information. It's a natural transition for them to access the web and shop.

Resellers often ignore the two age extremes—seniors and the youth markets. In actuality, these are the two groups with the highest growth potential. Baby boomers will influence the senior market enormously and represent untapped potential. Teenagers have purchasing power and are your mainstream customers of tomorrow. Building their loyalty to your branded store today will ensure continued profitability over the long run.

The average age of online purchasers in the U.S., Australia, and Canada is over 40, while in most of Europe it averages around 35. As usage becomes more mainstream, the population buying online will be more reflective of the actual population.

We can only make general predictions about age in the future, but the point is to look for generational attributes and then determine how they affect your target customers. Age influences our expectations, how we interact with the web, and how we approach the process of shopping.

Gender

If you're going to put yourself in your customer's shoes, you need to know whether the shoes are men's or women's, oxfords or heels. It's easy to stereotype gender differences, so it pays to spend some time truly understanding shopping behavior, Internet interactions, and attitudes that may influence your success.

How Men and Women Shop

Paco Underhill, inventor of the science of shopping and noted author of the best seller *Why We Buy; the Science of Shopping*, explains the differences:

"Stereotypically, we think of males as being the ones at the personal technology frontier—building stereo components from kits, or shelling out five-figure sums for speakers. More recently, personal computers and cell phones all began life as toys for boys. But the fact is that often, women are the earliest adopters of new technology. When business began using computers, the female office workers had to learn first about operating systems and software. The women, crunched for time on their lunch breaks, were the earliest enthusiasts of the automated teller machine.

How did we not notice? Because men and women use technology in very different ways. Men are in love with the technology itself, with the gee-whiz factor, with the horsepower and the bang for the buck. Back before cars had computerized innards, the commonest sight in America was three or four guys assembled around the raised hood of a car, watching its owner adjust a carburetor or install a generator, and offering copious advice on how it could be done better. Today those men are gathered around the barbecue comparing the size of their hard drives and the speed of their modems. As they say, it's a dude thing.

Women generally take a completely different approach to the world of high tech. They take technologies and turn them into appliances. They strip even the fanciest gizmo of all that is mysterious and jargony in order to determine its usefulness. Women look at technology and see its purpose, its reason—what it can do. The promise of technology is always that it will make our lives easier and more efficient. Women are the ones who demand that it fulfill its promise."

— Paco Underhill

Both men and women react emotionally to subtle elements on a website, including color, movement, and even punctuation. But it's not just the way men and women approach the functionality of a website—it's their *attitudes*. Men and women solve problems differently.

Men spend nearly 25 percent more time online in the home than women. Men also view nearly 40 percent more pages than women. It would be a simple deduction, then, that men dominate the Internet. However, spending more time does not equate to ringing up more sales.

Shopping Behavior on the Web Is Atypical

". . .men and women switch sides when shopping the Web: Men spend lots of time surfing from site to site while women go directly to their destination, click only enough to buy what they want and then log off.

It's pretty much the same way men and women behave with the TV remote control – he restlessly jumps from channel to channel, which leads her to fantasize about strangling him so she can watch just one program all the way through."

— Paco Underhill in Why We Buy

Online shopping sites were developed initially with the male shopper in mind. Developing a more female-friendly shopping site can help you attract these buyers. Historically, women dominate shopping in general.

While conducting customer testing, explore these positions individually as they relate to your store. Observing how men and women navigate the site offers only one dimension of their needs. Ask *why* they make each selection. Then determine their preferences by interviewing them about each subsequent element on the site.

Men still dominate the online shopping scene outside the U.S. In Spain, Switzerland, Germany, and France, over 80 percent of web shoppers are male. Women, however, are shopping online with more frequency in the U.K., and they represent nearly 50 percent of shoppers in Australia and Canada.

Income

Of course, every company wishes all high-income people would covet its site. But learning how income influences interactions is more than that. Variations in income affect the access to different experiences. Income, though, is not static. Today's millionaire can become tomorrow's pauper. Will his expectations change? Probably.

The advertising industry categorizes income by set increments. Income, by itself, may not be indicative of the views and beliefs of the consumer. Coupled with other information, it may be used as an indicator. The customer's hierarchy of needs may be very different for individuals or households making $25,000 a year from those earning over $100,000. At lower levels of income, basic needs like shelter and food are in competition for the wallet. Disposable income for discretionary purposes is limited. Upper income customers may choose to allot a percentage of income merely to items that bring them pleasure.

Income and lifestyle are usually somewhat linked but values can vary. Tracking spending history—how much customers buy, what they purchase, and how often—will give you clues to maximize their investment through add-on purchases. As you develop your database, it will be the analysis of customers' behavior that will help give insight into their potential.

Worldwide, online shoppers have middle-class incomes and are beginning to be more representative of average retail shoppers.

Education

Educational levels have been linked to certain preferences. You can examine your particular store's categories and determine how educational levels might be relevant. More highly educated customers tend to be more affluent and more predisposed to purchase particular categories. Technology products, for example, draw highly educated shoppers. Wine drinkers also tend to be more highly educated than beer drinkers as a group.

Take it a bit further. Track each and every purchase, and then cut the data with each attribute. It could be that education is the primary driver, not age. Knowing the combination is the magic key. Otherwise, you might miss something obvious. Remember, the person purchasing the product is not always the end-user or the one who determines whether a purchase is to be made in the first place.

Educational systems vary around the globe. A high-school education in Europe may be the equivalent of a community college education in the U.S., depending on the course pursued. Japanese education is very intense, competitive, and also equal to a higher education. Be sure to check on equivalencies, because all educational programs are not the same.

While shopping online used to draw highly educated buyers, this is no longer true. The majority of shoppers worldwide do not have a college degree. The educational level of your customers helps you determine how to communicate with them online.

Lifestyle

Some research companies focus exclusively on determining lifestyle segmentation. They slice and dice the data according to gender, geography, income, and other demographics and then apply lifestyle influences. Secondary research is available from these agencies and may augment your data. You may also try to create lifestyle information of your own as your database grows and you are able to interpret and analyze the data succinctly.

Lifestyles vary from person to person. Some people are athletic, while others are career-oriented. Some prefer quaint towns, and others prefer major metropolitan areas. Some like to entertain; others like to be couch potatoes. Some want to keep up with the Joneses, and others need to blaze their own trails. Some people are traditionalists, and others are non-conformists.

Lifestyles are dependent on individual personalities and preferences, and this affects attitudes and purchase behaviors. It also affects how a person relates to a website. If your target customer is non-traditional, he may not feel comfortable with a traditional website.

Lifestyles dictate what people have in their homes and what products they are likely to purchase from you. Because all online customers are Internet users, they have access to technology products. Knowing their level of traditional versus risk-inclined attributes can contribute to determining the product mix and how and why customers may use a product. This gives you insight into add-on sales and the ability to understand the primary uses of the products they purchase. Lifestyle methodologies may also identify items that are relevant to customers' particular circumstances.

Remember that lifestyles vary by region. While Americans may understand the concept of a "soccer mom," it is unlikely that someone from China will use the same definition.

Life Stage

Life stage segments track age thresholds and revolve around a person's marital status, profession, and family status. Other identifying designations, such as "student" or "pensioner," influence attitudes and behaviors. Family patterns also affect preferences. Consumer purchasing patterns vary considerably between families with infants and small children and those with teenagers or grown children.

In addition, non-married adults are growing as a segment in the U.S. Singles represent a wide range of economic choices and spending patterns. Singles, traditionally, have been more interested in entertainment, while couples of childbearing age have been more focused on establishing or providing for a family. Each stage in life influences the products they purchase and the stores in which they shop.

Each decade of life, along with income changes, brings new product preferences. Health changes may determine reliance on medicines, health foods, or health aids. Empty nesters may choose to give up their large homes and SUVs for smaller versions of each. Identifying these stages for target individuals will help categorize and give insight to possible motivating influences.

The following example illustrates some fictional segments:

Segments
Rural, student, 20-year-old male
Urban, professional, middle-aged female
Suburban, blue collar, 30-ish male

After the basic designations are determined, possible product usage may be assigned to each:

Segments with Product Usage Assigned
Rural, student, 20-year-old male—cola drinks, orange juice, milk
Urban, professional, middle-aged female—premium decaf coffee, iced tea, red wine
Suburban, blue collar, 30-ish male—microbrews, cola, hot chocolate

Household Size

The number of people in the household also determines attitudes and behaviors. Family size and related needs influence required activities for the household unit to function. It is generally understood that more family members in the home means more demands on the head of household's time. Also with more members, the need for more shopping instances naturally occurs. Shopping on the web can be a convenience for large families.

But household size is not just an indicator to predict the quantity of shopping. It also may help determine the types of products selected. Customers without small children will most likely be inclined to purchase fine china and crystal, for example.

Ethnic and Cultural Background

Connectivity to the Internet may be higher for some ethnic groups than others. Nearly 70 percent of Asian-American households, for instance, are connected—a very high rate. Comparatively, close to 50 percent of Hispanic households, a little over 40 percent of white households, and about 30 percent of African-American households have Internet connections.

Purchasing behavior does not necessarily correlate with connectivity, but the potential for interaction is real. Awareness of social and ethnic preferences along with global cultural differences will increase your ability to customize information to each individual. Americans of Cuban decent in Florida, for example, differ from Mexican-Americans in Texas. Attitudinal research should be coupled with demographic studies to explore attitudes, preferences, and perceptions. Racial and ethnic identity is key to individualization.

Cultural differences can present even greater challenges when communicating internationally. Language may be misinterpreted—especially slogans and brand names. Colors and images should be unique to the culture. A picture of a cow, for instance, might be inappropriate in India, depending on its usage, while applying the same image in the U.S. could be perfectly acceptable. Regional preferences for colors may be subtle but may trigger unconscious discomfort.

Campaigns and slogans designed for one culture may not have the same meaning in another culture. It's important to verify these with a native speaker of the target country. Chevrolet introduced a campaign several years ago for its Nova brand. But in Spanish, "No Va" means "it does not go." Always consider the implications of global descriptions.

Cultural differences also affect the predictability of loyalty. Some ethnic groups have extremely strong ties to relationships. Identifying those customer segments and balancing them with the other demographic factors targets your customers for loyalty programs.

Geography

It's not an accident that Seattle became the coffee drinking capital of the world. It's somewhat dreary and wet during the Northwest winter, and the warm beverage is a favorite to soothe chilly residents. But if you live in New Orleans, daiquiri bars far outnumber the coffee carts.

Our environment tends to influence our habits and opinions, and regional variances show up in food, clothing, language, opinions, and social interactions. Retail shopping in the U.S. focuses on the shopping mall, but in Europe "high street"—shops located on a major street—shopping is the norm. In Asia, small independent shopkeepers thrive on very specialized merchandise. To some people and cultures, shopping is a social activity. To others, it is a personal activity, such as browsing books. A creative challenge for the web designer is to simulate both activities and products online. Texture and feel are difficult to create online, whereas presenting product specs is very easy.

Customers are more likely to shop on their lunch hour in Europe than in the U.S., venturing out on foot or using public transportation to run errands. Large cities in the U.S., such as New York, are closer to the European model.

When conducting primary research, it's important to include a variety of test subjects representing the geographies that you intend to study. Geographical differences and varying time zones also affect web purchasing. Adequately staffing customer support centers at potential peak hours can ease the wait time for the customer.

Psychographics

Understanding customers is more than mining demographic data. There is a psychographic element as well, as shown in Figure 2-1. Psychographics include the activities, attitudes, values, opinions, and interests of the consumers. They ultimately affect motivations, needs, and personality traits that affect buying behavior. Some businesses actually name a person in a target segment to replicate an actual customer. If "Jane" is their target, they will continually ask what "Jane" would think about each program or service they propose. This technique certainly brings the staff closer to thinking about the customer, but it doesn't help that only "Jane" will benefit and "Jim" may not.

Psychographics address the emotional aspects of the consumers. What they believe can affect how they behave and what they purchase. For instance, are they health conscious, environmentally concerned, or politically active? Understanding your consumers' "hot buttons" will help you to avoid using offensive material in your website and to include relevant information. You may also appeal to their preferences, thereby gaining loyal customers.

Psychographics are made up of all the psychological variables that shape each person. The following are five key psychographic elements:

- Social styles
- Religious beliefs
- Career choices
- Attitudes
- Perceptions

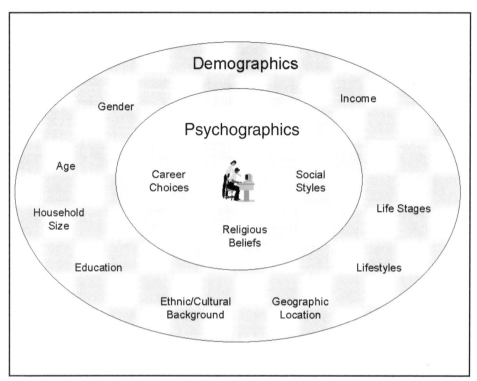

Figure 2–1 Each demographic and psychographic element adds a dimension to customer understanding.

Social Styles

Everyone has his or her own social style. Understanding the different styles gives you clues on how best to present information in a website. It also assists you in creating the right kind of information in a manner to which they can easily relate.

There are four main personality types into which a person can be classified:

1. **Type A's:** "Type A's" get things done and make quick decisions. These are visionaries and risk takers. They assess situations quickly and synthesize information that is relevant. This type tends to be of a "perfectionist" nature and can be hard to please. They likely will not have the patience to continue searching a website if it takes too long.

2. **Analyticals:** These people require lots of facts and information and are typically indecisive. They are very much risk-averse and require lots of reassurance before making decisions. Even when they ultimately are pressured to make a decision, they require lots of hand-holding and validation that they made the right decision.

3. **Sociables:** This style type reflects people who are very socially active and community minded. Decisions are typically based on opinion or group consensus. This style makes

up the majority of personality types. It is an important style to consider, because they can influence and be influenced through the opinions and perceptions of others. They are also risk-averse; yet, this aversion can be mitigated by a testimonial or trusted opinion of another.

4. **Competitives:** These are communicative and competitive people and generally are in professions such as sales and entertainment. They are creative, animated, and enthusiastic. They tend to make emotion-based decisions and can be impulse-driven. They aspire to public acknowledgement and seek the "audience" and approval of others. They also tend to get bored easily and will shop on sites that are interesting rather than informative.

Each person is different and your customers will no doubt be an unpredictable blend of varied kinds of behavioral styles. Most people have a dominant style that is easily recognizable, but they have attributes in the other styles, depending on the situation. For example, a person may have a type-A style at work, managing a department, yet have a sociable style while coaching children's basketball after school.

Knowing the personality types of your key customers gives you clues about how much information to provide as they shop your website. For example, the analyticals require massive amounts of information. While you wouldn't want to hinder a type-A—who makes decisions quickly—you would want to provide depth of information to satiate the voracious hunger of those people who study, compare, and deeply research prior to making a purchase decision. Technical products are a favorite of this group and may require additional coverage and information in your site. This can be done with links and readily accessible layers of information. Providing toll-free support in pre-sales is necessary for this personality style and type.

Anticipating various behavior styles influences web design to accommodate how people make decisions. If a large part of your customer base is of the amiable style, then testimonials, endorsements, and other referrals can be provided to motivate the shopper to take action. Too much information can get in the way of a "driver" who will make a quick decision based on critical, "bottom line" types of information. The web designer's task is to provide relevant information, while at the same time, limiting the information through which a customer must sort, depending on the customer's personality style and shopping preferences.

Understanding styles becomes more important in relationship marketing activities, whereby communications can be structured to converse with customers on a repetitive basis. If your customer has an expressive style, sending him announcements of new products that are filled with specifications can turn him off. However, announcements like this would be of interest to analytical types.

Religious Beliefs

Religion strongly impacts a customer's psychographics. Similar to cultural differences, dominant religious beliefs and behaviors are deeply instilled. More than 70 percent of the world's population is non-Christian, so global selling motions must accommodate this diversity of beliefs.

Global websites that leverage content and images across countries must aspire to consider and deliver respect for each group's citizens. Direct marketing activities must also consider global religious implications. For example, some religions prohibit selling and buying on holy or festival days, so the timing of a new product offer must be calculated. The Sabbath varies from religion to religion. Be aware that sending e-mail promotions during a religious holiday may cause offense.

Holy Days vary in different religions and cultures. Winter holidays include Christmas, Christmas Eve, Kwanzaa, and Hanukkah, among others. Spring religious holidays include Easter and Passover. Specific celebration dates vary from year to year. Most brick-and-mortar stores close in the U.S. during these times. Staffing a web-center operation may be more profitable to accommodate those who don't practice a particular religion during these times.

Religious holidays may be a boon to shopping as well. Gifts, flowers, and other remembrances are frequently exchanged during these observances. By knowing how each is celebrated, web designers can invite shoppers to select appropriate items for the occasion.

In addition to specific holiday times, be aware of symbols that may conflict with a person or country's belief structure. An asterisk poorly imaged on a screen may appear to be a swastika. An old hieroglyph may be considered a demon by some cultures. The number 666 may be offensive to some groups. The usage of hands in images in the U.S. is acceptable, but in some countries, it is offensive.

Careers

Career choices affect the market in which people work and, for retailers, the opportunity to have a business customer. Career choices can be vocational, professional, or trade related. Some members of professional groups identify with each other culturally. Doctors, police, and fire fighters, for example, share experiences unique from others in the community. You may create segments based on known professions or titles. Also, careers typically map to income. Income is an indicator of spending and disposable income.

There has been a gradual shift to white-collar occupations. The labor force has been in transition—moving from manufacturing to computer and service-related industries. The trend is also shifting toward knowledge workers—those occupations represented by teaching, law, engineering, programming, and management.

How People Process Information

How we choose, internalize, process, and store information has an effect on how we learn and use information. Customers ultimately make purchase decisions based on bits of information. People select the information they deem important or relevant and ignore the rest. Then the information is simplified and stored in the brain. We transform concepts as well as sensory data.

After the information is locked in our memory, it is then categorized. The categories help us classify the information even further and manage the information in a complex environment.

Information is melded with our own experiences and perceptions. This is the process of inserting new information into the categories we have already created in our minds. When communications are exchanged between businesses and individuals, the resulting beliefs will be based on the information provided plus the prior experiences we have had with that business or a similar business.

It is this ongoing matching and judging that contributes to the learning process. People do not learn about one concept independent of every other category stored in the brain. That's why the concept of integration is so important. People learn about products and shop for them in an integrated fashion, not in an isolated mode. The communication between the buyer and seller is not a one-way model either. It is a bi-directional process.

There are four information-processing responses:

- Attention
- Learning
- Acceptance
- Motivation

Shoppers use these responses to process and evaluate information about products and, ultimately, to select and purchase. Customers also determine their preferences for companies and brands in the same manner.

Attention

Attention is a response that can be stimulated either involuntarily or voluntarily. Involuntary attention is initiated by external stimuli, but voluntary attention is more goal driven. A store can be the recipient of either.

Advertising, promotions, sights, sounds, smells, and other sensory elements can stimulate shoppers. But initial intention induced by these lasts only a fraction of a second. That's why advertising requires many exposures to be effective.

Customers may also be influenced by the need that brought them to the store in the first place. In order for the consumer to fulfill his goal, however, the store must find ways to facilitate his actions.

Learning

Passive learning engages the brain in an unconscious way. This rote form of learning is the result of repetitive stimuli. Usually, associations are formed in the brain as a result. Advertising depends on this sort of learning because most consumers do not consciously choose to learn about many of the products promoted. A purchase should not depend on a customer's need to learn a new technique.

Brand or store association and recall will link to the established associations in the consumer's brain. The stimulus, in this case, must be the store, and the association is the store-specific value proposition. All stores should maintain the association over time.

Acceptance

The customer must accept that a shopping need exists in order to make a purchase. If he agrees with the association that the brand or store presents, he will accept the value proposition or benefit statement and be more likely to make the purchase at that website or store. Personal disagreement with the association leads to rejection. That's why the benefit belief must be based on knowledge of the consumer and his lifestyle and category needs.

Motivation

In order to achieve motivation, the customer must manifest learning and acceptance in an emotional response. Emotional elements stimulate the customer's purchase motivations automatically. They are deeply ingrained and not a factor of conscious learning. Color, music, pictures, sound, and movement all stimulate to elicit various emotions. Each of these can lead to a variety of emotions from "anxiety" to "pleasing" to "exciting."

Emotions linked to motivation may include problem removal, disappointment, or convenience. The store has the power to influence each. Emotions must be fostered to correspond with the motivation linked to satisfying a shopping need.

Attitudes

An attitude is an acquired predisposition or feeling toward a product or service that can reflect customers' values. Their reactions to products, services, brands, and stores will influence their purchases. Because people develop and learn attitudes, attitudes can change with time depending on each person's experience.

Opinion research is used to determine what people believe about their shopping interactions. Each brand will represent an association in the consumer's mind. A store, product, or website should reinforce a positive association with each shopping encounter. Attitudes can be shaped by the customer's family, the community, employment, economics, and education.

It's possible to measure attitudes even though they are a form of behavior. But because they are dynamic, they cannot be measured for more than a snapshot of time. Although continuous measures can be taken and predictions made about future behavior, we can't say with certainty how attitudes will be used when it comes time to make a purchasing decision.

We can, however, try to develop approaches to shape behavior. Because attitudes are learned, they can be changed with external communication. Consumers' attitudes about brands, companies, and products and how they interact can determine their purchasing habits. Integrating positive communications and customer-focused programs will help shape attitudes and behaviors.

Perceptions

Perceptions reflect selection of information to create insight and discrimination. Filtered through the five senses, information is screened and processed to filter out that which does not interest the receiver. Perception differs from opinion only in degree.

Retailers want customers to retain and agree with messages sent their way. Unfortunately, when customers are bombarded with information daily, they retain only a small fraction. Online merchants' objectives will be served by limiting messages to quality information in a selective way, rather than cluttering the web with too much stimuli—especially billboard ads.

Commitment

Consumer commitment is the demonstration of interest in a product or brand and can be manifested at several levels. A benign level of commitment can be surfing a website. When the customer actually looks for more information, settles on a website, or makes an inquiry, he is showing a level of interest upon which a business can act.

A more serious form of commitment is an actual purchase. Even when a customer purchases a related product, the commitment is made. For instance, if a customer purchases a set of skis, he has made a commitment to ski. Resellers can assume, then, that he may need other ski equipment – poles, clothes, gloves, and hats.

Each inquiry has the potential for commitment. Each response, request, or visit to a store or website must be handled in a responsive manner. It's important to follow up with inquiries as quickly as complaints. Every effort should be made to turn the prospect into a customer.

Types of Research

Research can be classified as primary or secondary. Primary research is new research either conducted in-house or contracted from companies specializing in the discipline. Studies may be qualitative or quantitative, and methodologies vary depending on the nature of the research. Qualitative research is usually conducted in small groups or individually because the intention is to probe for opinions and reactions. Quantitative research requires large sample sizes to validate the findings and usually presents results with some degree of numerical certainty.

Secondary research may be purchased from agencies, consultants, or other research providers. It is also available by contracting on an annual basis with any number of data firms. General or specific information is available on your competitors or customers both locally and globally.

Most often, secondary research can provide general demographic information. In order to capture intimate knowledge of the consumer, primary research is conducted to provide psychographic, attitudinal, and behavioral research.

It's important to differentiate between a customer's attitudes or beliefs and his actual behavior. Normally, asking the respondent about his feelings in a study or focus group—a small gathering of targeted participants—will reveal his opinions and attitudes. But to determine his behavior, he must be observed as he is performing a task. It is most effective to observe the subject when he is unaware he is being watched. This behavior can be observed in a usability testing or other research facility or in an actual shopping environment.

Research on a Shoestring Budget

Not all research needs to go through the formality of focus groups or purchased demographic information. "Next bench" research—what typically happens in an engineering environment when a developer asks the person at the "next bench" to do an impromptu or informal test— gives first-pass insight and creates a "best guess" consideration for a model. The model is not perfect, yet it is better than asking no one at all. This method is used more extensively when the product is a technological breakthrough and can relate to new ideas in web design. Later in the process, though, it's important to gain real customer response to the model.

Use caution when testing or researching strictly in an engineering environment, however. Research becomes tainted with "feature creep" that may provide elegant solutions for problems that have yet to be discovered.

This kind of research can be used when budgets are small or non-existent or when timing is short. "Next bench" research in today's environment can be extrapolated to talking with your neighbors, friends, or business associates that most closely resemble your target customers. It can be as simple as asking someone in your office or a parent of your child's friend to give her honest opinion regarding ease of use on a simple website task. For example, you can present a scenario, such as the following example, to test websites that sell clothing and have her search, find, and purchase a product based on the task's directions:

"You have a 14-year-old son who is six feet tall and weighs 135 pounds. On the website (yours, if you have clothing), find a pair of pants that have waist and inseam measurements of 29x34." People search with specific attributes in mind. Most clothing sites do not allow for a search by size. Determining the difficulty through personal testing may help you refine your prototype before moving on to more expensive testing.

Misusing Research

Research is intended to provide information to make decisions and strategically influence the programs you design or implement based on new insight. It is not intended to substantiate a given position. If the research you conduct contradicts your prior data, you must be open to reevaluating your results.

Research helps you not only target and design the website for the right people, it also helps you to predict the chances that a particular customer will purchase future products. Synthesizing the right insight from customers is an art that requires careful analysis to extract the nuggets to motivate people to purchase. Success depends on the questions you ask and how you ask them.

Grouping individuals into arbitrary categories or isolating one specific example are the two extremes of the spectrum. The best way to think like a customer is to surround yourself with actual consumers. You can talk to them on the phone, conduct web conversations, see them at trade shows, go to competitive retail stores and watch them—any activity that will enable you to understand their issues. Of course, it's best to observe them in their natural environment—their place of work, their home, or wherever they use the products and services you sell.

Shoppers vs. Customers

There's a difference between shoppers and customers. Shoppers are browsers, searching for information on products and services. They may or may not become buyers. That's why measuring the number of clicks on your site may not lead to profitability. Lots of browsers or even a few shoppers clicking more than once can wreak havoc with your statistics. The only way to accurately measure a current customer is by her level of purchasing.

Shoppers have the potential to become customers. The lasting value is gaining the loyalty of a customer for repeat purchases. You will need to assign targets to each in your investment model. And don't forget to examine your potential customers in the same way that you evaluate your existing customers. Those you ignore today could be your target customers tomorrow. When segmenting, determine the group that has the most future potential and put some programs together to cultivate them. You may choose not to invest in groups that have moderate current activity if their potential is minimal.

Three Types of Shoppers

Just as with traditional sales, e-tailers must accommodate a variety of shopper types. Internet users are not just "techies" anymore, and their behavior mirrors traditional retail and catalog shopping behavior.

There are three main categories of shoppers. It's incumbent on the merchant to determine how entering customers fit into each category.

1. **Data-shoppers**: The majority of customers shopping for products online seek information before they determine the "store" in which to purchase. Depending on the product, data-shoppers may investigate online and buy at retail or call a toll-free number to complete the transaction. This typically occurs when the customer lacks the necessary and required information to make a purchase decision online.

2. **Browser-buyers**: These people browse online stores and will purchase if they find a product they want or need. They trust the store, and they usually have a successful experience and are provided the right information that helps them make a buying decision.

3. **Decision-buyers**: These customers are task-focused. They already know what they want and balance price with the integrity and trust in the online merchant.

In addition to different types of shoppers, there are various shopping models to take into account. Whether a customer is a first-time buyer or a repeat customer, your site must accommodate the diversity of customers who hunt, browse, and purchase. Some shoppers use navigational category links in a linear path, while others use the search option. Repeat purchasers are most likely to belong to the decision-buyer category.

Shoppers can have a great deal of influence even if they don't turn into buyers in each instance. They can share their experiences with others, recommend your site, or destroy your reputation.

Buying Behavior

The customer employs different decision-making processes depending on the involvement required for purchasing each product. Some products are routine purchases and require little preparation or thought. Others are high-involvement purchases and take deliberation and even research.

Most customers spend little effort selecting and purchasing a pencil. Sometimes, these low-involvement purchases are even made on impulse. However, buying a high-priced item such as a car or computer will take more thought. The customer will need to search for information, evaluate alternatives, and decide where to purchase; he may even need to arrange for additional support functions, such as financing.

Although the information process is often conducted on the web, the goal should be to integrate this process with the purchasing site selection. Customers may select a brand and then find a store or site that offers it, or they may select the retailer first and select from the available brands. Combining information, services, and products gives the e-tailer an advantage in the selection process.

Lifetime Customer Value

A customer's first purchase begins a cycle of sales opportunities. This cycle is the Lifetime Customer Value (LCV), and it is core to an ongoing customer relationship. Cultivating the most valuable customers and measuring their potential sales over time delivers the relative value of their lifetime worth.

Using the LCV as a benchmark, you can determine the level of investment you need to make in your most loyal customers. Compare this with the cost of gaining awareness and preference of new customers. New customer acquisition costs are higher than those related to retaining a customer. You'll also be able to determine the loss to your business if this customer should abandon his shopping cart. An LCV cycle depicting the value of repeated purchases is reflected in Figure 2-2.

The LCV is based on the average shopping cart purchases over time, the frequency of purchases, demographic and target customer data, and the type of products purchased. Depending on the product lines, it may also include the number of products or units purchased and usage

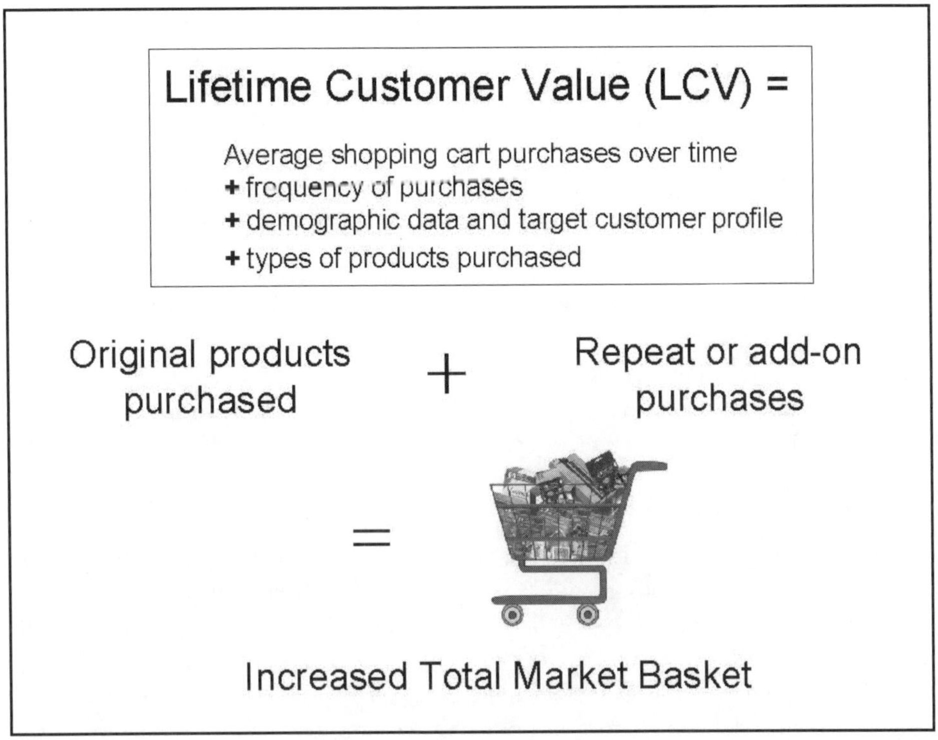

Lifetime Customer Value (LCV) =

Average shopping cart purchases over time
+ frequency of purchases
+ demographic data and target customer profile
+ types of products purchased

Original products purchased   **+**   Repeat or add-on purchases

=

Increased Total Market Basket

Figure 2–2 A repeat customer is more valuable than a one-time buyer

rates. By monitoring customer purchases, you can evaluate the likelihood of repeat, routine, or add-on purchases.

Building Customer Relationships

Consumer loyalty and retention begins with the value proposition you provide to your customers. To know if you're on track with your value proposition, you need to take the following steps. Here are four ways to generate unprecedented customer satisfaction:

- Listen to your customers, and create a dialog with them.
- Capture and analyze information about them.
- Know customer retention methodologies, and practice them.
- Develop and implement loyalty programs for your key customer segments.

Understanding your customers and linking your value proposition to their needs, develops stronger and longer lasting relationships. Ensuring that all customer information is incorporated into plans and programs will help develop loyalty.

Listening to Customers

If your web store or company is fairly large, you can monitor chat rooms designed to share information about your goods. You may, however, get an earful. The most informative sessions are those **not** sponsored by the merchant.

Complaints can be annoying, but your firm needs to ask if the complaints are warranted and if resolution is possible. It's easy to dismiss a complaint and make excuses, but this may be your most valuable research.

Look carefully at complaints—most often, they are based on legitimate customer concerns. Remember, having a focus on the customer does not provide a license to sell poor products or conduct poor marketing campaigns. Providing good quality is the baseline. Great customer programs build on the basics.

If you can satisfy customer concerns, you can gain the loyalty of most customers. If they are ignored, the issue may not go away, but your customer will.

Greasing the Squeaky Wheel

At retail, customers vote with their feet. Online, customers may vote with a click to another website. If you're lucky, however, they will tell you first what bothers them and give you a chance to resolve a problem. Unless they take time to tell you, you may never even know that something is wrong.

One method of investigating customer complaints is to log the top ten issues with your customer service or support department. What repeat questions are they getting from customers? If you can fix those, then it's possible that you have resolved problems for a good portion of customers that have not taken the time to contact you. However, you should expect that after you fix the top ten, another crop of ten surfaces.

After the issues have been identified, it's necessary to put a plan in place and create solutions—even if they're costly. Knowing there are issues to solve and not acting will never help you occupy the preferred place in the customer's mind. And that's exactly the position you need if you want to own a top brand—whether you're a manufacturer or online retailer.

For example, one customer-focused online retailer actually increased prices on the website until a major link in the value delivery system was fixed. While this act affected short-term sales initially, the retailer won long-term sales by limiting exposure of its customers to potential dissatisfaction.

Timing also is key. The optimal point in time to address customer needs is before your site has been developed or your programs or services defined. Conducting customer research needs to be part of your earliest activities and should be a cornerstone of your strategies.

Dissatisfying a Customer

You can alienate a customer forever with one word—spam. Spam is unsolicited e-mail. There is so much spam today that people are afraid to open their in-boxes. This practice is so unwelcome that companies sending spam should be prepared to lose that customer for life.

Unfortunately, the prevalence of spam is rising. E-mail is a legitimate tool if the permission of the recipient is obtained—although we don't recommend inundating customers with messages. Spam, however, is not acceptable under any circumstances. The company that sends spam does so at its own peril.

Managing Customer Relationships

There are many ways that companies manage the relationship with the consumer. One newer methodology, Customer Relationship Management (CRM), has taken hold of the marketplace.

CRM focuses on the consumer as the center of a business. It involves the customer at every stage of business development—from product planning through customer service. CRM is intelligence-based to understand what, where, and when the customer buys. The data is transformed into improved programs, products, and services. The risk to a company managing a CRM process is to become successful at collecting the information, but then either analyzing it incorrectly or, worse yet, never using the results.

Many companies decide to implement CRM programs only to manipulate customers in order to increase profits rather than truly addressing consumer concerns. Increasing profitability is obviously a goal for business, and creating effective customer programs is the best way to deliver profit. But to mask non-customer focused company objectives in customer clothing will lead your company astray. The best way to increase the bottom line is to actually improve your actions.

Let's look at an example. A telephone company prided itself on its consumer-focused programs. This company offered the best incentives in the industry—to both attract new customers and retain existing customers. If a heavy user made an overture to switch providers, they quickly offered him a financial reward to stay with the company.

This strategy seemed to be successful, and this company can point to the number of customers they have "saved" from the competition. They are happy with their programs and know they are customer-focused. But what is the customer issue they were solving? Were people switching due to high costs? If they were, a one-time payment would not save them from their high monthly bills.

If this company had only examined a customer chat room, they might have gained some insight into the true customer problem. Their per-minute charges were a little more than the competition, but the site revealed customer wrath well beyond any pricing issue. In fact, the company had a huge problem with its customer service. It turns out that billing inaccuracies caused customers to call and complain about being charged for calls they didn't make.

Once in the company phone tree, they were consistently notified that the wait for service would be 45 minutes. They received this same message any time of the day they called. After waiting 45 minutes, customers would then be treated to service representatives who were rude and arrogant. Complaints were never resolved in the customer's favor.

Chat rooms and websites revealed paper trails as well. Letters to customers portrayed a company that clearly wasn't reading customer messages. Responses were by form letters and ignored customers' issues. Still oblivious to the problem, the company continued to hand out large checks to entice customers to remain loyal. This begs for a definition of loyalty.

Capturing Customer Information

One-to-one marketing or CRM programs are usually anchored by a database used to consolidate information from multiple sources. CRM strategies are dependent on the ability to collect consumer data, determine the profiles of selected customers and their value, and deliver individualized services to customers. The database component merges information from sales, service, marketing, and other functions. The ultimate objective is to obtain a 3-D view of the customer at every touch point.

The best CRM programs are interactive for use by sales associates, service personnel, marketing staff, IT designers, and others who come into contact with customers. Databases are designed to instantly retrieve the latest information about shoppers—their purchase history, their segment profiles, their value to the company, outstanding service issues, preferences, and current orders.

It's not enough, however, to collect information. A true CRM program is dependent on how the information is managed and used for customer interactions. The number and quality of contacts, personalization, the relevancy to the consumer, and timely updates measure effective implementation. The database also needs to address future capabilities for the customer, not just operational efficiencies.

Each time the customer logs on to your site, she can be greeted by name, asked if she would like to buy any of the items in her purchase history, given a status report on any outstanding orders or repairs, and provided with ideas for future solutions based on the information she has provided. She can be rewarded with a thank-you gift or promotion for being a most-valued customer.

CRM programs offer the ability to differentiate visitors as they interact with the site and each should be managed individually. Each contact must be customized for the consumer based on what you have learned. To be targeted, this requires identifying their personality types so you know and can deliver their preferred method of communication. Through analysis, you can learn how to influence shopping preferences.

Globally, online shoppers are still predominantly purchasing books, CDs, tickets, and electronic equipment. Moving them to buy softer items will largely depend on building trust, but it represents a significant opportunity. Product offerings will evolve over time as consumer purchases redefine the product mix.

Some organizations use CRM stepped features to gather more information from customers. As visitors provide additional information, they are allowed access to further content. Gaining customer information is integral to the database, and consumers can also provide instant feedback for improved service. But CRM programs need to implement safeguards against badgering the customer or restricting access to key information. A customer benefit may be turned into dissatisfaction through mismanagement.

Retailers are beginning to take advantage of CRM as well. They are gaining expertise in electronic data management and are integrating Internet-enabled kiosks in actual retail stores. Ultimately, they will be able to replace outdated point-of-purchase programs with true CRM capabilities.

The e-Store Advantage

E-stores are more uniquely positioned to take advantage of interactive customized relationships. Most online shoppers worldwide made purchases that would otherwise have been made in traditional stores. Over 90 percent plan to make online purchases in the next year.

It's still difficult to greet the customer personally and instantly access past shopping behavior in a store environment. It's also difficult to get people to spend their shopping time at a retail kiosk. Many of these units, containing an Internet terminal and a printer, only offer coupons. But in the next few years, as many as a quarter million kiosks may appear in retail locations. Traditional retailers have also aligned with online retailers to provide more sophisticated online shopping. Strategic alliances could provide easy access for retailers hoping to offer both clicks and mortar. About a third of shoppers prefer to purchase at sites that offer a physical outlet.

There are challenges for the future. Nearly 80 percent of online visitors research products or services on the web and ultimately purchase in both retail and web stores. By tracking e-shopping exclusively, important information about web usage may be missed. Combining customer intelligence, retail customer information, and online customer information provides a complete view of the customer.

Internet purchases are expected to reach the levels of other alternate channels in the next few years. It will be key to track whether the increased sales will pull from catalog, direct mail, or cable television, or from traditional retail channels to understand whether customers are actually modifying their buying behavior or merely cannibalizing similar shopping methods. In the past, it was easier to identify a typical Internet user, but today's web use may represent any of a number of diverse behavior types. Characterizing customers and keeping their information current will be the challenge.

Measuring Customer Programs

How do you know when your CRM program has achieved success? First, you must know what you want to achieve before you begin. The right time to identify the correct metrics is at the inception of your program. The exact measures will depend on the specific objectives you want to achieve. However, limiting your success to cost savings may be shortsighted.

A CRM program is a long-term strategy to grow customer loyalty. Linking it to an annual budget will diffuse its impact. Focusing on customer value, process improvements, service improvements, retention of high-value customer segments, and market share will provide more accurate measures and allow the program to gain strategic importance.

Several years ago, companies focused on quality management programs. These were diffused when the economy worsened. Then firms became dedicated to efficiency programs. Historically, commerce and manufacturing have cycled between the two—quantity and quality—depending on financial security. Customer-focused programs must be neither a fad nor a cycle. They are the basic tenet of business that firms are merely rediscovering—especially because the customer seemed to be lost in the rush to achieve profit. However, companies now recognize that profit is unachievable without the customer component.

Measuring your success is the only way to ensure that the customer is central to your business strategy. It will also serve to encourage true progress and not merely limit a CRM program to "lip service." It's critical to gain internal company "buy-in" to ensure that the CRM program is not degraded.

Analyzing Shopping Habits

Internet shoppers may not actually be more price-sensitive than other shoppers, but they do have instant access to price comparisons. Nearly 50 percent "promotion surf" to find the best deals. The Internet has actually fostered this behavior. By line-listing products, goods that could be differentiated have turned into commodities. Online brokers have added to the impression that all products and services are equal, and price is the driving factor. However, it would be simplistic to characterize Internet shoppers as simply cost-driven.

There is a fundamental shift in consumer behavior and shopping habits in this blended shopping environment. It's difficult to determine how fast-moving goods are purchased through complex channels. Your goal is to convert shoppers to buyers and visits to sales transactions. Also, shopping habits vary from country to country depending on their level of development. Surveys and questionnaires must be customized to reflect country differences.

Internet usage continues to increase. But most visitors still favor using the web for research and e-mail. And e-shoppers use the Internet for shopping research but may not make their purchases online due to a variety of factors. Security, trust, issues with returns, problems with ordering mechanisms, the need for immediacy, and technical issues all create barriers to purchasing.

Worldwide, the issue of high shipping costs is the primary reason that customers abandon their shopping carts. Shipping costs, though, are trade-offs for convenience and may ultimately be worth the extra charge.

Although online consumers are not necessarily price-driven, they expect online goods to cost less than in a retail store, where the overhead is perceived to be much greater. Minimum advertised pricing (MAP) policies level the playing field for all types of selling motions by advertising products no lower than the set price. MAP policies cause e-tailers to look at other ways to show differentiation for their store from another's, such as superior customer service or an intuitive and easy-to-use website.

Most CRM programs focus on conducting primary research online to determine the identity of the customer. It's common to select a few significant questions and query customers as they enter a site. Here are some questions to ask your customers:

- Why did you choose to visit?
- How did you get to this site?
- What do you want to accomplish here?
- What are your expectations?

But it's also important to determine the customer's overall shopping behavior and attitudes. These questions illustrate how you might design your survey to capture their channel choices:

- Where else do you shop—retail, mail order, catalog, TV?
- How frequently do you shop?
- What else do you buy?
- How urgent is your proposed purchase?
- Have you purchased online? How often? Have you experienced difficulty?

Customer behavior is a moving target. A database will be outdated the instant it is completed. Understand that this is a science and a continuing effort that doesn't end with the first deliverable. Predicting consumer behavior depends on a combination of querying the customer, using secondary sources, and tracking current actions. Identifying specific sets of actions will determine their propensity to purchase.

With technology innovations and industry intensification, market trends are for consumers to stay connected and expect simplicity, control, speed, privacy, security, and customized solutions.

Customer-Retention Methodologies

Most companies focus their activities on acquiring a customer. For example, they may provide a toll-free number for pre-sales information. However, after the customer purchases, she may be required to pay for any support received from the company—including asking questions.

True customer retention and relationship marketing address the entire purchase and support cycle throughout the lifetime of the product and the lifetime of the relationship with the customer. When products need replacement, the hopeful intent is for the customer to return to the company that stood by her side when she needed help.

Good Customer Service—A Customer Requirement

Good customer service is not only a customer requirement, it is also a fundamental methodology in a store's customer retention strategy. Nearly three-fourths of online customers surveyed said they would discontinue conducting business with a company if they experienced poor customer service.

For multi-channel stores, this integration becomes imperative. If a customer has a problem with a catalog order, he will not understand why the same company's physical store will not take the item back as a return. But this is still often the case. Now with online shopping, ease of returning products—no matter what the reason—is essential, and some retail outlets now provide for this customer need. They recognize that a customer's bad experience with a store's online business transfers in the customer's mind to all of its sales channels.

Privacy and Security

Customers need to know they will be protected while accessing your website. If they feel at risk, they can't offer their loyalty. Guaranteeing their protection is crucial if they are to provide personal information.

Building trusted relationships depends on delivering secure credit card transactions, protecting the consumer's privacy and personal information, gaining permission to contact customers on the web, and preventing virus activity.

There is a direct correlation between offering a strong privacy policy as part of an overall CRM program and increased profits. This information that customers provide is the cornerstone to developing strong customized programs.

Emotionally, the online customer needs to feel safe. Selling names or lists for use by other websites will degrade the trust that your customer has built with you. It may also violate some legal regulations globally.

Credit card transactions must be secure as well. Companies offering ways to circumvent posting card numbers on the web are perceived as providing an extra service. Some creative ways to manage credit card privacy include establishing codes, pre-authorizing by phone, or setting up an Internet or company-only card that will later transform to the authorizer's credit card.

Determine your risk vulnerability frequently by auditing your site. Hiring independent security firms will give you the best results. Verify your system internally often to ensure that your security systems are intact, and find ways to reassure the customer. Anyone can claim that transactions are secure. You must prove it.

Many companies now employ chief privacy officers (CPOs) who operate on the same level as COOs and other executives. Their primary responsibility is to protect the privacy of their customers' personal information. Establishment of the position is in direct response to increasing legislation to protect consumer privacy—especially their medical and financial records. In addition, reports of corporate abuse of personal data has put pressure on companies to ensure that records are not misused and that there is no intrusion into the privacy of their customers.

Employing privacy programs requires companies to conduct complete audits of their systems to determine what information they hold and what they ultimately do with the data. These programs have also been extended to ensure employee privacy and link with suppliers to create seamless protection.

Online stores have access to customers' names, addresses, credit card numbers and other sensitive data. It's prudent not only to protect the information from web hackers, but also to secure the information within the company itself.

Hostage Programs or Loyalty Programs?

The most popular loyalty program among retailers today is the loyalty or affinity card. Consumers are issued a card with the promise of rebates, access to special prices, or promotional merchandise. In exchange, the customer furnishes personal information to the company and allows the monitoring of future purchases.

Since the programs have proliferated, consumers are now inundated with wallets full of plastic or cardboard affinity cards. Each time they make a purchase, they have to search for their "special" cards in order to get discounts that they were able to receive without cards before the programs were enacted.

Few companies have been able to use the data collected effectively. Hallmark has been at the forefront of the movement and is an exception. The card manufacturer created a "Gold Standard" rewards program. Purchases at Hallmark stores are credited to an account developed for each customer. At certain dollar thresholds, consumers are mailed certificates redeemable for merchandise.

Many of these programs, however, have fallen short of their objectives. It's true that companies have been able to collect consumer data. Unfortunately, by the time systems have been designed to utilize these databases, the information is usually too dated. Some firms never even get that far and wind up in a perpetual collection mode, while consumers keep digging for the cards.

In the 1950s and 60s, green and blue stamps were offered with many purchases. The stamps were redeemed for merchandise at special redemption centers. Popular with consumers, the stamps did not differentiate merchants because they were so widely distributed—even gas stations presented them with each purchase. But customers did notice when they were *not* available. They looked forward to pasting the small stamps into specially provided books so they could ultimately exchange them for luggage, lamps, and dishes. Consumers were disappointed when the stamps were no longer offered. Banks, gas stations, and other industries vying for the same customers supplied them with gifts and cash as substitutes.

If affinity cards disappeared tomorrow, would customers be outraged? Not likely. Some, such as frequent flyer airline programs, enjoy popularity. However, supermarket and drug store cards are often viewed more as an annoyance. The key to profitability is building long-term relationships with customers, and that requires connection and interdependence.

The true measure of loyalty as opposed to a hostage situation is if the customer would continue to purchase or use a service if there were no monetary incentive. With the lure of valuable hotel points and frequent flyer miles, how would a company know that the customer would stick by them if those programs were no longer available? Is the customer loyal to the company or loyal to the program? It could be that a customer is just waiting for something better to come along, and when it does, he will switch.

Measuring loyalty helps you track results over time. An index based on value, intent to recommend, and intent to repurchase is a good indicator of the degree of a customer's loyalty. Current loyalty program offers must be factored in, however, because programs may or may not be ongoing. Comparing the loyalty index during and after a program gives you a more precise loyalty metric.

The Customer Lifecycle

How do you monitor your customer throughout the lifecycle? Each customer enters the buying process at a different stage. This is most apparent with technology products and is not necessarily transferable to a commodity.

However, the Internet is, in essence, a technology product from an adoption perspective. Understanding how the customer interacts with your site or your products and when will help you target the correct intervention point. Pinpointing your communications to lifecycle stages will avoid a shotgun effect and will solidify your relationship with your customer as an evolutionary process.

Identifying Your Most Valuable Customers

You can identify your top customers by analyzing historical sales for dollar volume and frequency of repeat purchases. The data must be carefully analyzed because repeat customers can be more valuable over time than one-time, large ticket item purchasers. This analysis must then be matched up with the demographics and other attributes and characteristics you've previously identified in your customer segmentation. Integrating all of these elements gives you a good picture of your key customers. You will also need to include customers you *want* to have in your cultivation plan.

The opportunity equals the combination of customer retention and the value of all future profit plus those customers you deem to be potentially valuable over the lifecycle—minus the investment required to keep and to acquire them. It also includes future profit made by referrals. Prospective customers who visit your website prior to purchase are much more likely to become buyers than to become non-visitors.

Investments in personalization, promotions, and communications depend on the ranked value of your customers. Once your customers are identified and ranked, you can apply communication and program levels appropriate to their value as shown in Figure 2-3.

It's equally important to establish the identity of the consumers that do not measure up. Spending time and money on this group drains the company of the ability to cultivate new and more attractive customers.

Direct mail companies use a similar technique to determine their mailing investment to each customer segment. After dividing the customer base into ten equal groups, they then rank based on profit potential. These companies must ensure the cost of catalogs is worth the ultimate customer value.

After customer segments are defined, the data are incorporated into future forecasts to make product selection, pricing, inventory management, and promotion decisions.

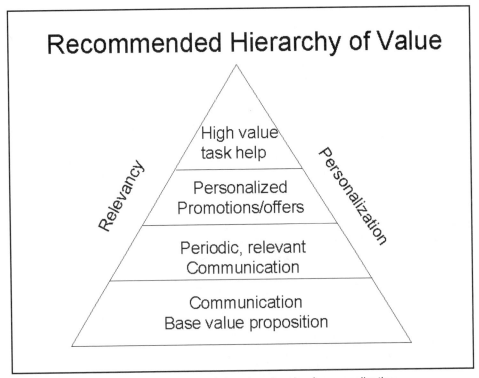

Figure 2–3 The value of the customer determines levels of personalization.

Business-to-Business Relationships

Up to this point, we have used the terms "customer" and "consumer" interchangeably. Consumer package goods companies normally focus on the consumer as the end user and reserve "customer" for other businesses, resellers, and distributors. Manufacturers and retailers with business-to-business relationships know that these customer relationships can be among the most profitable.

A one-to-one system with a company must still focus on an individual. Each functional area will approach the relationship uniquely. Depending on whether you're dealing with a professional purchaser, a technical specifier, or an administrative assistant, the customer's needs will vary. Simplifying routine purchases by offering custom lists or access to prior purchase invoices is critical for those tasked with frequent purchasing responsibilities. Ordering expensive or technical products may require justification and additional information.

Environmental information should be easily accessible along with health and safety materials data. Customized web pages address individual company requirements and purchaser needs. Automated ordering and delivery systems can be linked to other systems for integrated purchasing, billing, and supply-chain management.

Many mid-sized companies worldwide will use or plan to use the Internet to purchase supplies and equipment in the near future. While personal calls by sales reps could be construed as true one-on-one marketing, busy business managers perceive time as money. They don't want a sales pitch: they want to order and receive services *their* way. Convenience, speed, and cost are the main drivers.

Usage Behavior

We've examined shopping behavior, lifestyle, demographics, and other factors that influence customer purchasing and loyalty. How products are used, at home or in business, may also have an impact on web-based shopping. For instance, if a web designer knows that a customer routinely purchases a spare product in addition to a regular order, he may bundle two products together or offer an online reminder. If segment data confirm that most customers purchase two products together, a promotion may be offered to customers still purchasing the single item.

Historical purchasing data will be useful to monitor usage behavior. The best way to thoroughly understand customers and how they use the products they purchase is to visit representatives of your top segments in their homes or offices. Following them for a day or two will give you invaluable insight that you cannot achieve in a sterile test environment.

The analysis of customer behavior over time must be measured to get an accurate picture of usage. This is best managed with a permanent program rather than a one-time research project.

Predicting the Success of the Customer Relationship

Relationships between customers and merchants are very much like other typical relationships between people. Understanding what makes a relationship successful with your employees, spouse, children, or co-workers helps you determine how to measure a good relationship with a customer.

Relationship studies conducted by the University of Denver indicate that marital failure is predictable to a surprising degree. This means that, for many couples, the seeds of divorce are present prior to marriage. The study was grounded in understanding how to prevent marital failure and determining how prediction can lead to better interventions designed to help couples reduce the risk of divorce.

Dr. Howard Markman, Department of Psychology at the University of Denver has identified the steps in a relationship and potential danger signs and patterns in his book, *Fighting for Your Marriage: Positive Steps for Preventing Divorce and Preserving a Lasting Love* (Jossey-Bass, 2001).

Once a relationship is established by two partners, problems can develop. Escalation occurs, which can be resolved, ignored or neglected. Continued neglect implies invalidation, and contempt usually follows. Negative interpretations, withdrawal and avoidance lead to indifference. These are danger signs and patterns of a relationship headed for failure.

The same patterns and principles can be applied to the customer relationship. By reducing risk factors and increasing protective elements, you can preserve a fragile relationship. How the customer "feels" at every point of contact with an online store influences the relationship. Points of contact can be shopping on the website, asking a question of the customer service department, returning a product, or tracking an order. At each of these touch points, a customer must feel important, appreciated and respected.

Having a Great Relationship

"Having a great relationship depends more on how you handle differences than on what the differences are. A great relationship is predicted not by your finding the right partner, but by your being the right partner."
— *Dr. Howard Markman, Department of Psychology, University of Denver*

The large group of people called "customers" must now be narrowed down to specific individuals. When you think of these individuals less as "targets" and more as "partners," you begin to get the idea of how powerful a relationship can be. The customer is not someone we do something "to"—the customer is someone we do something "for." It's a symbiotic relationship in which we have to give something of value.

Shrinking the World

If e-commerce mirrored the actual composition of the world, it would be very diverse. Marianne Williamson, noted author and speaker on world issues, presents a new way to look at the people of the world:

"If we could at this time shrink the Earth's population to a village of precisely 100 people, with all the human ratios remaining the same, it would look like this:

- There would be 57 Asians, 21 Europeans, 14 from the Western Hemisphere (North and South), and 8 Africans.
- Seventy would be nonwhite; 30 white.
- Fifty percent of the entire world's wealth would be in the hands of only six people. All six would be citizens of the United States.
- Seventy would be unable to read.
- Fifty would suffer from malnutrition.
- Eighty would live in substandard housing.
- Only one would have a college education.

As web shopping gains adoption throughout the world, human factors engineering becomes even more critical. The Internet used to be a domain of technology aficionados and game-playing teens. Truly understanding the customer and designing for the future demands that you stay abreast of the changes in the population at large as well as feel the pulse of the shopping environment.

Major changes are usually addressed at the strategic level of a business. Yet, as soon as a belief about the customer is ingrained in a corporation's culture, it tends to be perpetuated. That's why many major corporations still believe that Internet use in the U.S. is dominated by men.

Subtle changes are even more difficult to acknowledge or track. Continual customer contact, whether through individual or group research, is the primary guard against complacency. Monitoring secondary research and staying in touch with customer advocacy groups will give dimension to growing customer needs.

Often, one channel will spot change faster than another. Even if your company uses only one channel—a pure-play web merchant, for example—it's still critical to understand how the customer shops in a variety of modes, what they prefer in each, and how a best practice can be replicated in another domain. Each channel can learn from the other because they take different approaches toward helping the customer have the best possible shopping experience.

Retail, Catalog, and Online Stores

This section takes an in-depth look at three types of stores: retail, catalog, and online. It looks at similarities among them and then offers in-depth examination of the best practices for each of these shelves. This section will also explain how to apply traditional success strategies of catalog and retail marketing to the online store.

Chapter 3 shares retailing secrets from professional retailers.

Chapter 4 covers catalog marketing and Direct Marketing.

Chapter 5 describes all the features of an Online Store.

Retailing Secrets:
Tips from the Pros

Commerce has been dependent upon retailing for hundreds of years. Retailers have concentrated on perfecting the in-store experience over the past 30 years in such a way that entire industries have developed to support the effort. Unique companies emerged to analyze register tapes, provide consulting services on furniture and fixture placement, and even research the consumer shopping experience with hidden cameras.

Selling on the web is not a completely unique function. It has many links to traditional selling techniques. Taking advantage of those lessons and extrapolating them to e-commerce will enable you to advance faster and understand the psychology of shelf selling—whether your shelf is physical or virtual.

Consumers evaluate new shopping encounters by comparing them with their own past shopping experiences. Although some of today's consumers may be very proficient at shopping on the web, the basic shopping experience for almost everyone is shopping in a retail store. Thus, e-shopping comparisons are more logically made to physical shopping than to another virtual site.

The customer may love the idea of shopping at home, but the reality of this mode of purchasing is not always as attractive as the promise. Once an obstacle is placed in the way of convenience, many consumers revert to the familiarity and comfort of the known—shopping in a physical store. The challenge is to overcome the obstacles and the uncertainty of shopping online and make it as close to normal shopping behavior as possible. Shopping online must be at least equal to or better than the current method. Shoppers often go online for product evaluation and selection, only to go to a store to make a purchase.

But what is normal shopping behavior? How is a favorable shopping experience at retail characterized? Understanding the unique techniques employed by retailers and integrating them into specific web-based patterns allows a holistic and artful approach to delivering the ideal experience.

Shopping at Retail

A typical shopper, Lauren will stop today at two retail stores on her way home from work. She will make a quick visit to a discount store to pick up some eye drops, and then she will go to her favorite grocery store to shop for something for dinner.

Lauren usually purchases her eye drops at a drug store, but it would be out of her way today. She parks her car in the vast parking lot and walks through the automatic doors. At once, she's confused—there's no clear path to enter the store. In front of her are rows of grocery carts but she will not need them for her small purchase. She needs to make a decision to go to the right or left around the carts. She chooses to move to her right, but it takes her through a narrow path cluttered with seasonal closeouts.

As she makes her way through the aisle, she finally spots the main thoroughfare. Now she has more decisions to make. Aisles grow out of the main arterial, and she must choose her path. She can read only the signage directly to her left, so she decides to navigate with her fingers crossed. She can see the cosmetic section on the left and wonders if the eye drops might be there. As she continues, she notices a likely section to the right. Shelved ahead are toothpaste, foot-care products, and hair spray. She mutters to herself that the hair spray really should be with the cosmetics.

She sees a sign for the pharmacy and takes a quick left, but then notices the sign at the window reads "closed." She wonders if eye drops would be in the pharmacy or in the section with toothpaste. Lauren decides to wander up and down the aisles until she finds what she needs.

Eventually, Lauren discovers the eye drops, but the store is out of her brand. She will not use a substitute and decides to see if they carry them at the grocery store. She leaves empty-handed.

On her way to the grocery store, Lauren makes a mental list—bread and cereal for breakfast and lunch tomorrow, fresh chicken and vegetables for a stir-fry tonight. She drives into the parking lot and finds a spot close to the door. She grabs a cart and hurries to select her first purchase—the cereal. Lauren wants something healthy for the kids, without sugar, but most seem too expensive. She chooses the nationally branded version of corn flakes, although there are cheaper generic packages on the bottom shelf. Heading for the bakery, she notices an end cap featuring cola on sale. She'd like to buy some, but she can't find the diet, decaffeinated variety. She knows the distinctive gold color of the package, but this display features only red and silver packages. She decides to skip it.

Locating the bread, Lauren grabs her favorite brand—good whole wheat that's not too expensive. She sees the large sign for the meat department and heads toward it. Beef, pork, yes—chicken—and she searches through the choices. She selects a whole chicken grown locally but pays a premium for the privilege. It's getting late, and she throws a few vegetables in her cart and heads to the checkout counter, forgetting the eye drops.

She must unload her own groceries onto a conveyor belt and laments the days when she could just push her cart toward the checker. As she waits in line, she is tempted by candy and can't resist the chocolate bar. Lauren finally gets to write a check after searching her bag for a coupon she was sure she had for the bread. It doesn't matter—Lauren is happy to pay the full price just to get out the door and head home. She'd like some help with her bags but rarely asks these days because the courtesy clerks seem so busy just bagging groceries. She loads her stash into her trunk and returns the cart. She hopes she won't have to repeat the process tomorrow night.

Lauren's trip to the store was a typical shopping experience and not entirely positive. Retailers have to deal with a variety of issues that shoppers face every day. Shopping can range from the pleasurable and recreational to the mundane and routine. Retailers have the ability to make the process fun, simple, functional, or exciting. Each day, retailers ask their customers to find their store, navigate around it, make product choices, stand in line, and finally pay for their purchases. Many retailers go beyond merely sticking products onto shelves.

The techniques that retailers use to guide consumers through the process have been planned and perfected over years of selling in large stores, small shops, and club warehouses. Some business owners, in a tight economy, have sacrificed sound retail practices in favor of cutting costs. However, the fundamentals have not changed and successful retailers focus on consumer-centered programs.

The brick-and-mortar store is still the channel of choice for consumer sales. According to the U.S. Commerce Department, online sales in 2000 accounted for less than one percent of all retail sales. Catalog sales average around ten percent. Although alternative channels are expected to grow exponentially, it makes sense to determine why most shoppers choose traditional stores. Understanding retailing techniques will aid in building multi-channel sales.

Ten Essential Retailing Techniques

The first impression of a store begins with its location. Its proximity to other stores that the consumer frequents, accessibility, and convenience are primary. But retailing experts know there is more to retailing than real estate. We will examine ten key retailing essentials that are transferable to web implementation:

1. Understanding how the consumer shops
2. Business planning and retail differentiation
3. Identifying key target customer segments
4. How to determine market structures
5. Merchandising and product placement
6. Planograms and SKU rationalization
7. Category management
8. Selectability
9. Refreshing the shelf
10. Retail advertising and promotion

These retailing elements can be leveraged to the online environment with little modification. Understanding traditional retailing basics will be the first step to connecting web shopping to the customer's most familiar shopping environment.

Understanding How the Consumer Shops

While each store is unique, consumers use some natural biological patterns to move through a store. The direction they turn upon entering a store, how they approach an aisle, or how long it takes them to notice merchandise after they walk into a shop are more a function of human nature than cognizant behavior. Harnessing this knowledge can transform your business into a store that's pleasurable to shop, whether it has physical or virtual parameters. The consumer's shopping experience is rooted in retail shopping and many of those patterns transfer to all shopping modes.

The retail shopping experience may begin with the expectations set by advertising, a phone call to the store, recommendations by friends, or by the first encounter in the parking lot. Often impressions are established before the customer even walks in the door.

The first key to success is to fulfill those initial expectations. Retailers will reinforce advertising through signage for advertising offers and booklets, samples of ads, or coupons by the front door.

The parking lot must be free of carts and provide ample parking. Store planners and employees try to remove any obstacles that may block the customer's ability to easily enter the store. But a new store starts as a blank slate, and creative retailers construct the interiors in varied and interesting ways. There are, however, basic retail navigation elements:

- Providing clear entrance and exit routes for ease of access
- Making it clear to the shopper which products and services the store provides
- Managing natural movement patterns within the store traffic flow
- Creating open visual paths to avoid clutter and confinement
- Providing clear signs and directions to help navigate the store
- Delivering a positive emotional experience through color, sound, texture, and light
- Facilitating ease of shopping with product information and selection assistance
- Providing store maps to assist locating a specific landmark or department
- Developing easy-to-find service centers for personal assistance

Your consumer will appreciate your directions and assistance. With less sales assistance available, both at retail stores and online, these will also help the shopper choose his selections independently, saving the customer time and saving the merchant money as well.

What Do You Sell?

Within one minute of entering a store, a prospective purchaser should clearly understand the products and services offered in that establishment. The customer should be able to logically determine whether a certain product can found in the store based on previous knowledge of a similar store. Even though some people come to the store only to browse, treating each encounter as a potential sale is the goal.

While it's not necessary to actually sell each product the customer wants, the store should represent, at first glance, a type of store category familiar to the shopper. If the store, whether physical or virtual, is a new or breakthrough format never before seen by the shopping world, the concept should be explained quickly in that first minute.

Product categories differ by consumer need. Destination purchases bring the customer in the store for very specific purchases. Convenience items are products required on a routine basis. Unplanned purchases are usually impulse buys—something the consumer may not need but may be enticed to buy—or reminder purchases.

Recently, stores have been branching into domains previously foreign to their environments. Drug stores sell milk (convenience), office product superstores sell soft drinks (impulse) and toilet paper (reminder), and grocery stores sell television sets. Again, it is not imperative that the customer understand this at first glance. But it is necessary that consumers know the main components of a drug store, office product superstore, or grocery store and might find the logical products therein.

Getting In and Out

Not surprisingly, we all want an easy way to get in the store and a direct and simple way to leave. This may seem intuitive, but it is one simple rule that can't be overlooked. Doors that are not marked clearly invite customers to push when they should pull. Exits in large department stores may look so similar that consumers may leave through the wrong door.

Clean, streamlined aisles at the entrance invite shoppers to take the time to walk in and assess their needs. Stores need to be navigated somewhat like a maze. Providing the clear "start" and "finish" marks on this maze help guide your customer to the goal.

Freedom of choice liberates the shopper. Trapping a customer will not make her purchase. Regardless of the format, she needs the ability to see and use the exit if she chooses to leave at any point in the shopping process. In fact, the *perception* of freedom works in much the same way. Shoppers want to be able to leave quickly once they have made their selections, even if they choose to stay. The purchase process must be simple, or customers will abandon their purchases. Store maps can solve the "Which way did I come in?" dilemma.

Stores used to feature turnstiles at entrances and exits. Today, they are replaced with electronic surveillance systems that enable the use of wide aisles and less intrusive hardware. Customers found ways to either avoid or disable turnstiles because they were perceived as obstructions.

Stew Leonard's, a large, successful grocery in Connecticut, uses a maze format to guide customers through the store. The company has packed the building with entertainment and the most enticing fresh produce and a host of luscious prepared foods. He provides frequent exits from the maze for the claustrophobic or those in a hurry to pick up one item. The store is experiential, and that is his unique value proposition.

Natural Shopping Patterns

Customers have certain ingrained shopping traits that are either natural or learned behavior. Working with these patterns help simplify navigation and avoid forcing the consumer to adapt to uncomfortable situations.

Whether a store is traditional or unconventional by design, honoring these behavioral patterns creates comfort and familiarity. Evaluate the following physical retail rules:

- People move instinctively to the right upon entering a store.
- Customers shop three-dimensionally.
- Music and audio cues can affect the shopping mood.
- Eyesight plays a key role in product selection.
- Over-stimulation creates confusion.
- Under-stimulation creates boredom.

Customers will react unconsciously to appropriate situations but will feel physically uncomfortable with unnatural patterns whether they are in the virtual or actual world. We will discuss how to transpose these rules to e-commerce later. For now, just recognize how subtle each retailing decision can be. The goal is to create an online experience that is natural and familiar.

The Battle of the Sexes

Men and women not only shop for different merchandise, their shopping processes are different. Women are the primary shoppers at retail and significantly outnumber men. However, social roles are changing, and men and women are shopping together more often recreationally. Taking into account gender preferences, retailers have used colors, images, and fixtures to appeal to both sexes in targeted categories. There is still quite a bit of work to do in this area to improve shopping interaction. Retailers are striving to develop one-on-one relationships while still categorizing the genders in a somewhat dated fashion.

Most men in the past had less patience for the many choices confronting them in the retail environment. They knew what they wanted when they walked into the store. Their goal was to find it and leave quickly. Now, women find themselves wanting to get in and out of the store due to the extreme demands on their time. Many are shopping after work and want to spend as little time as possible in a store. Though women still enjoy recreational shopping, less time is available for most activities in their lives.

Though there are distinct natural differences between the sexes, they are not static. Merchandisers change formats frequently to accommodate the fluidity of these changes. Physical structures take into account the size and shapes of men and women, their ability to reach products, and their preferences for privacy.

Excuse Me—Where's the Mustard?

Shopping is not always about choice. It is often the process of elimination. Signage can help narrow down the selections and serves two purposes. First, it's directional and helps shoppers find their way through the store. Next, it separates a variety of products into logical categories. The same ability is available online. Virtual signs can direct the shopper through the store and create groupings to facilitate navigation.

In either a physical or virtual store, it is not always possible to offer personal service. In fact, most stores now have elements of self-service, and some are completely dependent on the consumer being able to self-select merchandise. Sales depend on how well customers can serve themselves, including finding their way around the store, selecting the correct product, and paying for the purchase. Retailers now even have systems that include self-service scanning at check out.

It's not up to the customer to determine how he will accomplish these. It is incumbent upon the retailer to guide the consumer through the process and anticipate every obstacle, question, or problem through research and task analysis. How well a company can do this depends on how much it must invest in personal sales assistance.

Each retailer should conduct an independent assessment to determine to what level self-service can be achieved. If a customer is successful 80 percent of the time, the retailer must staff for the 20 percent eventuality that the consumer will need assistance. Leaving it to chance might result in the inability to find products 20 percent of the time, resulting in a loss in sales. Of course, retailers may need to staff for a level that provides more personal assistance regardless of the customer's shopping effectiveness.

In the virtual world, most shopping must be achieved independently. But it is inconceivable that consumers will be able to find their choice of products correctly 100 percent of the time. Virtual signs, directional cues, sample questions, and contact phone numbers will all serve to enable a successful shopping trip. Physical retailers have invented new techniques for guiding customers through the store. Floor graphics and electronic maps are two of the newer products. Online sellers can develop the same type of directional and visual cues to guide customers through an online maze.

Not all customers have the same expertise with the web. Some don't even know how to use search functions. Using large arrows and explicit directions will help them find the next level of information they require.

Color, Light, Sound, and Texture

Sensory aids add to the ambience of the store and help put valued customers in a pleasant mood. Nordstrom is famous for live piano performances—a real treat for shoppers. Reaction to sound,

Figure 3–1 The store entrance sets the ambience.

light, and color are more metabolic than conscious. The person affected will merely feel relaxed or mellow. Customers who feel good will purchase more. Figure 3-1 shows how the store's atmosphere can enhance the shopping experience.

A dark store, unless intentionally setting a mood, is neither inviting nor interesting. When a store does not have sufficient light, customers may infer the store is old or dated. Reflective light helps customers see their choices more efficiently, read fine print, or discern colors. Fluorescent lighting, while bright and cheerful, shifts colors—especially blues to purples.

Dressing rooms at retail stores are often dark and have insufficient mirrors, making it difficult for customers to accurately assess their choices. Lighting and color should enhance the buying experience and help selectability. Online, there are no virtual dressing rooms. Merchants must explain how garments fit, state whether they run large or small, and describe colors and textures.

Audio stimulation is essential in a store and is usually in the form of background music. Sometimes, small retail shops merely use a radio, and the station selection is left up to the employees. But more often, music is predetermined or piped into a store.

Audio cues are underused on the web. Music, shopping help, even announcements for specials can add to sales and attract customers. When grocers announce bakery specials, sales add up. These have been especially useful for freshly baked goods coupled with the aroma of baking bread. Even the "blue-light specials" used by Kmart in the past had people flocking to a rotating blue light to catch the latest bargain. Piano music at Nordstrom sets a mood and creates an ambiance for customers. Shoppers want to feel good and enjoy beautiful settings while they browse—even if they are in a hurry.

Consumers like to feel the textures of various goods—from apparel material to paper. In most cases, physical retailers provide consumers the opportunity to use their tactile senses to examine and touch products—or at least samples of products. Customers are less likely to purchase abrasive or harsh textures even if the product's appearance is pleasing. Corporate buyers require samples to determine all parameters of a product to predict sales. Small businesses must also take these issues into account.

From the moment a shopper enters a store, color, light, and sound have an impact on their first impression of the environment and, ultimately, their opinion of the store as a place they choose to shop.

Online, retail simulation can be achieved by using crisp, descriptive copy, enlargeable photos, zoom capability to see details and texture, and colors that are pleasing rather than jarring.

Each year, graphic design associations conduct studies to determine which colors they should use in advertising and brochures. These colors are often used the following year in home design products, so the research is relatively leading edge. Color preferences don't remain static from year to year. Olive green, orange, and harvest gold were fashionable 30 years ago but are not the current fashion colors of choice. Colors should be contemporary and reflect cultural preferences.

Selection, Eyesight, and Information

With an aging population, more customers have difficulty reading small print or reaching products placed on low or high shelves. Consumers routinely have to reach for glasses to decipher product information—especially inconvenient when shoppers are loaded down with packages or are trying to control small children.

Older Americans, 65 years of age or older, numbered 34.5 million in 1999, and the population of seniors increased by 10.6 percent since 1990. That accounts for one in every eight people in the U.S. Since 1900, the percentage of men and women 65 and over has more than tripled. By 2030, there will be about 70 million seniors, more than twice their number in 1999. Retailers are gearing up to provide new services, new methods of displaying products, and more convenient access.

In the age of self-service, data on packaging or merchandising can be the only information a customer has to make a purchase decision. Smart retailers use a variety of aids such as selection guides, demos, and samples. They also use lower merchandising fixtures, shelve key products at eye level, and allow manufacturers to provide a variety of shopping fixtures.

We'll address selectability later, but be aware that all information-providing tools need to work holistically with the environment. The position of the data must be in close proximity to the intended products, the print should be large enough to read without a magnifying glass, the fixture should not cover up or detract from any other product, and the format needs to be consistent through the entire store.

By building a system throughout the store, whether physical or virtual, consumers can anticipate the aid provided in each section and will know how to use it without relearning a format for each aisle. In addition, efficiencies of scale keep down the cost of creating new systems in each section. Remember, the entire category should be addressed, not merely one product.

Often, the leading category manufacturer—or category leader—will offer to create a guide to aid the consumer. Categories requiring selection aids vary, but some categories are clearly difficult to shop. Product categories such as halogen light bulbs, vacuum cleaner bags, inkjet printer cartridges, and automotive parts require additional information.

A Store Is Three-Dimensional

Customers shop as they walk, looking at both sides of an aisle, observing the front and sides of a product. No one faces the aisle and side-steps parallel to it. The aisle and the approach to the aisle are three-dimensional, but retail planograms, web designs, and product packaging are usually designed one-dimensionally.

Shoppers pick up products, turn them over and examine them, feel fabrics and textures, read ingredients, and feel the weight. Therefore, customers expect either an actual or simulated shopping encounter that provides a similar experience.

Sampling is a popular retail technique that offers a sample of the actual product at no risk. The technique works not only because of trial, but also because the shopper can experience all aspects of the product, including the packaging, instructions, and usage ideas. In the virtual world, pictures can spin to show the back of the product, and sample usage ideas can help the customer determine new ways to use the product.

Some online stores provide the shopper with product rotation capability or multiple photos showing different views and angles. Because online shoppers may have a variety of older PCs with limited capabilities, usage of new applications to display products is not yet widespread. This will change, however, as consumers replace aging machines with speedier computers that include expanded memory and as broadband availability is commonplace.

More Help Is Available

How do you plan to assist your customers when self-service just doesn't work? Consumers have questions, and part of the business strategy must be to offer additional help when all else fails.

Whether the assistance is provided by a person in the store, a phone number to call, or an e-mail to address, the key to satisfaction is timing. The window for a purchase is very short, and if you don't provide the answer, someone else will. Planning for prompt assistance will help you keep your eyes on the consumer and help him complete his purchase.

Consumer loyalty is dependent on obtaining service, having a wide selection of products, finding the intended or destination product, having a good location or good accessibility, and trusting the retailer. By offering excellent service, you also may also create trust in the process.

We recommend "live" assistance and toll-free numbers, recognizing that these solutions are expensive. Keep the contact personal. A service desk with a 15-minute wait or a phone tree that won't allow easy access may negate any positive relationship that you attempt to build.

On the web, put your phone number and address in a prominent position on the first screen. Many customers will go to your site for product information but prefer not to purchase online with a credit card. Providing another purchase method up front will boost sales and possibly gain a future customer relationship.

The web also offers the unique capability of providing a virtual sales force. The feature is explained in Chapter 1.

Retailers vary in how well they provide customer assistance. Some are outstanding, while others have succumbed to cutting costs for extra profitability. We strongly recommend maintaining this consumer link to both retailers and e-tailers. Cutting costs in this area has consequences that will be difficult to regain later.

Business Planning and Retail Differentiation

Retailers don't merely rent space, stock it with goods, and open the doors. They engage in extensive business planning, customer analysis, and competitive evaluation. Without an effective business and marketing plan, it is very difficult to establish metrics and to evaluate the success of the business. We'll discuss some specific retail techniques such as category management and SKU rationalization later in this chapter. The essential components, then, of a sound business plan include the following:

- Identifying the current situation, issues, or problems
- Creating objectives, strategies, and a mission statement
- Determining, analyzing, and selecting target customers
- Identifying the customers' needs
- Analyzing current and potential competition, other customer alternatives, and the role they fill
- Determining the differentiation strategy and the value proposition
- Creating the tactics including supply chain management, warehousing and inventory plans, personnel and training, stocking, promotional programs, and other retail issues
- Projecting financial needs, forecasts, and cash flow
- Staffing and training
- Developing a legal plan
- Measuring results

The extent of the plan depends on the size of the business, the extent of its services, and the scope of its programs. An in-depth assessment of the business environment and business opportunities is essential in any planning phase.

Pre-planning begins with location analysis in the retail world, but with the growth of Internet sales and even a rush to provide "clicks" with standard brick and mortar retailing, businesses often forget to create a separate business plan for their virtual stores. Both shopping modes merit an in-depth examination of potential business to avoid cannibalization. Although you may assume all e-shoppers have experience with retail shopping, it is not safe to assume the reverse. Therefore, adopting synergies between the two is efficient, but duplicating plans may not be reasonable. Creating a holistic approach really means bringing together the best of all shopping worlds and developing coordination while maintaining separate and distinct strategies.

Of course, our objective here is not to discuss every detail of a business plan but to stress the importance of connecting your selling channels—retail, online, or both—to your business plan. Integrating consumer needs into the plan at every level and measuring all programs, services, and employee actions ensures success. Retailers avoid the pitfalls of stocking inferior merchandise, cutting customer service, and focusing only on pure margin if they understand and provide for their target customer's needs.

Differentiation—Your Competitive Edge

Retailers typically differentiate by price, customer service, brand, specialty products or services, or a unique customer experience in the store. A few, including Wal-Mart, have differentiated geographically by building stores in smaller cities.

The first step to creating a unique position in the retailing world is to scope out the competition. By understanding which positions have been secured, retailers can then claim a position that no other company owns. Of course, not all retailers have taken this first important step. There are many "me too" companies in the market.

Most retailers know that their competition extends beyond the obvious. Department stores don't simply compete with other department stores. They compete with discount stores, specialty stores, warehouse clubs, catalogs, mail order companies, and the Internet. Sears competes with other department stores like JC Penney, but also with the JC Penney catalog and online store as well as club stores like Costco, discount stores like Target, and a host of Internet merchants.

The low-price position is often attractive to adopt but difficult to sustain. Even though some resellers check competitive ads every morning and adjust their prices accordingly, few go down this path for very long. Most choose to offer better quality, create an appealing store format, or specialize in unique attributes or products. Wal-Mart, even though it advertises low prices, is still very concerned with offering name brands and quality merchandise to its customers.

Companies that offer sales both in physical stores and on the Internet often offer the same merchandise and the same value proposition in both modes. Shopping can be interchangeable, allowing the consumer to order on the web and return items to a store. Of course, these companies are very aware of the risk of cannibalization to either of their outlets. While cannibalization usually results in losing the sale entirely, when outlets compete, this may be the net effect. Synergy between the groups will build sales.

Some retailers also participate in complementary businesses. An office product superstore may also conduct business as a copy center, contract stationer, or even a wholesaler.

Whatever the differentiation strategy, it must complement, enhance, or mirror the value proposition. The similarity in today's online stores makes differentiation even more challenging. More e-tailers can take advantage of the customer need and desire for specialized services.

Creating a Tactical Retail Plan

The tactical plan will vary greatly depending on the type, size, and structure of the business. Retailers, though, usually require specific performance by each store in a chain if it is a multistore organization. Smaller businesses with one or two outlets may have less formal plans. In any case, the plan must be clear enough to measure results.

The tactical plan is usually developed for the fiscal year but, due to the nature of some retail businesses, this period may extend to 18 months or longer for adequate planning. This will take into account promotional windows and seasonality.

Retailers with more than one channel should write separate plans for each with an overarching, integrated business plan that balances products and resources. Independent channel decisions vary depending on the customer base and business structure. Internet planning must take into account the global nature of the channel. In addition, the physical flow of product distribution, promotions, and consumer targeting must all be adapted to the Internet. Retailers must use caution to avoid channel conflict if they offer both click and mortar sales.

Here are some sample topics for the tactical plan:

- Stocking and inventory levels
- Promotional programs
- Future store openings
- Employee hiring and training plans
- Product assortment and pricing
- The services mix
- Profitability targets and forecasts
- Press relations and communication plans
- Advertising

Creating and managing an online business is dependent on leveraging a basic plan. Click-and-mortar companies must integrate their online plan into the overall business plan. Two separate plans, independent of each other, will prove to create a dichotomy in the business, and the online version of the store is likely to suffer.

Smaller online businesses often sacrifice the planning stage. It's difficult to move to higher levels of customer-centered planning without the baseline plan.

Measuring the Plan

Retailers obviously measure sales in each store. But they also measure stores in comparison to each other. They must analyze existing store sales separately from new store sales. Retailers also measure each SKU's (stock-keeping unit or individual product) performance along with category performance.

While much of the retailers' measures are financially focused, they are also concerned with service levels and employee performance at the store level. They employ a variety of techniques, including "mystery shopping," to determine how well they are meeting customer needs. Every element in the tactical plan should have a relative measure to determine if the company is meeting its goals and the expectations of the consumer. The measures may be different for various selling motions. To be truly effective, most retailers couple management performance with attaining objectives. Figure 3-2 provides some sample metrics to help evaluate retail goals.

Retailers vary in how they implement these measures. Some retail chains will actually fire a store manager for allowing excessive levels of shrinkage, store loss due to retail theft or mismanaged inventory, while allowing the manager to have low store sales. Store managers, in this case, may just lock up key items to avoid loss and meet their goals. Retailers must then deal with poor sales and unhappy consumers. Each measure will depend on how retailers value each attribute. By putting the consumer first, retailers' choices are clearer.

Retail Short-term and Long-term Measures

Long-Term	SKU	Product Line	Category	Store
Return on Management Investment (ROMI)				
Internal Rate of Return (IRR)				
Return on Assets (ROA)				
Income from Operations (IFO)				
Cash Flow				
Sales Dollars				
Margin				
Case Sales				
Short-Term				
Income from Operations (IFO)				
Cash Flow				
Various Promotion Measures				
Sales Dollars per square foot				
Margin Dollars per square foot				
Case Sales				
Franchise Measures				
Share of Market (SOM) actual & relative to competition				
Category Growth				

Figure 3–2 Sample measures for retail evaluation.

Retail success is measured by gross margin, sales/gross profit dollars per square foot, inventory turns, and total store performance. Segments are compared to similar segments, and categories are measured against total store performance. Individual SKUs are measured by overall performance and gross margin, value-to-size ratio, and turns. The actual dollar margin multiplied by inventory turnover, or how many times the company's average inventory is sold out or "turned," generates a retailer's revenue.

Mystery Shopping

One method of checking on routine business transactions is called mystery shopping. Mystery shoppers pose as normal customers, make several purchases, and evaluate the experience. Usually a contracted firm is hired to conduct these shopping audits.

Usually, the emphasis at retail is on service and the professionalism of the staff. But this is an excellent way to evaluate how well the brand promise is delivered in any shopping mode.

Mystery shoppers can be given priority assignments to evaluate overall store performance, individual clerk performance, or comparison measurements between stores in a chain.

Competitive Intelligence

Competitive intelligence may augment the business plan and may help measure how well a retailer is doing in relation to its competition. Understanding potential competitive actions also protects against emerging threats.

Competitive intelligence is predictive in nature, and this discipline is used to answer specific business questions. It is not intended to provide a dissertation about every business aspect of every competitor.

Of course, retailers check competing ads frequently and often adjust their prices accordingly. Price competition is difficult to sustain because competitors can always lower their prices. Successful retailers use a combination of competitive measures, and the most effective of these is winning over the consumer with an excellent value proposition. Competitive intelligence can assist with the scorecard to help assess market share and other key measures.

Methods for competitive intelligence vary and include checking business-reporting functions and local and national media, monitoring business results and emerging technologies, and frequenting trade shows. There are many other techniques, and the value of competitive intelligence is in the analysis, so it is best left to professionals with experience. Small retailers may use the web and search local media to stay abreast of competitors.

Online intelligence is easy to conduct on a frequent basis but cannot be completely reliable because deliberately misleading information may be published on the web.

Identifying Key Target Customer Segments

In order to truly understand the customer, it's important to determine who you're targeting, their characteristics and demographics, their relative value to your business, and what they need and want to purchase. Even more important to know is *why* they are purchasing an item. Their root motives can help you organize your store in more relevant ways and can give you more context for cross-selling. Several segments may be relevant to your business; however, it's important to focus on only a few. Trying to be everything to everyone usually results in being mediocre to most.

Customers may be segmented on a variety of parameters as discussed in detail in Chapter 2. Usually, retailers know if a customer is a home consumer, a small business, or a corporate entity. They also may be segmented geographically by zip code.

Retailers approach segmentation through rooftop targeting and store clustering. By examining the trading area surrounding each store in concentric circles at specified intervals—five or ten miles from a store—they achieve a relatively good idea of the store's customer base. Combined with analyzing store register tapes, used to understand which items in the store are the most popular, and buying patterns, this research provides insight that helps the retailer stock the most appropriate items and forecast sales. By knowing what people purchase in a particular geographic area, retailers boost sales through focused ads and promotions.

Clustering examines purchase behavior, lifestyle, and other demographics, such as income, to find commonalities between consumers. Grouping and prioritizing segments brings focus to targeting key consumers with promotions, pricing, product mix, and shelf space. Then each store is customized to the target segments with improved assortment and merchandising. Chain stores then group similar stores and adjust the product mix and promotions accordingly.

Identifying the Customer's Needs

After retailers have identified the target customer, they set out to define his or her shopping and product needs. The same demographic and lifestyle research conducted to determine the target audience can offer clues to the customer's retail requirements. From a product perspective, retailers use sales data to analyze products and determine customer preferences. Determining service and future product needs is more difficult and best managed through qualitative research. Store surveys, promotions, and other research techniques are employed to understand how consumers respond to programs and services.

The shelf itself is used as a testing function to try out new planograms, the store's layout, and merchandising fixtures. Large chain retailers usually have a flagship store that serves as a trial outlet. Before new implementations are rolled out chain-wide, they are tested in these stores. Some programs are tested for a specified time in a handful of representative stores as well. When stores are grouped by type—similar target customers with common demographics and psychographics, store size, and geographic similarities—planograms and test data may be assigned accordingly. All "A" stores, for example, may have the most square footage, contain additional departments, and target higher income brackets. By rolling out a test in "A" stores only and examining results, retailers may be able to extrapolate performance across the chain.

Retailers may choose other parameters for different types of research. An in-store observational program may be executed in geographically diverse stores with high sales performance.

Selecting dissimilar stores will ensure that a wide variety of customers are included in the study. Stores with high levels of traffic are selected to ensure that enough representative customers are included.

Manufacturers may conduct studies in stores, as well, to examine a particular category's performance. They may also offer the retailer results of product research utilizing a variety of research techniques.

How to Determine Market Structures

The market structure can be described as the skeleton of the store and the precursor of markets, categories, segments, and sub-segments. Basically, it is how the consumer *perceives* fundamental groupings of products. Dissecting a grocery store, the customer expects to find departments comprised of certain types of food—produce, meat, bakery, and dairy, for example. Then, each department can be broken into sub-groups. Figure 3-3 shows a sample market structure hierarchy.

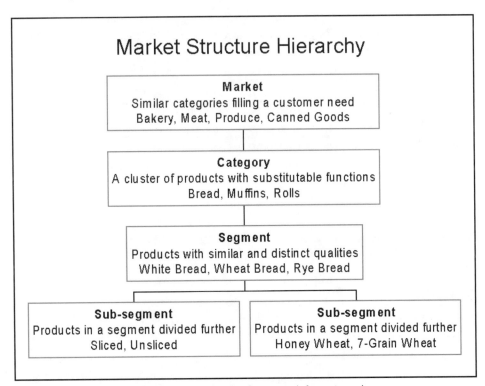

Figure 3–3 The market structure creates the framework for categories.

If you took a close look at the bakery department, you would find breads, cookies, cakes, donuts, and various other baked goods. Breads can be divided further into wheat, white, pumpernickel, rye, and other grains. There may be other choices as well—diet breads, sliced or unsliced, pre-packaged or fresh from the bakery, sweet breads, breads with raisins or other fruit, and so on.

A category is determined by the customer's perception of how these products should be grouped. Products might be grouped by brand, model, color, technology, size, occasion, weight, or gender.

Selling products in groupings that are not natural to consumers will confuse and frustrate them and hamper the purchase process. Imagine mixing housewares, women's shoes, and men's dress suits. Shopping would be an impossible task. Poor choices may be more subtle but still disruptive. Unfortunately, many manufacturers create categories based on the selection of the products they sell. They might believe, because they manufacture vacuum cleaners and vacuum cleaner replacement bags, for example, that these are in the same category. Usually, products within a category are the same or serve as substitutions.

The basis for a market structure is consumer need at a given point in time. Purchasing coffee is a routine task, while buying a new coffee maker is predicated on a completely different need at a different point in time. It might be nice to buy some coffee for the new appliance, but you certainly wouldn't expect to be asked to purchase a new pot each time you buy ground coffee or freshly roasted beans.

Each category's elements need to be defined by the customer to be correct. Adjacencies, or related categories, will be determined as part of the research process. Add-on sales are dependent upon shelving co-dependent categories in close proximity.

As an example, let's examine paper and stationery to understand how the consumer might segment this market. The market is defined as "paper" but, from that point on, the structure is quite diverse. Segment levels include plain paper, stationery, specialty paper, and so forth. Specialty paper may include cards, which then may be further segmented into greeting cards and business cards. If we took these down a level, the consumer might select based on size, weight, color, and other factors.

The same structural analysis may be applied to the grocery store. Meat is segmented into chicken, beef, pork, and lamb. The next sub-segment may be particular cuts of meat, including ground beef. Once ground beef is selected, the consumer must choose between lean, extra lean, or regular fat content. The next step involves deciding what size of package to purchase—family size or individual portions.

Every product belongs to a market hierarchy that the consumer must define. On occasion, a product may fit into more than one category. Online selling allows products to appear in more than one place without a large investment. It must be done sparingly, however, because the practice can easily dilute the value of distinct categories.

Merchandising and Product Placement

Merchandising and product placement are essential retailing staples and control much of how the store looks and how it functions. When they are managed effectively, they increase sales, enhance the customer's ability to shop the store, and serve as implementations of the natural market structure.

Usually, retailers have entire departments focused on these two disciplines that work closely with the buyers, planners, and even manufacturers. Because product manufacturers contribute merchandising fixtures to large retailers and even some smaller retailers, they are an important quotient in the merchandising strategy.

Online merchandising incorporates graphic design and layout in the same way that retail merchandising utilizes fixtures. The design enhances the shopping experience and influences sales.

Planograms and SKU Rationalization

Stores are physically space-limited and, therefore, cannot accommodate all SKUs. SKU rationalization is a method for selecting, listing, and placing key products on the shelf.

The physical store allows for only the most profitable SKUs to be placed in prime locations. Other products are relegated to the bottom or top rows of the shelf that are shopped less frequently—and many don't make it to the shelf at all. Customers dislike getting on their hands and knees to find items and often disregard products placed in odd locations. Some stores, such as grocery chains, charge manufacturers stocking fees to place their products on the shelves. Premium placement commands higher fees. The practice may discourage placement based on consumer needs.

SKU rationalization also is the process of evaluating each SKU at frequent intervals to determine profitability in relation to other store SKUs. Other factors, in addition to profitability, can also enter into the equation. Marketing fees or merchandising displays provided by the manufacturer can sway the retailer. High shrinkage products may be pulled from the shelf regardless of sales.

Individual product performance is evaluated through scanner data analysis to determine how each relates to overall performance market-wide and to the category itself. When a product performs well in the market but poorly in one chain, the category manager needs to determine why. Competitive stores may offer deeper discounts or more frequent promotions. Other products may need to be taken from the shelf to emphasize the stronger product.

Manufacturers have a great deal of consumer knowledge at their disposal. Some provide layout recommendations, category expertise, and merchandising fixtures. Brand manufacturers may also suggest special ways to feature their products to grow revenue. These techniques may be factored into SKU rationalization. Applying these concepts online will be discussed in Chapter 5.

The Planogram

The store layout, or planogram, is the map to the store and the basis for merchandising, product placement, category management, and promotion implementation. It indicates the placement of every aisle and every product. Good planograms offer familiarity, ease of shopping, and comfort to the shopper. This diagram is refreshed or even completely changed at least once a year and sometimes more often. Each shelf, category, and aisle is mocked up in a prototype store and tested before the new planogram is rolled out to the entire chain.

Often, there are several store formats with varying planograms. Large retailers may implement physical planogram tests for entire stores in preparation for holiday sales. Each new rollout can be based on square footage availability in each store.

While shoppers like familiarity, updates are necessary to make room for new products and new categories and to eliminate some as well. It's important to complete research and usability testing thoroughly before making extensive changes to a planogram. After the basic structure is sound, changes for seasonality, clearances, or design enhancements can be made on a more regular basis, as long as navigation remains constant.

The category manager usually determines the assortment on the shelf. Space planning is usually handled through specialized software with pre-loaded information on each SKU.

Category Management

A few years ago, retailers, in an effort to rectify some major retail issues, devised a new way of evaluating merchandise and streamlining the supply chain. The foundation for category management depends on cooperation and sharing between manufacturers and retailers. In the past, buyers were responsible for entire categories but were still managing each SKU individually. Category management treats the entire category as a profit and loss center.

Grocers were the first to adopt the concept and tasked certain manufacturers—category leaders—with actually managing their individual categories. This meant these category leaders had to recommend stocking data based on a set of financials and consumer information. By evaluating the category as a unit rather than as a series of independent products, manufacturers were forced to prove the financial viability of a category. It was even possible that they could list a competitor's product and de-list their own based on objective consumer data.

Category leaders needed to understand the category through fact-based knowledge rather than resort to selling products on features or margins alone. The result was a new-found dependence on the consumer's needs. It was necessary to determine how the category was shopped, and understand consumer preferences and interdependencies.

Both retailers and manufacturers have achieved a greater level of knowledge about the category and the consumer as a result of this practice. Larger retailers are best able to implement category management because extensive research is required. Smaller retailers benefit by using whatever fact-based analyses are available to them and by observing how larger retailers treat key categories.

Category management at retail depends heavily on scanner data from cash register tapes. Manipulation of the data must be managed by third-party consultants to maintain sensitive information.

Category management has several benefits for retailers. It helps them manage their product mix, inventory, shelf space, and capital. By managing each category to a detailed level, more information about the category, individual products, and the consumer help them make difficult business decisions and gain competitive advantage. In addition, category management enables the retailer to determine the impact of one category to another category. Category reviews are usually conducted annually. Category management, though, is not a replacement for other good business planning and should be combined with fundamental business programs.

The greatest competitive advantage that any retailer can achieve is to understand how consumers shop and why they select one site, store, or product over another. It's not necessary to implement a full-blown category management program, but some basic research is involved. The focus of category management has been on streamlining the supply chain for improved availability and increased profitability. Much of this can be corrected with improved inventory management systems.

One limitation to category management has been the reluctance of some retailers to share scanner data. Grocers and consumer packaged goods retailers routinely share data, while other retailers consider the information too sensitive to provide widely.

Some consultants are touting new systems that are supposed to be even more evolutionary than category management. Solution selling, aisle management, and other programs have been advertised as the next system to embrace. The focus for most of these expanded programs is the physical store as opposed to data management.

While category management and other similar techniques were designed for reseller efficiency, consumers benefit from improved organization at the shelf—whether virtual or physical—and improved product availability and selection. Figure 3-4 illustrates how the category management process creates efficiencies.

The Category Fact Book

A category fact book serves as the primary reference tool for the category. It contains information about the market, the consumer, products, and programs. Essential as background information, it consolidates business information in one convenient document. Each section or page may be used in a mix-or-match fashion in presentations, in sales tools, in PR discussions, or as a backgrounder for business and advertising programs.

Topics depend on the type of business the book material will cover. Typically, a category fact book will cover the following information:

- **Market and consumer research**
  - Consumer knowledge
  - User profiles

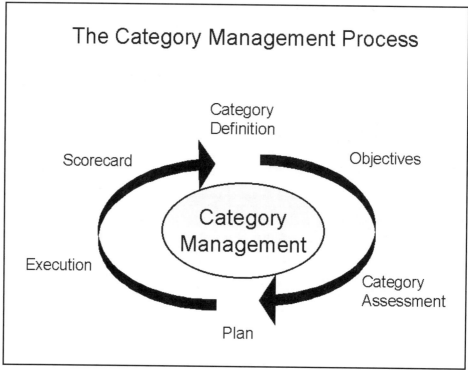

Figure 3–4 The category management process is data-driven to deliver efficient shelf
replenishment.

- – Product usage and potential usage
- – Market potential

- **Category trends**
  - – Category profitability
  - – Category dynamics
  - – Competitive/category analysis

- **Marketing programs**
  - – Advertising and promotion
  - – Reseller marketing
  - – Packaging
  - – Point-of-sale materials/merchandising

- **Product innovations and technology**
  - – Product line
  - – Individual product information

- **Reseller marketing**
  - Reseller marketing strategies
  - Space management and assortment
  - Location

- **Classes of trade**

- **Key opportunities**

The category fact book may also include training materials, technical support information, and other specific topics. With category and market information at their fingertips, marketers are able to access consistent information to avoid discrepancies in public or sales information. As a training document, it is an excellent vehicle for the sales force.

From a retail perspective, using fact-based category information helps both the manufacturer and retailer base decisions and programs on objective data. Because category management depends heavily on category and consumer information, a fact book can provide the baseline for all category development.

Merchandising

Merchandising helps consumers make product selections and guides them through the store. Retail merchandisers use any combination of the following fixtures:

- Signage—outside signage, directional signage, category signage
- Floor graphics—directional, product specific
- Spinners—rotating free-standing racks holding a specific product or entire category
- Shelving—standard shelving; custom-made usually for a specific brand or category
- Shelf talkers—small signs or animated graphics promoting a brand or offer
- Clip strips—long plastic strips holding small products hung in an aisle next to a category
- Cabinets—either locked or display; protect or feature high-end products
- Furniture—ranging from tables to chairs and variety pieces used functionally or for display
- Mirrors—for product enhancement or to view garments or accessories for fitting purposes
- Interactive shelf displays—electronic tools featuring demonstration, information, or for promotion
- Selection guides—electronic or static compatibility guides
- Kiosks—free-standing merchandising units, often electronic

While there are many other merchandising tools, most have just a few purposes in common. They display or promote products to their best advantage, explain or demonstrate, aid in selection, protect, or direct.

Merchandising is used to define each section of a category. Consumers identify the category selection criteria through the market structure definition process. Fixturing should emphasize each level of the hierarchy. If consumers depend on the brand as a selection element, for instance, manufacturer's brands should be clearly identified and shelf fixtures should enhance the brand. Placing this product into bins would be inappropriate because labels are difficult to see when shelved in this manner.

Milk almost always was shelved at the back of the traditional grocery store to make shoppers walk through several aisles to encourage impulse purchases. Now grocers understand convenience shopping and are beginning to position these goods at the front of their stores. They believe consumer loyalty will outweigh any additional sales gained through coercive practices.

Effective presentation includes gaining a prominent position on the shelf, sufficient information to make a purchase decision, reminders to purchase, and fixturing that enhances the product and brand through color, graphics, and product-dispensing facilitation. Promotions and collateral material may be included.

Discount stores or club stores operate on a model very different from department or specialty stores. Customer expectations vary depending on the store model as well. When shopping at Costco, for instance, customers know they will buy larger sizes of each product or, often, bundled offers. Merchandising displays must accommodate twin packs and giant product sizes. Large bins may be designed to hold clothing. Small specialty stores may require fewer signs but may need specialty cases for small display items.

Merchandising, then, needs to support the category's special needs as identified by the market structure. Let's examine the paper market, how customers view it, and the special ways it might be merchandised both at retail and online.

According to the defined hierarchy, all plain paper should be shelved together. For instance, consumers expect to find reams of copy paper and printer paper in one aisle. Ideally, merchandising should give a clear indication of each SKU's size, weight, and color so the customer does not have to examine each individual package. However, the customer still wants to be able to see and touch the package, so merchandising should never cover up the product or substitute in any way.

Cross-shelving at retail spurs additional sales. Kodak film may be located in as many as 10 to 15 locations in one store. Camera film is usually an impulse purchase, and locating it in many different parts of a store can help a shopper remember to put a package or two in the shopping basket. Products that have a symbiotic relationship are good candidates for cross-shelving. Small items may be placed on "clip-strips" or hanging strips next to sibling merchandise. When it is not practical to shelve items together, written reminders in the section serve to jog the shopper's memory.

Retailers prefer simplicity in merchandising and want fixtures that do not take up much room or require electrical outlets. They often frown on literature at the point of purchase. But for a complicated product category, literature often helps sort out confusion and aids the sales associate as a selling tool. The same is true for selection guides. Our observations confirm that sales associates, to respond to customer questions, use selection guides consistently. Because salespeople must be responsible for hundreds of purchases, guides that help them at the shelf are effective aids as well as training tools.

Securing a prime position for a retail display is key. Retailers seeking to capitalize on in-store real estate sell end caps, the preferred end-of-aisle position. Sometimes, these positions are purchased for an entire year and are furnished with elaborate displays. Both retailers and manufacturers have conducted consumer research indicating that shoppers notice end-caps more than other positions in the store. However, these positions are limited.

Merchandising serves a functional role. Apparel retailers know the placement of mirrors and fitting rooms is important if they want to move the customer to try on a garment—and customers rarely buy unless they are sure of the fit. Chairs must be placed strategically for the elderly, children, or others who wish to sit and rest. Aisles need to be wide enough to provide a degree of freedom and accommodate wheelchairs. Clothes must be grouped in ways to logically find sizes and styles.

Selectability

Selectability is a term coined to represent the increasing complexity in selecting merchandise. Issues at the shelf include sizing, compatibility, language, technical information, and brand clarity. Selection is a process of elimination.

Figure 3-5 shows a wine shop featuring hundreds of similar bottles of wine. The wine merchant has first categorized them into whites and reds. If the consumer wants a red wine, for instance, he can immediately eliminate half the choices. The secondary selection element is the type of wine—Pinot Noir, Merlot, Burgundy, or Bordeaux. Now the shopper can select through a much narrower field of choice.

Selection Hierarchies

Shoppers use hierarchical selection processes. After customers eliminate products that do not fit their choice criteria, they then begin selecting based on specific attributes beginning with the most important. When selecting a red wine, for instance, a customer can eliminate all white wines and then narrow the choice to simply Merlot. Then she must choose between all the bottles of Merlot on the shelf. While she selects her bottle of Merlot, she will then formulate a hierarchy—country of origin, brand, age, and so forth.

Presenting the product category appropriately depends on understanding these criteria. If brand is the number one attribute, it will be important to shelve the products by brand. If it the country of origin is more important, all French wines should be grouped together. You can see

Figure 3–5 Selection at the shelf requires hierarchical organization.

Photo by Kreta Chandler

how these groupings will facilitate selection. Instead of searching through every wine bottle on the shelf, the customer can immediately go to her brand of choice, pick the appropriate bottle and pay for her purchase.

The selection process, determined by the customer, does not usually vary between channels of shopping. Whether shoppers choose a product through a catalog, in retail, or on-line, they will benefit from a streamlined hierarchical presentation.

Becoming too tied to your database can be a real problem. Users can get lost in a structured hierarchy when items are "cross-shelved." Following a link may jump the customer to a completely different part of the hierarchy and the resulting confusion can be very disorienting.

Sizing

Although many clothing sizes are similar within country boundaries, there is no global standard. There may even be significant variation in clothes marked within the same system due to manufacturer variances. More expensive clothes, for instance, may run larger than bargain clothes. Some companies even create their own sizes and may use systems that substitute for compatible sizing.

Small, medium, and large may have completely different values depending on the origin. Asian clothing is typically smaller than garments made in the U.S. European sizing also is somewhat smaller. The fit of shoes varies according to manufacturer as well.

It is incumbent upon a retailer to explain these differences to the consumer. Online merchants must take special care to assist because the online shopper is unable to handle clothes.

Compatibility

The compatibility of some technical products is difficult to determine without assistance. Computer and automotive parts and some supplies are manufactured as part of a system. Packaging at retail may use numerical or color codes to easily distinguish a familial pattern. Merchandising aids are required to complete the task.

Categories with many choices—hosiery, toothpaste, cosmetics, and soup, for example—use other methods to discern differences. Soup, usually branded to look the same, may be shelved alphabetically. Women's hosiery uses package color as a differentiator as well as distinguishing marks on the packaging. Merchandising racks and dispensers with selection information are also usually used in this category.

Technical Information

It is incumbent on retailers to explain the differences between technology products. Generic products are not always identical to the original products that they are intended to replace. Consumers need to understand technical comparisons before they decide to purchase compatible products. The product brand should be prominent and the reseller should never mislead the consumer to believe the substitute is the original product. "Compatible" should not imply "identical."

Be sure to be truthful and up front with the consumer and explain the differences between the products. Performance, quality, price, warranties, and other important attributes vary between original and generic products. The customer should understand the trade-offs before making a choice.

Brand Clarity

Customers want to know the manufacturer of the product they intend to purchase. Each package or fixture should clearly identify the brand associated with the product. Substitutions or generic brands should be identified as such and never confused with an original brand.

Merchandising provided by a manufacturer is intended for that manufacturer's product only if the brand name is clearly identified on the fixture. Category merchandising is the exception. It is never acceptable to shelve a competitor's merchandise on a branded shelf.

Language

Some countries have legal language requirements for product packaging. Canada, for instance, requires both English and French on any product sold within the nation. Optimized sales may depend on broad use of regional languages. Products sold in the European Union usually require at least five different languages. Asian countries may require even more.

Global marketing requires customization and the use of international graphics for clear selectability. The best solution, of course, is to use the local language wherever possible.

Refreshing the Shelf

Refreshing the shelf requires shelf management or "detailing" on a regular basis. Typically, retailers or manufacturers hire firms to come to the store on a daily, weekly, or monthly basis to restock, clean, and generally manage the physical retail presence. Some retailers prefer to perform this service internally.

When companies refresh the shelf at retail, they ensure that the presentation is good—products are facing the right way, torn or damaged products are removed, and the pegs or bins are restocked.

Products should be replaced when new packaging is released. Consumers are confused when two or more identical products feature different colors or images. Consumers also expect older products to be discounted when new versions are released.

One of the most important aspects of keeping the shelf current is to make sure that items are currently in stock. If a product is temporarily out of stock and it's a destination product, consumers may shop elsewhere taking their entire market basket with them.

In a retail store, customers can usually assess whether or not a product is physically available. Some substitute retail methods can confuse consumers. The take-a-ticket system provides a paper "ticket" with the product number or description printed on it. The consumer then takes the ticket to a counter for redemption of the actual merchandise. Retailers use this system to protect high shrinkage items and to reduce the amount of space that products take on the shelf. These items are usually high value items such as electronic games or large products such as TVs or bicycles.

Unfortunately, the tickets don't allow for inventory tracking. Therefore, customers may select a ticket, take it to the customer service counter and wait 15 or 20 minutes only to find out the product is not available. Also, take-a-ticket systems don't allow for tactile examination of a product. Retailers, however, find the system is much easier to re-planogram than actual physical merchandise. The trade-off is creating merchandising systems for the convenience of the retailer or developing methods for simplified consumer shopping.

Retail Advertising and Promotion

Brick and mortar retailers use every medium available to them—radio, television, print advertising, outdoor/transit, direct mail, and the Internet—to deliver their messages. They are adept at finding new ways to advertise and offer promotions. The ability to approach advertising diversely gives them an advantage because retailers in other channels often promote only within their channels.

Advertising's functions include awareness, preference, and direct sales. The concepts are the same whether advertising a store or a branded product. The goal is to gain store loyalty or brand conviction rather than merely brand familiarity. This is achieved through differentiation.

Advertising decisions are easier after you have determined your target market. Media choices should reflect your customer target as well as other buying dynamics including demographics—age, income, educational level, preferences, and purchase patterns.

Retailers focus on certain retail windows to move products. Holidays, tax-filing deadlines, and back-to-school opportunities are targets for the retail calendar. Planning takes place months in advance. Christmas planograms and advertising might be finalized by April or even earlier. Of course, advertising deadlines close several months before publication as well.

Pictures are more powerful in advertising than words. Regardless of the channel, visual images create a strong emotional response and communicate in any language, especially effective for the Internet. Visual thoughts are also easier to remember, are simply more persuasive, and get the message across more quickly.

While an effective advertising program is based on clear communication objectives, promotions are grounded in trial. Retailers encourage trial through sampling, coupons, contests, and other promotional programs. They also take advantage of every tool at their disposal including inserts in billing statements, phone promotions, and shopping cart advertising.

Demo Days

Personal demonstrations are popular for promoting technical products. Representatives from the original manufacturer staff store aisles during the promotional period. They answer questions, give technical demonstrations, and sell products.

These product representatives usually have expertise not available to retail sales associates. In addition, they may bring additional equipment with them, offer specials, or provide free incentives.

Implementing a "demo days" program provides additional benefits for the manufacturer. By participating, technical employees are provided the opportunity to meet and speak with customers personally. They also are able to work through customers' problems and understand the customer's point-of-view.

Hewlett-Packard has participated in demo days with a variety of retailers. The newest products are demonstrated for each individual customer visiting the shelf during the event. The company encourages technical and product experts to help customers learn more about each category and how to use the products, and to assess the customers' needs.

Seasonality

Special sections are created in many retail stores for seasonal merchandise. As soon as one promotional season is complete, the next is set up. Some retailers use freestanding kiosks on wheels for rotating seasonal merchandise.

Planning for seasonal sections occurs months in advance of the actual event or holiday. Usually, merchants prefer temporary and disposable displays—pre-packed shippers—or bins that can be removed quickly and easily.

Dating on products limits their shelf life and requires shelf management to rotate the merchandise. Both end-of-season and outdated products are usually marked down for quick sale.

Holiday seasonal merchandise is most often featured through special promotions. The products must be sold quickly because storing the goods for an entire year is costly and retailers prefer to offer new selections.

While special areas in a retail store are usually reserved for seasonal merchandise, an online merchant is free to put these products anywhere in the site. Special holiday products can take priority over regular merchandise without sacrificing fixtures or being forced to reset the section. The flexibility that online selling offers is uniquely positioned to take advantage of special and seasonal programs.

Using Retail Tips to Increase E-tail Profits

How can you make the most of retailing expertise if you sell online? Become familiar with retailing techniques and learn how to apply them in your virtual store. The following tips can serve as a checklist:

- Know the customer. Approximately two-thirds of consumers prefer to shop in traditional retail stores. The psychology of the shelf is more than usability. Test frequently.
- Know your competition. Your competition is retail and every other selling motion.
- Understand the categories. Retailers know you can't just put products on a shelf—you must learn about each category.
- Borrow retail expertise. Incorporate more sophisticated techniques in your plan. Don't limit your plan to e-commerce.
- Create the familiar. Customers want a site they can relate to, and they expect personalized service.
- Merchandise the e-shelf. Line listings don't work.
- Refresh the virtual shelf. Keep it fresh—"detail" the shelf often.
- Promote your site. Remember, retailers advertise in many mediums to promote a store or chain. Don't limit yourself to your website or the Internet at large.
- Measure your progress. Retailers evaluate their stores frequently—use the same rigor.

The retail and e-tail shelf require the same diligence and commitment to stocking, organization, and selection. Customers require many of the same services regardless of the shopping method. Both will require new techniques as shopping requirements continue to evolve and customers are crunched for time.

Know the Customer

More customers are complaining about the Internet—at nearly the same rate as mail order and telemarketing channels. Because most customers prefer shopping in traditional stores, e-tailers need to understand and meet the customer's expectations.

We all know consumers want convenience, and e-tailing should be a preferred method of shopping. After all, shoppers don't have to leave their homes, use their gas, and spend precious time shopping. But there are some issues to overcome.

Retailers have moved from just putting products on the shelf to advanced retailing management. They also know the high cost to the business when shoppers abandon their shopping carts. Because abandonment is an even greater issue on the web, developing a detailed analysis is the first place to start.

Retailers employ firms to come into the store and observe customers actually shopping at the shelf. Interactions with products are timed, hesitation is monitored, selection roadblocks are determined, customer service is gauged, and category analysis is performed. While some analysis is measured on the web, the research coverage is less qualitative and more focused on the number of hits and sales.

Data should be gathered to give insight to customer frustration, confusion, ability to obtain service, and the time it takes to make a selection, make a purchase, and exit the site. For example, even though there are many different types of pet food to choose from, it takes less than 30 seconds to select a can of dog food at retail. If the same product were purchased on the web, how long would it take for the customer to purchase the product? Testing regularly with real target customers will provide insight. Testing early in the process will add the most value.

Even when selection is simplified, the checkout process can be a nightmare. It is the purchasing process where most shopping carts are abandoned on the web. Abandonment carries a high cost to e-tailers. Normally, at retail, when consumers can't find what they want at the shelf, they leave the store, taking the entire value of the shopping cart with them. Unfortunately, when customers remove the shopping cart at e-tail, they may also take the entire channel with them. If they have one or two bad shopping experiences, they may never again attempt to purchase on the web.

What do consumers really want from their retailers? They want a combination of vintage shopping services and technological advances. The warmness of yesteryear's shopkeepers who greeted their customers by name, helped them select their purchases, and then wrapped and delivered even inexpensive items at no cost is now perceived as a luxury. The ideal model combines value, selection, and comfort shopping with exciting new technology, fun, and entertainment. It's personal, convenient, benefit-oriented and almost impossible to achieve at retail today.

If web retailers can offer a set of these features and provide shopping methods to rival retail, consumer loyalty will shift.

Over the years, the shopping environment has transitioned to self-service. Even when sales assistants are plentiful in the stores, they are often poorly informed, because many of them work at any given retailer less than a year. Retailers also hire students and temporary workers and often pay low wages. Companies that have branded service attributes, such as Nordstrom, tend to attract career employees because they offer higher wages and incentive programs. But these are the exception, not the rule. Service should be one of the first attributes to tackle.

Offering toll-free phone numbers on the first page of your site will help consumers who are uncomfortable with cyber shopping. It will give them a way to get assistance, place an order over the phone, and help them overcome technophobia.

You should not only be prepared to manage these basics, but also to keep an eye out for ways in which the retail community is advancing. You will need to be able to match or even exceed these improvements.

Hybrid retailers are easing customers into e-shopping by giving them options and choices to mix-and-match services between traditional retail stores and the Internet. All e-tailers will need to turn the Internet into an active shopping mode rather than an advance information-gathering device for retail store sales.

Put some rigor into understanding why consumers prefer physical stores. By solving problems like high delivery fees, security, and service, Internet retailers can increase their market share.

E-commerce could create an environment that is personal, targeted, convenient, and entertaining. Cyberspace holds the key to personal customer relationships. Selection can significantly exceed that of the retail store, and preferences can be recorded for future shopping ease. Offering targeted and personalized merchandise during every encounter is simplified on the web because the customer reveals his or her identity during each purchase.

Retail Trends to Watch

The future is difficult to predict. But the following trends are in progress and will continue to pick up steam as time progresses. Some, like CRM, will become a condition of doing business in the future rather than a trend.

One-to-One Marketing/Loyalty Programs

One-to-one marketing programs or customer-relationship management programs (CRM) are the latest trend in retailing, web-based marketing, cataloging, and manufacturer relationships. Retailers have jumped on the bandwagon, looking for new ways to create connections with individuals.

One goal of CRM programs is to provide singular insight of all customers and every interaction they have with a retailer. The main goal, however, is to act with this information in mind every time a customer visits a store or makes a transaction. That will be the major transformation in retailing in the future. Any loyalty strategy, of course, will need to employ offline and online marketing. In the future, customers most likely will refuse to provide their information to more than one agent in the same company. This will force businesses to integrate customer information.

Customized Programs and Services

As an adjunct to their CRM programs, retailers will be adding customized programs and services, and manufacturers will be creating customized products. As a result, retailers will have to modify their supply-chain processes to meet the demand. Logistics and warehousing will need to evolve to remain competitive.

The demand for customized products will result in shorter product lifecycles and smaller production output. Because it will require more flexibility, retailers will need to respond as well. The cycles for resetting the stores may need to move from the traditional fixed dates and seasonal planning to responsive, just-in-time planning. The store of the future will have to be very different to accommodate real-time consumer demands.

Aggressive Differentiation

In the past 20 years, retailers were very aggressive in expanding their chains through the building of new stores and consolidating with other companies to become larger and more powerful. In their haste to build new stores, some stores have almost become clones of one another. Warehouse-type superstores, for instance, all tend to look like one another. Other "big box" formats and club stores are hard to tell apart as well.

Now retailers realize they must close some of the stores they built so quickly and differentiate the rest of the stores in their chains. They will be adding more interactivity and special services. In order to be successful, retailers will need to help the consumer associate a unique benefit with their stores that is different from their competition.

In the future, customers will want to be able to experiment in the store, enjoy face-to-face interaction with a variety of demonstrations, and participate in entertainment. Retailing will need to become more active than passive. Stores will incorporate interactive technologies and offer instant training rather than classes. Of course, retailers will have to conduct research to determine which technologies customers prefer. Some shoppers dislike using a handheld scanner that tells them which product matches their personal profile. But the same shoppers would like handheld scanners to conduct price checks, verify sizes, or place orders. Just because a tool is electronic does not guarantee its acceptance.

Increased differentiation will include these new tools and new techniques. But the main emphasis will be on building brands to gain recognition of store value and service.

Channel Blurring

Channels aren't as distinct as they once were. Drug stores sell milk, and grocery stores have pharmacies. More than 40,000 products are now sold in supermarkets. Consumers just want convenience and shopping speed. Retailers know that if they are able to satisfy most consumer needs in one shopping trip, there will be less need for the consumer to shop at another store. Retailers would like to capture as many of the day's shopping dollars as possible.

Watch for this channel blurring to continue. While consumers today favor European-type shopping, being able to purchase fresh foods daily or satisfy other needs without pre-planning, retailers may replicate the hypermarket concept to provide all needs under one store roof.

Customers are also moving toward using more than one channel to make their purchases. While online sales are just a fraction of traditional retail sales, the web complements all sales by providing supporting information for purchase decisions. Retailers will increasingly rely on the web to learn more about their customers and offer specialized services and promotions. It's important that the customer has a consistent experience across all of the channels.

Channel blurring has extended to the Internet as retailers have pushed customers online with web-specific promotions. Many companies still pursue web sales for the immediate cash return and low overhead dollars, rather than building the channel or contributing to a brand. The Internet customer relationship in the future will be perceived as a long-term asset, not a short-term sale.

One retailer can span channels within its own organization. Kroger owns chain drug stores, convenience stores, supermarkets, and mass merchandisers. Wal-Mart has its conventional mass stores, supercenters, Sam's clubs, and Neighborhood Store supermarkets. The future may include more blending among these.

Security/Trust Focus

Over the past several years, there has been an increasing issue with security and trust of both merchants and manufacturers. When appliances break before their time, when services cost more but provide less, or when fashion designers force new fads on the public without alternatives, the retailer is often the one to take the blame.

Cybercrime is also rising. An unprecedented number of websites have been infected with some type of computer virus. Other attacks have ranged from defacement of a site to disabling a site entirely. Victims include e-merchants, manufacturers, and financial institutions.

Higher costs, more self-service, and crowded checkout counters don't contribute to furthering trust. Retailers are trying to re-establish themselves as trusted advisors and service providers. Both resellers and manufacturers have dedicated resources to ensure that the products they sell and the environments in which they sell them are safe and secure. This trend will become more critical to conducting business.

Problem Solving Programs

Home discount centers used to be merely warehouses stocked with remodeling materials like countertops, sinks, and faucets. Now these companies provide a consultant to work with the consumer not only to select these products but also to recommend entire remodeling services. In addition to the products, home discount centers offer contracting services to install the new kitchen fixtures.

Retail solution centers will increase in virtually every store. Instead of staffing with sales associates, retailers may add category experts to their stores in major metropolitan areas. The trend will extrapolate to virtually every type of business.

Category Expansion

Over time, categories tend to divide as more specialized products are developed. The paper category used to consist of writing paper and typing paper. Then the advent of the computer created the need for printing paper. Now, the category has expanded to include specialty printing paper as well—glossy, resume, and brochure paper to name a few.

While companies are merging and integrating, they may mistakenly believe they have gained synergies in categories. The opposite is true. More categories are being offered in each store, and more categories are being created as they divide and multiply.

The result—for traditional as well as online stores—is the ultimate capping of product assortment. Offering too many types of products only confuses the consumer. The retailer will have to carefully prioritize even more in the future.

Store Expansion/Remodeling

Stores are running out of room. It is always a struggle for the retailer to determine which products go on the shelf due to space constraints. There are now more than 50 versions of Crest toothpaste, and other brands offer nearly as many. Only consumer-preferred variations will be placed on the shelf.

But store expansion is limited and not merely focused on making more space for more products. Retailers are updating their stores to create meal solution services and interactivity. Grocers feature more prepared foods and have expanded the perimeter—the most popular area of the store—to focus on high-profit, interesting products and services.

Watch for all types of retailers to concentrate on creating ambience and entertainment. Because e-merchants will provide convenience, retailers plan to stress that in-person shopping is fun and an activity that you can share with friends and family.

Of course, some of these are not just retailing trends. Trends in the past have started with retail and then gradually moved to the other shelves. Now, with channel and program integration, some trends may evolve concurrently. Internet companies can take an active role in adopting those trends that improve web shopping.

Know Your Competition

Most retailers use the Internet—one way or another. They either embrace it as a tool, see it as a secondary channel, or track e-tailers as competitors. Because they have a great deal of experience in retailing and own customer preference, it will be important they do not define Internet shopping as a passive medium. The good news is that customers are looking for solutions that brick-and-mortar retailers cannot provide with physical solutions alone.

Taking advantage of the unique capabilities of the Internet will set web retailers apart. No other medium can offer personal and customized consumer interaction so quickly and with every transaction.

By embracing a strong differentiation program, implementing services currently offered only at retail, and solving Internet-related problems, e-tail's competitive position will strengthen. As with any competitive program, it's important to analyze current competitive issues and predict potential risks. That means understanding what retailers are currently undertaking and why, and determining what they might do in the future.

Understand the Categories

We discussed category management as a retail discipline. But there are aspects of category management that can be adopted at the virtual shelf. Understanding category dynamics can be the key to more effective selling on the web. Information for both the reseller and the consumer is available through fact-based selling. Understanding how the customer perceives and approaches certain products may change the structure of the online shelf. SKU rationalization prioritizes the most desired as well as the most profitable products, simplifying the consumer's search.

Category management may be used to integrate a site. The entire online store should be more than simply a collection of disjointed pages and should have the same continuity as a store. An online furniture site we visited used "chairs" and "tables" as designation labels. Unfortunately, the site missed the opportunity to sell furniture collections. Customers often shop for entire room settings of furniture that feature the same or compatible design.

By developing a market structure to define categories, you can design your store's categories with the customer in mind. Organization of the site can flow directly from your virtual map. Web page navigation is discussed in Chapter 5.

Borrow Retail Expertise

Why reinvent the wheel? Retailers have years of experience that are there for the borrowing. In fact, many retail systems can be adapted to the virtual environment. Some are quite sophisticated. It will be interesting to monitor click-and-mortar hybrids to see if they are able to leverage these systems to their e-tail divisions.

While some retailing techniques are complicated, others are simple and fairly easy to implement. The same information, demonstration, and even personal attention can be handled on the web with a fraction of the investment. It's even possible to provide seminars or tutorials online and reach large groups of people. This is a simple implementation of a complex retail issue—providing service with fewer employees.

Other programs, such as cash register tape analysis, are simplified online as well. Much more information can be tied to a sale, including an online database that will give data in real time. The issue, for both retail and e-tail, is using the collected information effectively.

Create the Familiar

The Internet was established by technicians and perpetuated by entrepreneurs who were more interested in start-ups and buy-outs than with building customer loyalty and establishing brand equity. Marketing knowledge, metrics, and solid business plans took a back seat to fast-paced financial wizardry. Now, in order to gain consumer confidence and comfort, Internet shopping must look and feel familiar. That means it needs to remind them of retail shopping.

That's why understanding the retail environment is so important. The details that surround a consumer's shopping trip are often subtle and ingrained deep within the customer's memory. These are areas we take for granted and may not replicate in an online system without giving them a great deal of thought. Ensuring that the basics are there will level the playing field and enable online merchants to expand into innovation.

Merchandise the E-Shelf

The days of delivering pages of product line-listings are over. Merchandising on the web is just as important as merchandising in a store. Retailers who throw products on a shelf and try to sell them find that they are relatively unsuccessful unless the store is a bargain basement. Consumers expect to find pleasing, well organized, and easy-to-use shelves at their disposal.

Virtual merchants should use large, colorful pictures—usually of the front, back, and sides of a product. Remember how consumers shop in a store—they pick up the product, turn it over, and examine it. Because the e-shelf is missing the ability to provide tactile senses, it must make up for the deficit through better imagery.

Sound is under-used to sell merchandise on the web. It can provide a personal touch with a human voice to guide the consumer through the shopping process. Product instructions, demonstrations, and even music will make the experience more interesting, informative, and pleasurable.

Don't forget that merchandising serves very functional purposes. Use it to guide the customer through your store with virtual signs, category delineations, and selection information. It also flags promotions, brands, and reminders to purchase complementary products.

Ask manufacturers to provide specially branded "fixtures" or "kiosks." Traditional retailers receive all types of merchandising materials to promote manufacturers' brands, and online merchants should be able to take advantage of these as well. Most manufacturers are happy to help e-tailers achieve their sales goals.

Some categories are very complex and require selection aids. It is essential to provide clear compatibility guides, extra information, and pictures to help sell these products. If misleading information angers and confuses customers, it can also affect their relationships with product manufacturers.

Virtual planograms will map the "store" to look and feel more like the retail counterpart. Partitioning obsolete or infrequently purchased products into separate units will help customers browse through the site. Selection is a process of elimination. If you limit the choices on the most frequently visited pages, customers are not overwhelmed. A search function will help them locate the odd product.

Refresh the Virtual Shelf

Nothing is as irritating online as connecting to an outdated link. Old information in a site reflects on the integrity of the reseller. Remember, establishing trust is the key to brand preference and sales.

If a consumer clicks on anything labeled "new" on your site, the product, information, or promotion should be no older than six months. There are actually laws in the U.S. that govern the use of "new" labels in advertising and promotion. Be aware of the restrictions.

Even information about your company should be current. If the latest press release is dated 1997, the customer may wonder if your company is still active. If you don't maintain your own site, the consumer may also have doubts about the service he will receive.

"Detail" your product offerings frequently. Update pictures with new packaging or merchandise as it is released, not months later. New information on products, seasonal promotions, or new fashions should be incorporated as quickly as possible. Provide the pull-date information for consumers on perishable or dated merchandise. Consumers look for these dates in the store and want to be reassured of freshness through any shopping mode.

Have professionals visit your site regularly to give you an unbiased opinion. Integrate mystery shopping into your capabilities. You can't really understand what a customer goes through in the purchase process if you use web designers to evaluate the site. Conduct focus groups or one-on-one sessions with actual customers to find out how well your site relates to their needs. Simulation of random shopping emulates the actual process.

Managing each shelf and each category independently will ensure that the entire site is kept up-to-date. Refreshing the virtual shelf does not mean changing the first page only.

Promote Your Site

Because retailers use every medium to promote their stores, advertising outside the channel will leverage sales. Utilizing direct mail, print advertising, and even broadcast advertising will reach an audience wider than those who frequent the web today. If web shopping is perceived as appealing, it will give others a reason to participate.

Promotion is more than using a dotcom designation as an afterthought. Most people can't remember the name of a website. Potential customers don't always have a pencil to jot down the site's designation, and even if they did, there is no guarantee they would later remember to visit. For those who have not been inclined to use the web regularly, the addresses are rather cumbersome. An ad, coupon, or other aid not only sparks interest, but also gives customers a physical tool to help them remember the site.

While web retailers want to drive business to the Internet for a variety of cost reasons, click-and-mortar businesses have upset their traditional retail customers by providing discounts online without giving the same advantage to their store shoppers.

Online merchants can give customers a choice to place an order on the phone and still receive a discount to avoid channel issues. Because many consumers are still reluctant to use the web due to lack of security, provide them with an alternative shopping method. Savvy retailers will let customers come into their stores, browse, and then call the store to order their products. Similar choices need to be available on the web.

Measure Your Progress

In order to compete with traditional retailers, web retailers need metrics at least as complete as those used to measure store performance. Virtual merchants have the opportunity to measure with more frequency than retailers who are dependent on physical systems and point-of-sale tapes. Each metric should reflect your plan's objectives.

Not all measures are quantitative. How are you relating to gender differences? Be aware that women now outnumber men who shop on the web. And their buying patterns on the Internet are different than at retail. Men frequently choose to browse and interact online more than women. Many women want to place their purchases and quickly leave the virtual store.

Evaluate the most significant obstacles for web shoppers—slow processing speed of orders, concerns over security, and high shipping and handling costs. Many shopping carts are abandoned online because the consumer cannot find a way to have questions answered.

The combination of shopping transaction technical data, business metrics, and qualitative information will serve to ensure a successful website.

Globalization

Few traditional retail companies are established as global enterprises. The Internet, by its nature, is a global tool. It has the potential to offer merchandise customized to individual countries and cultures and with localized language. True one-to-one marketing not only takes into account the product needs of the consumer, but also his or her social needs.

Manufacturers have been able to create products on a worldwide basis. Internet resellers have the potential to manage sales at this level, but customization is the key. Using U.S. pictures and formats for European or Asian implementation does not work. Color preference and other attributes vary widely by country. Translations alone cannot localize a site.

Establishing partnerships in other regions offers localized merchandising, retailing, and marketing. Customizing a site requires all three.

Retail Excellence at the Virtual Shelf

Retail techniques, shelf-management strategies, and consumer behavior change frequently. Any strategy to excel at the virtual shelf should incorporate frequent monitoring of the retail industry to stay abreast of new approaches.

Retailing in the 1950s or even the 1980s was very different than it is today. But beware of the newest fads that promise to revolutionize shopping. Often, these programs are meant to improve the life of the retailer rather than the life of the consumer. Shoppers are reluctant to adopt new shopping methods unless they really improve their lifestyles.

The future of e-tail lies in understanding consumers' preferences and meeting their expectations.

CHAPTER 4

Catalog Marketing: Taking the Best and Leaving the Rest

Who hasn't heard of the "wish book"? Entire families used to sit by the evening fire and thumb through the glossy pages, choosing any number of wonderful items they'd like to order. While the Sears catalog is now defunct in the U.S., the catalog industry has been rejuvenated in the last ten years. Rather than large, 400-page books, many of today's consumer catalogs reflect vertical, or specific, industries with specialty catalogs ranging from hard-to-fit shoes to new-age remedies.

In fact, the catalog business is growing. In the U.S., only about 10 percent of households *didn't* purchase from a catalog within the year. And catalogers are moving to the Internet with amazing velocity. More than 80 percent of all catalog companies now have websites.

The catalog "shelf" entices consumers to browse in the same way that a retail store invites a customer to walk through the front door. It's not even necessary to have a product in mind to enjoy opening and browsing a catalog. Turning the recreational aspect of catalog browsing into sales is dependent on capturing the consumer's interest and urging her to keep turning pages.

A retail store offers instant gratification. It's easy to pick up a product, walk to the checkout counter, and pay for the merchandise. The shopper is able to obtain the merchandise immediately. Catalog shoppers may merely mark a page, intending to order later. The catalog, though, offers the convenience of shopping at home. It's simple to pick up the phone, dial a toll-free number, and place your order. The shopping process may be abandoned with either shopping mode, though, so it's important to determine how customers interact with each shelf and what motivates them to purchase.

Catalogs, direct mail, and retail all can differ from Internet shopping in a significant way. Using a "push" strategy, they take advantage of sending frequent mailings, promotions, and advertising that have not been requested to reach customers in their homes or places of business and bring them to their "stores." But many e-stores must depend on customers entering the web before they can attempt to promote their wares—a more passive form of marketing. Although e-merchants are adept at using the Internet and sending e-mail messages, most have not used all the traditional marketing vehicles at their disposal. Catalogers are pros at finding, enticing, and keeping their customers.

The Catalog Shopping Experience

Renee was excited to finally get the latest version of her favorite catalog. She looked forward to sitting in her comfy chair, watching TV, and browsing through the pages to select her favorite products. She had to admit, though, she was a bit annoyed at having to purchase the catalog. Why, she thought, should she have to pay for the opportunity to browse through someone's store? Even though the company gave her a coupon to redeem with her first purchase, she equated the practice with paying a toll to enter a retail store. If you purchased something in the store, the retailer would give you back the toll. Otherwise, you'd have to pay.

Nevertheless, Renee knew she would pay the price again to get the catalog. She didn't always purchase out of each catalog but when she did, her purchases were usually large. She seemed to favor the winter edition of the catalog, but she didn't know why. Her purchases tracked with her preference—she ordered twice as much from the winter book.

After Renee settled into her chair and opened her catalog, she immediately turned the pages to her favorite section in the book—the home furnishings. She decided to browse but quickly remembered that she would like to purchase a cabinet to hold her videotape collection. She looked in the index but couldn't decide whether to search under "furniture," or "electronics." It was not listed in either location.

Renee decided she would have to look through each section. Finally, after turning numerous pages, she found a cabinet. Unfortunately, it was not available in the finish she desired. Then, to her surprise, she spotted another one she liked at the top of the next page. She was pleased to find it offered in an ebony finish to match her bedroom set. She wasn't sure if the black finish was gloss or matte, however, and the description offered her no clues. She hoped it was the dull finish.

The cabinet could hold 108 videotapes according to the catalog copy. The accompanying picture showed the cabinet with the doors closed so it was impossible to determine how the inside of the cabinet was organized. Did it have shelves in the doors? Were the internal shelves adjustable? She wouldn't find out unless she had the heavy object delivered. If she ordered it and it didn't work, she would have to figure out how to lift it, repackage it, and send it back.

Renee decided to take the risk and picked up the phone. Although she had the page turned to the object she wished to order, she realized the phone number of the company was not on the page. She had to turn the book to the front cover to obtain the number.

She dialed and a rather tired voice came on the line. "May I have your catalog code?" Renee wasn't sure what a catalog code was, so she asked for clarification. When she found out it was in a box on the back cover, she turn the book again and nearly lost her place. She made a mental note to remember where the code was located, although she wondered why it was even necessary. Weren't the product number and the price enough to find the item? Did the company use duplicate numbers in each catalog?

Renee furnished her personal information and was informed there would be an extra shipping charge due to the weight of the item she selected. She hesitated because the price became quite high when the extra charges were added. But she consented to complete the order because she knew she would probably have as much trouble finding a black video cabinet in a store. She was thanked for her order and told to expect her cabinet in two to three weeks.

Renee returned to browsing through her catalog. She decided to take a look at the clothes, although she really didn't need any. About half way through the section, she found a sweater she couldn't resist. She realized she forgot to use her coupon for the order she just placed, so she called back to adjust her order.

A different operator answered this time. When asked for her catalog code, Renee knew exactly where to turn. But she still almost lost her place in the catalog. She asked the sales assistant if she could add the sweater to her order and also redeem her coupon. The representative told her she couldn't adjust an order after it was placed. She would have to place a second order.

Renee consented and placed the order. She was told she would have to pay another fee to have it delivered. Couldn't she just add to the other order? It was a very light sweater and wouldn't weigh anything compared to the heavy cabinet. But, again, she was told there were no adjustments and she would have to pay the extra charge. Renee decided to have it delivered to the store to save money and she would have to drive the ten miles to pick it up. Maybe she should have done the same with the cabinet, she thought.

Catalogs are fun to read and are a convenient way to shop. Ordering from one, however, is not foolproof. Buying products, other than impulse purchases, requires using the index. Indexes in some catalogs are becoming briefer and more cryptic to save pages and avoid locking in products to specific pages. Smaller indexes allow for more production flexibility because the index must be completed last. The complexity of navigating through catalogs depends, of course, on the size of the book. Very small catalogs require only a quick search. But larger, complex, or business-to-business catalogs are somewhat ineffective without the index.

When placing a catalog order, the customer must be prepared. She will need the phone number, the catalog number, the quantity, and perhaps additional information, such as the color, size, price, or finish, in addition to her credit card. Unlike ordering online, the customer doesn't have unlimited time to place the order if calling on the phone. She may place her order by mail or fax; however, she will not be able to ask questions.

Whether your business is online or offline, any direct ordering process can be improved by following a few key recommendations:

- Help the customer find products through an expanded and relevant index.
- Prepare the customer before she places the order. Ordering information with simple instructions should be prominent.

- Try not to "surprise" the customer with unwelcome news—high delivery fees and out-of-stock products, for example.
- If possible, standardize delivery fees or deliver for free. Don't base delivery fees on the cost of the order—with higher fees for increased spending. One very small $100 item should not cost the same to deliver as ten $10 items. The process penalizes the customer who spends the most.
- Minimize the need for customers to provide you with internal codes.
- Keep key ordering information available on all pages.
- Provide alternative methods for ordering—phone, fax, mail, and Internet.

Although not everyone reads unsolicited catalogs, many catalogs are welcomed and even requested. If the shopping experience begins in a positive vein, catalog experts know it's important to keep it that way through the entire ordering process.

The Direct Market

Direct marketing employs a variety of methods to reach the individual customer. Although the industry has a reputation for sending direct mail, there are actually distinguishing elements within the market:

- Direct Mail—an advertising medium
- Direct Response—an advertising technique
- Mail Order—a marketing methodology

Direct Mail

Direct mail is an advertising medium similar to TV, newspapers, magazines, and radio. In the same sense, the web is also an advertising medium. Direct mail is dependent on customer lists and inquiries. It is used for prospecting to the home consumer as well as to the business-to-business consumer.

Direct mail may be used in conjunction with any other channel. For instance, retailers use direct mail extensively to entice customers to come to their stores. They realize many sales begin long before the customer walks into the store.

Similarly, Internet stores can take advantage of direct mail to bring their potential customers to a specific site without relying on web browsers. By using a very specific list, they can target customers with a high likelihood of purchasing.

Because direct mail is a prospecting tool, it is often termed as "junk mail." While the online movement may transform all modes of shopping and advertising, junk mail is as unwelcome online as it is sent through the mail. The safety of mail has been questioned and some respondents are unwilling to open unfamiliar mail. However, unfamiliar e-mail may carry viruses and may pose a risk to equipment.

Direct Response

Direct response is an advertising technique that manages the call-to-action element of an ad, mail piece, TV commercial, magazine or newspaper ad, or a catalog with a coupon. Customers call a toll-free number, send in a coupon or postcard, or respond by logging in to a website to obtain more information or place an order.

Other forms of advertising may focus on building awareness or preference. Direct response is the most active form of advertising and asks the customer to take an action.

Mail Order

Mail order is a method of marketing that uses the mail or telephone to sell or enable delivery of products. Catalogs are a form of mail order.

Mail order pieces sell the actual product as opposed to creating a lead or promoting an offer. Customers usually place an order via a toll-free number but may send an order by fax or mail.

E-mail Marketing vs. Direct Mail Marketing

There is essentially no difference between e-mail marketing and direct mail marketing. One uses the mail for prospecting, and the other uses electronic mail. However, e-mail is dependent on a narrower prospect list—those who have connectivity. In addition, marketers must have an actual e-mail address as opposed to a reverse phone listing—which must be provided by the individual. Most people are reachable by traditional mail but it is difficult to keep lists current.

Direct mail recipients must take the step of opening an envelope. E-mail customers must open the message. Both are subject to the wastebasket. The direct marketing industry has learned to send "lumpy" packages to entice and tempt customers. The theory behind this technique is that most consumers enjoy receiving something for free. Lumpy packages are impossible to send online. In fact, messages with attachments are the worst possible implementation.

The future of e-mail marketing may lie in conducting a transaction entirely through e-mail. Because many customers are tired of surfing, e-mail marketing is effective for direct transactions to repeat customers. Routine purchases made through e-mail are easy to place, especially if the consumer is not required to go to a link. It's best used, however, with routine or repeat orders or key category products because it is not effective in selling many diverse products.

Combining Direct Marketing with Other Marketing Techniques

A variety of marketing elements may be combined with both direct mail and e-marketing. Traditionally, a mix of telemarketing and direct mail has been very effective. The telemarketing portion of the program provides direct, personal interaction with the customer, while the direct mail provides a lasting physical presence of the company and its products.

The best combinations couple long-term and short-term programs. As with any advertising or marketing promotion programs, the most effective programs are continuous and provide steady contact delivering reasons why the target market should do business with your company.

The Character of the Catalog

Along with other cataloging techniques, we'll cover the five "Ps" of cataloging:

- Positioning
- Presentation
- Production
- Personalization
- Persistence

Understanding these will give you insight into how the industry operates and the unique advantages that catalogers have built for their companies.

A catalog, in retail terms, is a "shelf" that relies on direct marketing techniques. It can encompass education as well as entertainment. This is not just due to the inherent nature of the catalog—the fact that it's a portable picture book. It's also due to the diligence the industry has given to effective presentation including compelling artwork and persuasive copy. Even several business-to-business catalogs have created interesting dynamics in their books and have added significant value over the years. Trade catalogs may include sidebars explaining specific techniques or procedures and are often perceived as reference materials as well as sales vehicles.

Because the catalog industry is so dependent on repeat sales, it has been critical to develop a rapport with customers by mailing frequently and using effective promotional techniques. Due to these techniques, catalogs have gained perceived value that other shelves have not. Customers often keep catalogs even when they are out of date.

The Catalog Market

The catalog industry is segmented into business-to-business (B-to-B) and home- or consumer-focused mailers. The two often differ in the size, complexity, and frequency of publication. The business-to-business market varies depending on the industry it supports. Frequently, the catalogs are large reference books designed to facilitate both routine purchases as well as those, infrequent, hard-to-find product searches. These catalogs are positioned primarily for the businesses they serve, and within an industry, it is sometimes difficult to tell them apart. They are often supplemented with more frequent catalogs featuring specials and promotions.

Home- and consumer-based catalog firms, however, have learned to segment along vertical markets and have flooded the market with specialty catalogs. Many catalog firms have decided to focus on more narrowly targeted catalogs for two reasons. First, catalogers have become more proficient at targeting consumers effectively. Secondly, catalog firms found they could cut costs and deliver more timely and relevant materials by creating smaller but more frequently mailed catalogs.

Specialty catalogs often feature only one category. There are catalogs specifically for popcorn, chocolate, shoes, hams, rings, and T-shirts. Sports and hobby catalogs specialize in virtually every activity imaginable. These catalogs bring new meaning to the term "armchair shopping."

Whether a business-to-business or a consumer catalog, positioning serves the purpose of differentiating in a crowded market. Historically, catalogs have evolved in the following ways:

- First, some companies have spawned vertical-market catalogs from their larger, more inclusive catalogs. Based on historical sales, they have identified opportunities to specialize and have positioned smaller catalogs to fulfill specific needs. They have, on occasion, separated low-volume specialty goods into catalogs that are updated less frequently and cut costs by removing these from the more expensive, larger book. JC Penney focused exclusively on its large catalog until the company separated several specialty categories into smaller flyers. Bridal, special-size apparel, and home & leisure are a few of the vertical specialty markets they serve.
- Next, retailers have given birth to catalog businesses, and, just as frequently these days, catalog firms have developed corresponding retail outlets—sometimes clearance houses for overstocks. The stores have pre-defined the business and are often the result of emergence on the web. Office product superstores created their own specialty catalogs for frequently purchased items, and sales are supplemented by larger contract stationer catalogs for hard-to-find items. Spiegel owned a thriving catalog business before opening retail outlets to sell discounted overstocks. True hybrids—stores with catalogs designed from the outset to compete on both fronts, are somewhat rarer because most establish one or the other first.
- Last, some vertical catalog businesses have been created to function in the specialty realm with only a website as an adjunct. Companies with special expertise in a market or those that have embarked on significant research to understand market opportunities are most likely to enter these niches.

Each catalog needs its own identity to create competitive distinction. This position must be firmly ingrained in consumers' minds and deliver a package of products, services, and promotions that meet their needs. Vertical catalogs—catalogs designed for narrow markets—may satisfy product needs, but they must also appeal to the specific customer segment for which they are intended. Because the catalogs are so specialized, the cataloger must know quite a bit about that particular product segment and the corresponding lifestyle of the consumer.

The personality of the catalog is apparent through the use of copy, images, the quality of the paper, and the quality of the products. Graphics and visuals are critical to convey messages. Customers usually browse catalogs rather than read them. Pictures and captions may provide the only opportunity for a cataloger to communicate with his audience.

Other, subtle characteristics, such as the selection of models in the apparel industry, give signals to your customers. It's difficult to gain credibility with older consumers, for instance, if 20-year-old models don clothing meant for the senior consumer. Relevance is key to positioning—especially in the catalog industry where one-to-one marketing is the name of the game.

Catalogs That Sell Catalogs

Today's catalogs are so varied that the industry has spawned a new phenomenon—catalogs selling catalogs. These flyers list a variety of unique specialty catalogs, and the reader can order any of them for a small fee. They fulfill two needs—they create awareness for specialty catalogs that otherwise would be unable to gain distribution, and the responses feed into a database qualifying consumers based on interest while updating current demographic information. In addition to receiving revenue from the sale of catalogs, these firms also receive advertising revenue from the feature placements and are able to sell their databases to other catalogers.

Business-to-Business Catalogs

It's fairly common for business-to-business (B-to-B) catalogs to be published annually or semi-annually due to seasonality, production expense, and the production lead time. Smaller flyers often supplement the larger catalog and may be mailed monthly or quarterly. The larger books tend to be organized as reference catalogs, line listing a variety of products. Because they usually feature many diversified products, it's not unusual for these catalogs to minimize product descriptions. In fact, B-to-B reference catalogs can be very expensive to produce. Manufacturers often must supplement their production.

The problem for customers, however, is first locating the correct product category. It's like walking into a large store and trying to find one item within two to three minutes. Then the customer must select, from the variety of products within a specific category, which item will fill the specific need.

For example, if a customer wanted to purchase a telephone from a retail store, it would not be a complex task—although there are many models currently available. At least the customer can pick up the phone and hold it in his hand, look at the features, or examine the box for more information.

Making the same purchase from a catalog, however, is very difficult unless each specification is listed in detail. If all phones in a category have only the same two features listed, they may all appear to be identical. Determining how extensive descriptions should be and how to differentiate similar products is critical to helping the customer make a decision. Each product description should include some unique feature that is proprietary to that product alone. This is the challenge that B-to-B catalogers have to deal with on a daily basis. Many of these are issues for B-to-B websites as well.

B-to-B direct marketing can be cost effective compared to other sales methods. While it costs between $250 and $300 to make an individual sales call, a contact with a business customer through direct mail can cost under $2. The average order size is more than $200. Catalog production is more costly, however. For this reason, many B-to-B catalogers are trying to move their clients to web-based ordering.

The business customer may be reached through direct marketing in a variety of ways. First, a distributor catalog sells goods for resale to other businesses. While repeat sales and standard inventories are common, it is especially helpful if a mechanism alerts customers to new or changed products to simplify the ordering task. Websites can also take advantage of this service.

B-to-B customers who make repeat purchases may automate their orders, changing one or two items as needed. These customers are often not the end users of the product, but employees who have ordering responsibility. They need fast, simple service with quick responses. Unless the customer is going to be using the product, he or she will not be as interested to merely browse through the pages. Organization and simplicity are the hallmarks of business cataloging.

Next, some catalogs are used in conjunction with continuous services. Contract stationers, for instance, provide catalogs to the businesses they serve for the selection of a variety of office products on a routine replenishment basis. Some also provide services to stock and maintain inventory for businesses, physically visiting a site for auto-replenishment purposes.

Business-focused catalogers are as aggressive as their consumer counterparts. In fact, B-to-B firms spent the most on direct mail in order to recruit new prospects and retain customers. They not only pursue customers within their own databases, they also purchase outside lists for prospecting as well.

Electronic Catalogs

Electronic catalogs were the precursors of today's websites. These are catalogs on disks or video. While electronic catalogs were common at one time, they are used sparingly today in the consumer market. They are still offered for high-end products and are common in the B-to-B arena.

Manufacturers often create electronic catalogs for resellers as a way to provide them with data that will eventually reside on their websites. These catalogs also frequently include training materials that feature new product presentations, graphics, features, and benefit information. Electronic catalogs can be web based or placed on a CD that is mailed.

Presentation—How to Define a Catalog

Retail stores have basic commonalities—a front door, aisles, and cash registers. But the presentation of each is what defines the store and creates a basis for differentiation. The overall presentation provides the structure, image, and personality of the store. A convenience store has the same basic format as a large hypermarket, but on a much smaller scale.

Within a chain, retailers maintain several different types of stores with corresponding square footage. Similarly, each catalog has a defined structure. While catalog models are dependent on the specific products sold, target customers, and other variables, there is basic consistency within the catalog industry.

Catalogers know that shoppers expect to find goods in a catalog in similar ways. You'll find the basic skeleton of the catalog is similar from book to book. Ordering materials are usually in the center of the book. Indexing can be found in either the center or the back of the catalog. And catalogs that are published from year to year usually maintain their structures to create familiarity for the consumer. The creative presentation, however, can be extremely varied and unique.

Structure of the Catalog

The structure of a catalog depends primarily on the targeted segment. Business-to-business catalogs are most often designed around products or product segments. Consumer catalogs may be arranged by products, either structured or random, or by topics.

The product formatting process usually divides products according to market structure. In a large catalog, apparel may be grouped together with separate sections for women's, men's, and children's clothing. Accessories may be in a separate section or may enhance each selection. B-to-B catalogs may drill down to very specific categories for ease of ordering.

Topical presentations group products according to a theme or function. A gift catalog, for instance, may organize products by holidays or occasions. Bridal catalogs may include apparel for the entire wedding party, accessories, guest books, and so forth. Everything relating to a specific occasion can be grouped together to maximize sales. These catalogs are usually reserved for consumer products and themes and are best implemented in specialty catalogs. Cooking catalogs may feature pots, pans, and utensils, as well as pasta, sauce, and recipes.

Random product groupings are the most confusing for customers. This format is usually used when the cataloger has many diverse products to sell. Product groupings must be as related as possible for cohesion. These catalogs usually sell a variety of gadgets and tools. An unbound version, with single pages sealed in shrink wrap, is a variation of the traditional catalog and cuts costs by eliminating expensive binding.

People read books methodically and scan quickly through websites, but they may take their time browsing through a catalog. Catalogs are often considered, by the home audience, as recreation. Although they are not necessarily "readable" as text, the layout and images help guide customers through the pages and keep them interested.

To gain consistency from one page to another, a grid is used as the basic structural design element. By grouping a series of lines on the page, a format is created from which the entire catalog achieves continuity. The grid usually allows some flexibility while maintaining structure. Grids may be either symmetrical and balanced proportionally or asymmetrical.

Designing to a grid does not limit creativity. Images may be sized to fit anywhere within the structure and are key to an interesting layout, especially if the sizes are varied. Graphic designers can create a look and feel that will enhance the brand identity and develop a link with the consumer. Designing technical or business catalogs need not be less creative. The same principles apply. Figure 4-1 illustrates a sample catalog grid.

Some high-end catalogers present only one product on a single page. This is really a brochure style, but it is very effective for products requiring large images, explanations, or when the cataloger has only a few specialty items. It's an expensive approach and is not suited to catalogs

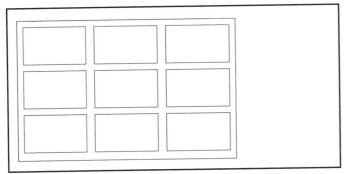

Figure 4–1 The catalog grid lends structure to each page.

that feature many products, especially if they are very diverse. But for those SKUs that bring in more than their share of profitability, dedicating an entire page in a catalog may pay off.

Unfortunately, a catalog is limited to a specified number of pages in the same way that a store is limited to its square footage. Catalogs are expensive to print, and a major cost is the paper itself. Designing to a specific size also predetermines mailing costs. As retailers need to invest in shelf fixturing to present their products in the best way, catalog production with effective presentation features products on the printed page to their best advantage.

Grids and images are important elements online as well. The first consideration for any catalog, whether electronic, virtual, or printed, is how the reader will access, read, and use the information.

Position Preferences and Covers

How the catalog communicates to the customer will depend on the target customer profile. As with advertising, a reader will first come into contact with the upper-right position of a page. This is the equivalent of the prime position on a retail shelf. The lower-right and lower-left corners are the least read positions.

Not surprisingly, the cover is the most noticed page in a catalog and the back cover the second most valuable position. Just as some retail store positions, like end caps, are more valuable than others, the inside cover, inside back cover and the first few pages are key to a catalog. The covers can be compared to the windows and front of a store. Products featured on the back cover can sell two to three times as many as items on the inside pages of the catalog.

When selling online, there's a time limitation imposed on the home page. The first page is similar to the window of a store or the cover of a catalog, but the customer wants instant gratification within a few minutes. Therefore, the first page of an online store must work harder than either of the other two shelves. It must clearly direct the shopper to exactly the right place in the online store immediately.

Another prime position for a catalog is the photo caption. Captions usually get two to three times the readership of body text. Essential positions in a catalog are at a premium just as in retail. Some catalogs even include advertising within their pages to subsidize the high costs of production, similar to offering ads on a web page. Others charge manufacturers for the space they occupy. Most often, though, catalogers research how their customers interact with their catalogs and maximize space for readership and profitability.

While you must walk through the front door of a retail establishment, there is no such restriction with a catalog. You can enter at any page. It's even possible to read a catalog from the back to the front if so desired. Catalogers have to be prepared to capture the customer at any encounter. Customers can go right to the section of interest and still interface with a catalog that is consistent throughout—finding a similar look and feel on each page. Good catalogs reinforce their positioning throughout the catalog as well.

Because catalogs are mailed frequently, catalogers can save money by changing catalog covers and re-mailing existing catalogs. New covers may also be customized for specific target customers or markets. The cover presents an opportunity to address a personalized message, offer a promotion, or provide key information about the company. They also give the appearance of a brand-new catalog even if the content is the same on the inside. Catalogers know that it often takes several impressions—similar to advertising—before a customer ultimately decides to purchase. Repetitive marketing works and the same technique can be extrapolated to any of the "shelves." Catalogs are usually "coded" with identifying alphanumerics to distinguish from which catalog the order originated because any given product may be featured in more than one catalog.

Indexing—What Do You Call It?

An index supports catalog use in the same way that a TV directory supports television channel selection. You can randomly search through channels each hour to find out what programs are being broadcast. Or you can refer to a printed or broadcast listing of all the shows.

Attempting to find something in a catalog is a hit-or-miss proposition without an index. Without a way to navigate the book, consumers can't find products they would like to purchase.

Creating a world-class index is dependent on understanding how customers will search for each product. The index is comparable to the store directory at retail, but is much more critical because the customer must rely completely on the index for all location information. It may also be compared to the search function on websites. It must help shoppers quickly find products that may be buried in as many as 500 or 600 pages.

Because many products have several alternative names, indexing is more of a science than an afterthought. Indexes may be arranged by product categories or by manufacturer. Some catalogs are separated into a series of mini-indexes featuring sections for furniture, apparel, toys, and other categories.

Customers don't always refer to products in the same way. In fact, the index should actually plan for incorrect use of a term and refer the reader to the accurate or selected reference. The following examples illustrate how common products may have several names:

    Comforter—bedspread, duvet, quilt
    Sofa—couch, sectional, love seat, davenport
    Range—stove, oven, cooktop

Pants—trousers, slacks, capris, jeans
Carpet—rug, floor covering, area rug
Transparency film—slides, viewgraphs, overheads
Inkjet printer cartridge—print cartridge, inkjet cartridge, printer cartridge, ink cartridge

Customers shop in different ways, and catalogers can't predict which method or word search they will employ. Therefore, an index usually covers all possible search choices. Also, because many catalogers today do not group all similar products on the same page, customers may find their selections spread out over ten or more pages. Jewelry, for instance, may be grouped with clothes or may be in a separate jewelry section. A typical listing might look like the following:

Jewelry 4, 12, 26-32, 46, 89

Listings like these make it difficult to select products because shoppers have to look in so many places. In addition, this listing is not very specific. The customer searching for a watch, for instance, would have to look through ten different pages to see if "jewelry" includes watches. Similarly, a jewelry shopper may want a specific piece of jewelry, such as a bracelet, or may need to distinguish fine jewelry from costume jewelry. This manual search is similar to an automated search online except images and text links replace page numbers.

Some catalogers hope their books will be "read" from front cover to back cover to encourage add-on sales. While they understand the need for cohesive indexing and grouping similar items together, they also want to present "solution selling" opportunities. By clustering pivotal products together, they offer the complete solution for the customer and maximize cross-selling opportunities. In order for this to work, however, customers need to "browse" the catalog instead of making a purchase of intent. While successful with discretionary categories, this approach doesn't work well for categories that are more functional in nature.

The latest trend in catalog indexing is the limited index. This version lists broad categories only with major sub-categories. It normally does not list each product. To facilitate navigation, this technique is usually coupled with color-coded and tabbed category sections. The following is an example of an abridged index:

Women's Clothing—career, casual, uniforms, maternity
Housewares—cookware, small electrics, linens
Electronics—audio, video, TVs, computers

Instead of listing skirts, blouses, and sweaters, this format simply groups them into casual or career. It will be up to the consumer to determine where a black skirt, for instance, will be found. Similarly, a customer can no longer search for a blender in the index. She must look through the "small electrics" portion of the housewares category, which may be several pages long. The computer section within electronics may carry peripherals as well as software. In this format, jewelry would be extremely difficult to find. Because it is not listed at all, the only way for the customer to find the product is to browse through each page.

While catalog indexing lists several alternatives for the root search, there's a bit of mind reading to developing online search capabilities. A catalog index allows a customer to peruse the list, and seeing the options can trigger a choice. Online, the burden is on the consumer to enter selections. If he cannot come up with the correct word, he can't search the database. Drop-down hierarchical choices help narrow the field. Seeking alternatives for keywords in the category provides more selections and creates more opportunity for a match.

The Order Form

In the past, when customers ordered from their favorite catalog, they filled out the order form and mailed it to the reseller. Today, the bulk of orders arrive via e-mail, phone, or fax.

Because a catalog is bound in the middle, the corresponding middle pages tend to hold the order forms and special offers. While the order form is still used, its functionality has been redefined. The section containing the order form also provides sizing, warranty details, and additional ordering information.

Today, the order form serves as a "planning tool" for consumers to capture their order information and make decisions before the order is placed. It rarely gets mailed. But the order form can impart useful information and can actually make or break a sale. Deal breakers such as high shipping and handling costs are encountered here, as well as other restrictions. On the other hand, free merchandise or free shipping can be an enticement featured on the order form. The order form also can feature specials and closeouts.

Consumers jot down part numbers to phone or fax. Catalog resellers usually use their own part numbers, which may be different from manufacturer's part numbers. Complexities may stall the entire shopping trip, so simplicity is critically important. This is true whether the order form is offered through a catalog, direct mail, or an Internet site.

Because the order form is used primarily for planning, catalog resellers sometimes insert more than one in each book—assuming the customer will order more than once.

The Production Process

Catalogs take time to develop. Large annual catalogs are often in production 12 to 18 months prior to printing. The product mix, then, is somewhat risky because product packaging and pricing can change during this long lead time. Even the actual product can change during the gap between initial planning and printing, and new product introduction schedules change with regularity.

The production process includes product selection, layout, artwork, photography, prepress production, and printing. Much of the production phase is in the hands of the graphic designer in the same way that the web development process is managed by the web designer. In order to achieve the best possible catalog, the designer must work with buyers, sales staff, and marketing professionals to understand how consumers in each category shop, the relevance of the products to the customers, and to determine their demographics to make the most effective presentation.

The Layout—The Planogram of the Catalog

You wouldn't lay out a grocery store alphabetically, so you certainly don't want to lay out a catalog or website alphabetically. Customers aren't trained to shop in a particular aisle for everything on their shopping list that begins with "A." It's important to know how customers shop in each category and vary product information to reflect their experience.

The layout may be compared to the planogram in a retail store. It helps the customer navigate through the maze of products and allows the store or catalog designer to add or subtract products as the SKU mix changes. Consumer catalogs are usually updated most frequently and are changed throughout the year. The layout selected will depend on the company's needs, the style of the catalog, and the customer segmentation.

The layout is the actual arrangement of words and images on a page and is reflective of customer needs in the same way that the merchandising process manages products for the customer at retail. In order to determine how each product will appear on the page, it is necessary to understand the following qualities about each SKU:

- The strength of the product, including its brand position
- The category in which the product is sold
- The target customer for the product
- How the product ranks in sales
- The type of presentation that will be appropriate
- How much copy or explanation the product merits
- Illustrations or photos that will show the product in its best light
- Compatibility information
- The product style, color, size, fit, and function
- Unique differentiating attributes
- Other products that are required to use the product (cables, batteries)
- Complementary products for cross-selling
- Technical data

This means it takes clear marketing savvy to be able to put together a good catalog. Most of the time, a buyer or manager inside the company is responsible for a particular section of the catalog. Unfortunately, the overall book may not be thoroughly coordinated from buyer to buyer, and the end result may appear to be a number of disjointed sections under one cover. The same is true at retail and now online. Buyers are responsible for certain combinations of products that the company sells. Therefore, the resulting catalog is sometimes arranged to reflect the company's organization, rather than by how consumers purchase.

For instance, while it may make much more sense to put transparency film with other printing supplies, the product is most often shelved with overhead projectors. When projectors were first introduced, it made sense to co-shelve the hardware with the corresponding supply. Today, however, film is purchased considerably more often than projectors. Customers want the printing supply category to be in one place in the store for convenience. The solution is to place products in multiple locations where the customer might logically choose to shop. Managing the overall catalog holistically ensures that customers will be able to locate and purchase products where they expect them to appear. The entire catalog, like a store, must appear seamless and demonstrate cohesiveness.

Customers want to know how each product benefits them and how each product is differentiated from every other product on the page. The presentation must take into account the strengths of the individual product and how it might be used, and it may even include sample applications. A cataloger who sells jewelry components, for example, can enhance sales by illustrating several finished jewelry samples made from the individual parts. One supplier even offers technical sidebars to feature special jewelry techniques to encourage new trial. By offering creative ideas, this catalog company increases sales dramatically.

While the overall "look" of the catalog defines its personality and is key to grabbing a customer's interest through dramatic impact, it's just as important to understand how the customer relates to each product and what they expect to get from each purchase. Art and copy work together to convey each of the benefits. Product information includes the following attributes:

- Height
- Weight
- Other dimensions (width, length, number of pages)
- Name of manufacturer, designer, author
- Color
- Pattern
- Contents
- Volume
- Fabric
- Country of origin
- Materials
- Sizes
- Texture
- Warranty information
- Accessories
- Functionality
- Compatibility
- Electrical or other standards

The manufacturer knows the product best and often provides information, data, and even artwork on request. Most will consult with the buyer to give clear direction not only for each product, but also for the overall category. Manufacturers usually are the customer and category experts and can be a valuable resource. Category leaders will have many tools to help manage the category effectively for the best profitability.

Consistency is critical to achieving an excellent presentation. Size of images, background colors, type styles, type sizes, and other physical elements are maintained throughout the book unless the designer is deliberately trying to achieve an avant-garde effect. In order to maintain visual space and avoid clutter, good catalogs employ a liberal use of white space. Both business-to-business and consumer catalogs average around five products to a page.

Trying to cram as much on a page as possible is a common mistake. Designers use white space as effectively as space they fill. Of course, there are instances when a catalog positions itself as a high-volume, high-discount book, and a crowded layout reinforces the message. But readability and interest are sacrificed. It's important to study the page, know where the reader's eye travels, and gain feedback from customers. Store designers avoid stuffing each aisle so full of products that it would be impossible to make a choice. Catalogers and e-merchants make the same trade-offs.

Using large images draws the reader to the page and to the offer. Nothing sells a product quite as well as a photo. In fact, a major issue for Internet sales has been the lack of good images accompanying product listings. Catalogers know that it's very difficult to sell a product through words alone.

Effective catalogs match art and copy with the overall presentation. If the products are casual and earthy, for instance, the copy, colors, and photos are designed to reflect an overall casual presentation. All elements—including the tone, copy style, and level—are synched together by the production staff. Catalogers can't even be complacent about business catalogs. They are competing fiercely on a variety of fronts—price, service, and delivery—and can't afford to produce catalogs that don't capture the attention of corporate buyers or office managers or, even worse, make it difficult to find primary products.

While it's tempting to avoid devoting prime real estate to compatibility charts or explanations, nothing alienates a customer faster than receiving the wrong product. It's a much safer investment to ensure that customers receive the right product each time they order. That's why catalogers devote extra space to selectability information.

The Schedule Is Key

Developing a catalog is similar to publishing any other printed document—it's a detailed network of schedules, reviews, and deadlines. But it's even more complex due to the variety of products involved. The schedule is critical to the success of the catalog. Slipping a date could cause a company to miss a major catalog seasonal release and, therefore, to lose out on one of the year's most profitable business opportunities.

The catalog industry is dependent on efficient production in a way that retail or e-commerce is not. If a shelf is not refreshed or a website updated, sales will not cease—although they will certainly not be maximized. However, if a catalog is not mailed, customers have no opportunity to see the cataloger's merchandise, and the result could be devastating.

Typically, the catalog schedule begins with the proposed drop date and works backward. Depending on the size, the number of products represented, the frequency of mailing, and the complexity of the design, it can take a few months to around 18 months to produce. Figure 4-2 shows a sample catalog schedule.

Large semi-annual consumer catalogs or annual B-to-B catalogs consume the most production and planning time. The latter often use consistent backgrounds for all photos—requiring that product samples or prototypes are sent to the firm before art production can begin. Manufacturers are also required to provide product information months in advance, including pricing data. New product information may not be complete this far in advance, but manufacturers must find a way to participate or wait as much as two or three years to include a major product introduction.

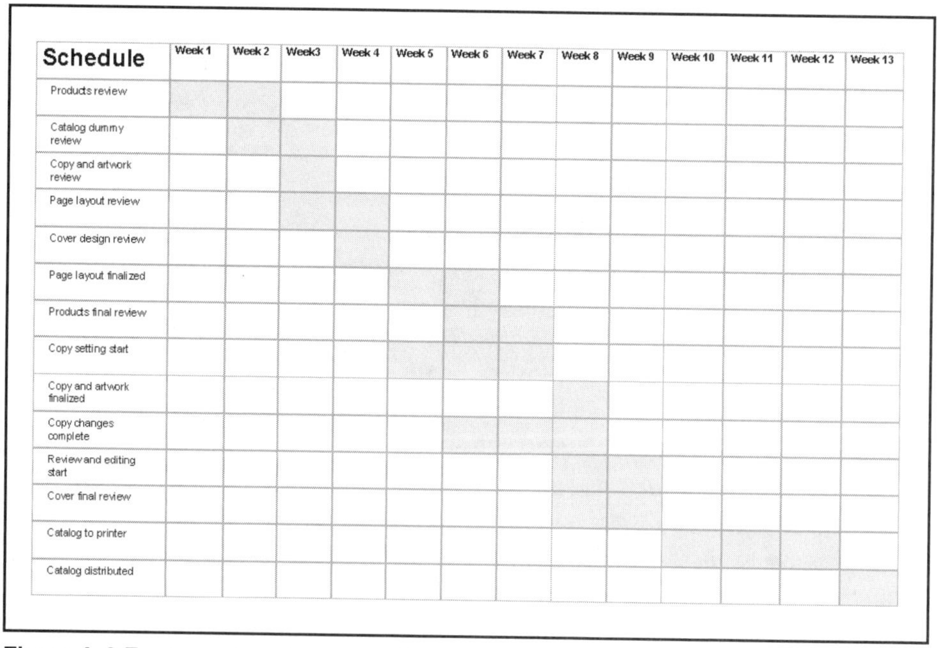

Figure 4–2 Example of a catalog schedule.

While not the norm, some manufacturers assist catalog companies by taking responsibility for producing their own pages, much in the same way that manufacturers help retailers with merchandising solutions. By providing the manufacturer with a grid and layout requirements, the category leader can help make decisions to determine the hierarchy of products, category groupings, product information, and even copywriting. The product manufacturer is also able to provide compatibility charts and other aids that assist in selection of products.

Seasonality—To Every Sale There Is a Season

Major catalogs usually have at least two primary selling seasons. The majority of all catalog sales are made in the second half of the year. Consumer catalog companies focus on the holiday season to produce specialty catalogs—many offering guaranteed delivery providing that orders are placed by a specified date.

Holiday catalogs are quite popular and allow the home consumer to avoid battling long lines at retail. A critical issue, however, is the availability of merchandise during this selling period. One of the most frequent consumer complaints is the proliferation of out-of-stock products during the season—especially annoying when customers, expecting to enjoy the convenience of ordering from home, must resort to going back into retail stores.

Back-to-school and other seasonal occasions present opportunities for catalogers to not only rack up sales but also to establish new customers. Some B-to-B catalogs are produced on an annual basis and take extra planning. Typical seasons revolve around business-purchasing cycles and tax time, for example. Of course, seasonality applies equally to online and retail sales.

Delivery—It All Arrives on the Doorstep

Consumers have more choices than ever. But whether they purchase through direct mail, call a toll-free number, or order over the Internet, they will receive their goods in the same way. Their orders will arrive via the mail or a delivery service.

While it is precisely the back-end delivery mechanisms that prevent remote sales from growing to huge levels, catalogers have the know-how for effective order fulfillment. Ironically, order fulfillment and service are the most pervasive problems for non-catalog Internet stores. In fact, many online orders were either delivered late or experienced some other delivery or fulfillment error.

Customers preferring to shop at traditional retail stores cite several reasons for continuing to avoid alternative shopping methods. First, they don't like their orders left sitting at their doorsteps when they're not home. They equally dislike receiving notification left on their doors informing them that a package was undeliverable. Some online companies have resolved this issue by including a printable form with an order that the customer can sign and leave on the doorstep to direct delivery requirements.

Other perceived issues include the following:

- Difficulty with returns

- Fitting problems
- High service and delivery fees
- Lack of instant gratification
- Out-of-stock products
- Difficulty in determining color or product quality from a photo
- Freshness
- Theft
- Damage

In addition, residents in certain geographies have problems with heat, cold, or humidity that can subject sensitive products to the elements. About five percent of all consumer catalog products are returned. Color and fit are the two main reasons products are sent back to the cataloger.

Catalog customers must also deal with receiving incomplete orders. It's quite annoying to get part of an order and have to wait several days for the remainder. Substitutions are not usually acceptable unless authorized by the customer. And out-of-stock items delivered at a later date are an issue identified by consumers. Catalog firms usually give customers the choice of canceling an order if the product is out of stock.

Despite the problems, catalogers have years of experience in meeting customer expectations in a non-perfect environment. Because delivering customer expectations is so difficult through a catalog, they had to learn to create opportunities and build relationships with consumers. They also had to become proficient in those areas that were precisely the most challenging—order fulfillment, database management, and efficient production.

Personalization—How to Keep the Connection

The catalog industry was spawned from direct marketing—a discipline that has used various forms of customer personalization over the years. Both catalogers and direct marketers have been using one-to-one marketing techniques even though Customer Relationship Management (CRM) is perceived to be a relatively new discipline. They know that if a customer feels acknowledged or special, he is more likely to purchase. The industry relies heavily on repeat sales and, therefore, values each customer.

Catalogers use several techniques to create personal contact with their customers:

- Personalized cover letters
- Personalized messages on catalog covers
- Personalized catalogs
- Personalized direct mail pieces
- Customized merchandise
- Special mailings
- Personalized offers
- Thank-you letters

In addition to using special messaging, some catalogers mail different versions of their catalogs to varying customer segments. They may also send abbreviated editions to entry-level or prospective purchasers and reserve full-length catalogs for their loyal customers.

Because mail can be highly personalized, direct marketers and catalogers are able to refer to a customer's past purchases. They also let customers know when they have not ordered for some time. Using these reminders, catalog firms gently point out that customers will lose their "special status" or may not receive a catalog in the future unless they order.

Some companies acknowledge special occasions, such as birthdays, by providing the customer with a gift—most often a coupon for several dollars off their next purchase. By integrating loyalty programs with personalized treatment, the customer is made to feel like a VIP.

Companies can no longer afford to reach shoppers through generic, mass-media communications. By targeting customers through their lifestyles, behavior, and preferences, catalogers, direct marketers, and e-merchants streamline their marketing efforts and use their promotion dollars effectively.

New CRM programs depend on obtaining a level of information only the customer can provide. As they "opt-in," or choose to participate in these programs, they receive in exchange special targeted offers and personalized solutions. These, however, are limited because the customer must provide the data—usually through e-mail or web surveys.

Both manufacturers and resellers expect programs like these to increase their promotion effectiveness, and most believe they will increase spending by high-potential shoppers. But the greatest hope is that catalogers and retailers alike will be able to retain their best customers.

Persistence = Increased Sales

It's no secret that mailing catalogs frequently wins customers. In fact, the most successful catalogers are the firms that are the most persistent. About 15 billion catalogs are mailed to consumers each year.

Average catalog shoppers tend to place repeat orders with frequency ranging between twice a year to every other month. That's why catalog companies identify target customers and stick with them. Giving up on a potential catalog customer—especially one who has ordered in the past—can be a grave mistake because confirmed customers have a predisposition to order from the "catalog shelf."

The same customer who is comfortable with alternative modes of shopping is also a potential e-customer. But, oddly, Internet sales have not seemed to hurt the catalog industry. In fact, the web has reinforced the convenience of one-to-one marketing and has actually bolstered the business. Over the past few years, consumer catalog sales have grown at twice the rate of retail sales in the U.S.

Tenacity is the backbone of the direct industry. With hundreds of companies vying for the same customer, the most aggressive certainly has an edge. Persistence is a major driver of profitability and focuses on retaining existing customers. But being persistent should not be confused with annoying the customer or sending spam e-mails. Nothing will lose business faster than alienating your customers.

How to Measure a Good Catalog

More than 15 billion consumer catalogs are mailed within a given year. How does one catalog succeed where another fails? There are some basic criteria for measuring how well a catalog communicates to its target customers:

1. Can the customer find what he needs quickly and easily?
2. Is the buying information for any given product sufficient to make a purchase decision?
3. Does the cataloger offer extra help and service?
4. Is the index up-to-par? Can you find key products?
5. Are the ordering, delivery information and instructions clear?
6. Are the products relevant to the target customer?
7. Is there sufficient product assortment?
8. Are the claims honest? Is there an attempt at deception?
9. Is the presentation compelling? Are there sufficient photos?
10. Are the handling and service fees within reason?
11. Is the company trustworthy?
12. Is compatibility information offered for products in categories requiring selection information?

Catalogers are in touch with their competitors' catalogs in the same way that retailers monitor competing ads. Each catalog will present the same information differently, so they know it's important to acquire competing publications to see how they present and price similar products. This is an opportunity to evaluate and measure each catalog to pre-established criteria. Because most catalog companies have websites and may have retail outlets as well, checking all "shelves" adds to comprehensive competitive intelligence. Whenever possible, catalogers need to test products to ensure that their own claims are accurate.

Ethical Content Considerations

It's just as much an ethical violation to be misleading in a catalog as it is to bait and switch at retail. Any action that deceives the customer is unethical. Merely omitting information is enough to cause confusion.

It's easy to imply, for instance, that a generic product is really made by the leading brand manufacturer—even if it isn't. But when the customer receives the product at his home and realizes the product's performance is not up to par, any short-term additional margin gained by the reseller turns into a long-term loss by sacrificing the customer's trust. Customer loyalty translates into long-term profit.

That's why it's so important to be clear and straightforward in the presentation. Even if there is no intention to deceive, if key information is omitted, the result is the same. It's more difficult to make a product decision from a photo and words than it is in a store where you can examine the product, view the packaging, feel textures, see actual colors, watch a product work, and try on apparel. Catalogers play the role of the store associate helping the customer select each item on each page. Loyalty is built through trust and service.

Catalog Lessons for E-commerce Sales

Is the Internet merely a distribution channel for catalogs? So many e-commerce sites are nothing more than line or alphabetical product listings on a page. But as we have seen here, that's not what constitutes a catalog. That's why the web, in order to gain parity with catalogs, needs to add sophistication in presentation and efficiency in delivery.

Today, customers are fluid. They will shop in a store, online, and through a catalog all in the same week. While they purchase "safe" products on the web—those that they are sure will materialize exactly as they envision them—such as books, CDs, and tickets—they are also somewhat willing to experiment as long as the result is in their favor.

Convenience is the major driver for web-based sales, but the desire to touch a real product is the main reason for shopping at a store. If convenience and simplicity are the catalysts for non-traditional sales, web resellers can emulate the catalog industry's success. But for home consumers, it's often easier and faster to pick up a phone and place an order than it is to log on to the Internet. The selling proposition must enhance the channel because the web, by itself, is no longer so compelling that customers will try it just for fun.

Shoppers love the web when they have a product in mind. They can run a search function for a specialized item and find a supplier. But the Internet is not conducive to browsing. Searching for common items will bring thousands of hits. This is like being confronted with an index for a catalog that is twice as large as the catalog itself. And it has no sorting capabilities, presents itself in random order, can be several years old, and may not even be functional.

But more than 30 percent of the U.S. population goes online every day, and well over half of all Americans have used the Internet during the year. There are nearly 130 million people in the U.S. connected to the Internet—representing a substantial pool of prospective buyers. The opportunity is huge for e-tailers who want to remove some obstacles for the common consumer.

Identifying the Obstacles

Unless the customer has a relationship with an e-retailer, he has to search through a maze of providers to find someone to take his order. But ordering through a catalog is a fairly standard procedure. And if a cataloger can afford to produce a glossy mailing, the company is most likely not a fly-by-night operation. Not so on the web. Anyone can set up a site, and the company may or may not be reputable. Before sending someone money or sharing a credit card number, customers want to be sure they will get their order.

- Customers believe quality of service is critical when selecting a catalog provider. Yet, they actually expect a higher level of service when shopping on the Internet than in traditional retail stores or through a catalog. Most e-merchants do not have a holistic e-service program that is integrated throughout their companies. The future will require a "live" person to help select merchandise and place orders 24 hours a day—as many catalogers now provide.

- Catalogs take advantage of imagery and have mastered the use of photographs. Photos are mandatory for selling products but often take too long to materialize on the web. They are usually too small to see a product in detail, but catalog photos are large enough to view and enjoy. If speed can be overcome, the opportunity for web resellers is to provide full-page photos with a click. Their progress will be hindered by inadequate consumer equipment, such as slow modems.

- Production diligence is the hallmark of catalog success. The intimacy of the printed page can be replicated on the web using the right techniques. Each web page requires micro-management to ensure that no detail is overlooked. The speed of the Internet should not translate to throwing a site together quickly.

- Cross-selling is a technique that catalogers adopted with relish. Web retailers can maximize sales by encouraging customers to add to their shopping carts. These sales cost less and bring in more revenue than an original sale. Rather than enhancing sales with banner ads, try adding a valued service with recommended compatible products from a "personal shopper."

- Catalog companies have become proficient at managing their catalog businesses and unifying them with their e-businesses. E-commerce must also close the gap by creating seamless websites and smooth transactions. Integrating all aspects of the business and delivering dependable fulfillment will ensure that there are no inconsistencies in operations for the customer.

- Trust is a major factor in catalog sales. Catalog firms have already predisposed customers to watch for marketing tricks. For example, a well-known floral company sent out a catalog that proclaimed there would be no delivery fees through a set date for any item ordered out of that particular catalog. Unfortunately, the price of nearly every item in the catalog had been raised an average of $10. "Free delivery" wasn't exactly free, and customers are not fooled easily. This sort of deception is not as common in the catalog world as in the Internet arena. E-merchants have to work even harder to regain consumer trust.

- Catalogers have learned how to present merchandise in the most effective ways. The interactive nature of the web lends itself to some unique capabilities that are under-used. For instance, clicking on an image could produce a video clip of the product in operation or a common application in use. One click could bring up an image of the packaging, another could show the product unwrapped, and still a third could picture the back of the product. Furniture could be presented in a mock room setting that the customer designs to replicate his own home. The possibilities are unlimited—but information, speed, and excitement must offer the customer more than a printed page, or there's little advantage to using the Internet over a catalog. The web offers the possibility of movement and sound—two sensory delights that catalogs will never be able to offer. Interactivity will drive websites in the future, and static environments will be passé.

Integrated Businesses

Because customers don't differentiate between separate divisions of a company, it's critical to integrate catalog, retail, e-commerce, and direct marketing functions. If these divisions are competing with each other, they are unlikely to share sales and customer information that will be essential to establishing a lasting relationship.

A customer may be acknowledged as a loyal customer on the web but may be ignored in a store. In order to build a true relationship, every point of contact must be reinforced through consistency. The customer should be "recognized" wherever she chooses to shop. Click-and-mortar companies have unique advantages. A customer's web history can be shared with the retail store nearest her home. Promotions and service should be the same, regardless of whether she conducts her business online or in the store.

Building Competency

Catalog companies have built competency over the years and have spent time perfecting their craft. They have a loyal following and offer consistency and compelling product presentation. When e-merchants fail to deliver basic services, confuse consumers with awkward ordering methods, or don't provide enough information to make a purchase decision, consumers walk away with their pocketbooks intact. Some not only stop shopping or purchasing at the website where they experienced problems, but they also will cease shopping online entirely. Building competency in the channel should be a concern for all online companies.

Many websites have been built in stages and lack the flow of a continuously designed site. Because they appear fractured, customers have difficulty following through the entire site with coherency. Designing and promoting are two different disciplines but must be integrated on a website. Conducting online research will help build expertise and customer knowledge. Benchmarking other companies with expertise in critical competencies will give insight into best practices and highlight success factors as well. Reading and critiquing catalogs will help provide the focus for competency basics.

Prospecting and Promoting

E-mail is a form of direct marketing and also a technique used by catalogers to provide lead generation. Online merchants are using e-mail as a prospecting tool. In fact, direct marketers of all types are using the vehicle as well—and most expect to increase the practice. The majority of direct marketing efforts are targeted toward acquiring new customers. In addition to e-mail, they're using traditional direct mail, direct response promotions, and other aggressive methods to both build their markets and retain existing customers.

The list is key, and catalogers manage their own databases and purchase names from select lists. These are widely available, but in order to choose the appropriate list, catalog firms must be very familiar with their target and potential customers.

Special offers and coupon insertion in catalogs bring in additional orders. Internet coupon use has grown by a third, even though only half of all coupon redeemers have Internet access. E-customers go to the web expecting to find bargains. These tools and others help remind customers of the opportunities awaiting them on the web or through a catalog.

Retaining customers may take different tactics than acquiring new customers. Of course, it's less expensive to keep loyal customers, but it will be necessary to broaden the customer base if e-tailing is to grow. Keeping the ordering process simple will ensure repeat sales. Customers should be reassured at each ordering step and given final confirmation for their orders. Otherwise, customers wonder if their orders really did go through or wound up in a "black hole."

The online population is changing and becoming less technical. Early adopters loved the technology, but today's customers are more concerned with convenience and are less technically sophisticated. The newest opportunity focuses on late Internet adopters. Techniques that e-merchants used two years ago may be outmoded today. Today's consumers have new needs and less patience for technological glitches. These customers want to emulate store shopping in the convenience of the home. They don't surf; they browse. That's why learning from catalogers, who have perfected selling to this same audience, is important.

Some Internet companies are promoting their websites through traditional methods such as FSIs, the freestanding inserts found in Sunday papers. With the website address printed for customers along with information and a coupon, new prospects are enticed to give the web a try.

A Case Study—Quill

Quill is a seasoned direct marketer that has been in business since 1956. The company offers a variety of office products for the B-to-B market through catalogs, direct sales (both outbound and inbound), and the web. Focused and dedicated to customer support, Quill's philosophy is to provide services wherever the customer wants to shop. That's why Quill customers can order on the phone, by fax, by mail, through e-mail, or on the web. Quill has integrated its operations to provide seamless options for the customer.

So how has Quill migrated from a catalog company to this hybrid? The company launched its first website in July 1996 as a scientific experiment, and in the last two years Quill focused aggressively on integrating it with its core business. Today, web sales represent 21 percent of the total business, and Quill expects they will grow to over 30 percent next year.

Quill's core target is the office manager or receptionist and is 80 percent female. Until last year, 40 percent did not have Internet or e-mail access. But, because most companies are now giving their employees increased connectivity, there's a growing interest among their customers to order through the web. It gains them flexibility and the ability to multi-task. Instead of being tied up on the phone for 15 minutes placing an order, the office manager can place an order online, handle another task, and come back to the order. Because Quill has added special capabilities to the web, customers can use quick ordering programs or save their favorite lists for reordering purposes.

Still, catalogs are a staple for Quill (see Figure 4-3). They believe that many customers order on the web with the printed book in front of them as a reference. They mail target customers anywhere from three to five direct mail pieces per month. These can be catalogs or flyers supplemented by a direct mail postcard or letter. They also manage weekly e-mail campaigns as a complement to print pieces. Quill still finds that direct marketing is crucial to growing the company. They also discovered that e-mail is a good trigger to help migrate customers to the web.

Figure 4–3 Quill produces a variety of catalogs.

Quill has 52,000 SKUs on the web. In order to help customers achieve success with their orders, the company has implemented extensive customer service. B-to-B customers are more demanding and less forgiving than their consumer counterparts. They expect low prices, good value and superior service. Quill's customer-relations team is integrated to manage anything from navigation issues to technology questions.

Internet ordering has helped Quill manage the timely business of catalog production and planning. Because catalogs require pricing to be locked in for a fixed time, cataloging has never been as flexible as store retailing. But the web gives catalogers such as Quill added flexibility. The company does believe, though, that the web is not unlimited. If a site carries more than 100,000 SKUs, it will overwhelm customers. The entire efficiency of the web is dependent on its simplicity.

Quill believes that the days of "mail it and they will buy it" are gone. Direct marketing companies like Quill depend on extensive promotion and make use of a variety of customer programs. Setting up a website with complete dependence on links is the equivalent of opening a retail store and depending on a Yellow Pages phone listing to bring in 100 percent of its customers. Proactive marketing is key to the success of any business, and e-businesses are no exception.

Quill identified the five top measures of an effective direct business:

1. Ease of use
2. User-friendly interactions
3. Simplicity
4. Customer service
5. Excellent overall product assortment

About 80 percent of all visits on Quill's website are converted to sales. The company attributes this to the extensive customer research they conduct and the assistance they provide to the customer to make each order simple. Quill purchases lists to gain e-mail leads but relies on its own database for mailings.

> At the end of the day, if you keep your customers happy and you do it cost effectively, you will be successful in the catalog industry.
> —*Sarah Alter, Quill executive*

Hybrid companies like Quill allow customers to choose their method of purchasing. While Quill is focused on the B-to-B arena, this can be extrapolated to click-and-mortar companies. Home consumers, like business customers, want to have choices, and the future will entail more switching between channels for convenience and for specific product needs.

The Building Blocks for Better Web Design

Developing a consumer-centered focus is not dependent on the sales vehicle. But each channel adds experience, best practices, and applied learning for online sales, the newest member of the team. Whether selling through catalogs, direct mail, a retail store, or website, the basic building blocks are interchangeable. The elements are consistent through the channel:

- Design
- Functionality
- Service
- Engaging the customer
- Uniqueness

Design

As we've seen from the catalog experts, a great deal of planning goes into the design. Successful catalogs are not just a list of products. They present the information in a compelling way and use photography as a cornerstone. They're also built on a grid that is consistent from page to page, but each page is unique. Online design is similarly a mix between graphic design, usability standards, programming, and imaging. Customer-centered design adds customer knowledge and advocacy and category expertise.

Functionality

Every website is designed to operate as intended. But how many are not completely functional? Customers leave the site when an element doesn't work. Just as regular maintenance is performed on sensitive equipment or an instrument is tuned periodically, a website requires checking at regular intervals.

Service

Ordering from a website is not enough. We've learned from catalogers that backend order fulfillment is as just as important. If delivery mechanisms don't work, the online merchant will not get a repeat sale. Catalogers have worked through customer fulfillment issues.

Engaging the Customer

If a catalog is boring, it will most likely not be read. The most compelling catalogs receive the most orders. Websites are no different. The belief that the Internet is "cool" and transcends everything else is no longer true. Websites can be boring, and customers aren't likely to stay very long when more interesting alternatives are a click away.

Uniqueness

Hundreds of catalogs are mailed out each year. Catalogers compete by offering a unique value proposition—better service, unique presentation, excellent selection, or even a socially conscious program such as environmental stewardship. The key here, though, is that the site must be different from its competitors, and the unique advantage must be something that customers find to be of value.

Integrating Catalog Techniques into the E-tail Mix

These catalog techniques are the "tried and true." The industry has perfected them over the years, and they await adoption by e-merchants. Although Internet businesses have used cataloging basics as the skeleton of most websites, most other elements have been overlooked.

E-commerce is a form of direct marketing. Although it competes with every shelf including catalogs, the greater issue is not meeting customer needs. Catalogers have determined how to capture the alternative sale and make it work. They have built a loyal following that accounts for a steady percentage of market share.

Catalogers don't expect customers to just order their catalogs and maintain sales. They manage their businesses proactively using a variety of promotional vehicles and advertising. E-marketers need to be as aggressive in adopting other forms of marketing to sell their wares.

Effective cataloging starts with the customer. Excellent graphic design is a major contributor to appealing to the target audience. Liberal use of photography is the most important element for capturing sales. Adopting these techniques will improve the e-commerce experience for your customers.

Catalog firms have revitalized their industry with new techniques and have combined the best of direct mail and the Internet. Catalogs are part art and part marketing expertise. E-tailers can learn some of these techniques—especially excellent graphics and marketing expertise—from the catalog industry.

In the next chapter, we'll show you how to integrate all the shelves. We'll start with the structure of the e-shelf to help you create the building blocks to improve or design your site.

CHAPTER 5

Anatomy of the
e-Shelf

With the race to get onto the Internet, most businesses focused on getting there as quickly as possible. They staked claims to cyber-assets by creating online stores. The Internet was a new creation and, in their haste, many stores took a "Frankenstein" approach. They pieced the store together with whatever parts were readily available—whether they fit seamlessly together or not—and most often they did not.

Some of these parts, electronic product catalogs, were related to structure and were developed in a variety of database-driven architectures. The online store that relies solely on a database-driven product database is weak and cannot withstand competition or support customer needs. These early electronic catalogs displayed long lists of products to online customers. They lacked intuitive organization and structure.

Other parts related to form and came from old methodologies and techniques associated with traditional advertising and catalog page layouts. While these forms work well in a printed format, they didn't translate effectively online.

A strong online store is dependent on having the right elements, which consist of structure, form, and navigation. It is also dependent on having the right product mix, sufficient customer research, intuitive navigation and ease of use, and a good delivery and fulfillment mechanism. Information must be adequate and appropriate. The basic elements of the store—the web pages—must fluidly guide the customers to desired destinations.

Customer-centered web design reverses the typical development order for websites. The typical method is to take an existing product database and build a user interface on top of it to accommodate the existing category structure. The customer-centered method starts with the user interface and builds the database structures and content to accommodate the page layout and content requirements of the customer and merchant. The user interface requires specific online merchandising techniques to influence effectiveness and design simplicity, which are discussed later in this chapter.

Shopping is a specialized form of navigation, and shoppers actually develop unconscious, ingrained purchasing patterns and shopping expectations that they attempt to transfer to this new shopping medium. The online store offers new convenience for customers by providing ordering capabilities at home, at work and in rural areas where physical retailing is sparse. The system structure and form, however, still need to reflect certain standards on which the consumer relies.

The Cost of Convenience

Depending on the channel, customers have shown a willingness to adapt to new shopping methods as long as the benefit outweighs the investment and the risk, either real or perceived. But if the payoff for shopping online is convenience and speed—and the process becomes frustrating and slow—shoppers will abandon the method. That's why developing the basic structures, applying new online merchandising techniques, and developing and using new tools specifically designed for this channel are survival requirements.

Many customers in our research studies commented that they would go to a retail store instead of continuing to search for products on a confusing website. Their willingness to do so indicates how much they are willing to do to avoid pain—in this case, the pain of shopping online at that unrewarding website.

What's a customer's time worth? What could be more convenient than ordering products from home or from an office and having them delivered to your doorstep or desk? Is it really easier and more convenient to get into the car, drive through traffic to a store, find a parking space, go into the store, locate the products, wait in line, pay for the items, and then drive through traffic to your office or home? That process is not convenient or time saving, yet that is what people are willing to do because they perceive that it is "easier" than shopping on some websites. Unless there is an immediate need to have a product, successful online shopping is clearly more convenient.

Shopping Online

A typical online shopper, Michael will shop and browse today at four websites. His first virtual stop will be to order office supplies for his two-person realty office because the part-time bookkeeper/secretary is on vacation. He knows that she typically shops from a couple of name-brand stores because they offer next-day desktop delivery service. That makes it extremely convenient, because he discovered the office has only one sheet of brochure printer paper left. Michael has an important open house in a couple of days and needs to print out the home listing. Besides the brochure paper, he'll also purchase a color inkjet cartridge—just so he won't run out—and boxes of staples, paper clips, and envelopes.

He doesn't bother looking for the supplies order folder that his secretary keeps, because he only needs a couple of items. He'll just pay for them with his personal credit card and reimburse himself from petty cash. He sits down at his computer to get this task out of the way before his first client of the day arrives for their appointment in 20 minutes.

He logs on to the Internet and types in the URL for the office products' website. "Whoa," he whispers to himself as the home page appears on his monitor. "Okay, where do I start?" The home page is densely packed with advertisement boxes and long columns of text links. As he squints and moves his face closer to read the small print on the screen, a product promotion window pops up covering part of it. Not even looking at its contents, Michael dismisses the box, thinking to himself, "That's annoying."

He scans the list of categories, scrolling down a couple of screens, scrolls back up, then clicks "paper," which takes him to a page that asks him to enter his zip code. He just wants to see if they have the product first, so he clicks the "continue" button. An "error" message fills the screen insisting that he enter his zip code. It tells him he must do this before he will be allowed to continue shopping. He looks at his watch—now he's only got 15 minutes until his client shows up. "That's it for that one," he says to himself and types in the URL for the second store.

Again he looks at a cluttered home page and anticipates that this will not go well either. He really needs the brochure paper, so he scans the list of links on that home page. He looks for something that will give him a clue as to what he should click. He sees a link for "forms and paper" and clicks the link, hoping he won't get one of those zip code demands again.

A list of 40 paper products appears. He hadn't realized there were so many different kinds of paper. He begins scanning and scrolling the list when the telephone rings. After the call, he has only five minutes left to prepare for his appointment. He looks back at the long list and decides to bag it and pick up the supplies on his way home from work. He makes a mental note to make sure his secretary orders extras of everything before her next vacation.

At home that evening, Michael goes online again—this time shopping for a new DVD movie. He just bought a new player and is building up a DVD library. He logs on to a popular website and is relieved to see that there is a "DVD" link easily visible on the home page. The home page has larger type and less clutter than the home pages on the websites he used earlier that day.

He clicks the link and is brought to a page that lists types of movies: comedies, dramas, musicals, and classics. He'd really like a comedy and is a fan of Steve Martin. He types "Steve Martn" into the search box and clicks the "go" button just as he notices he misspelled the name. Michael is pleasantly surprised when he is presented with a list of four Steve Martin movies instead of the "sorry, no results" page he anticipated.

He clicks the add-to-cart button next to his favorite movie and proceeds through the checkout process. "That was easy," he thinks to himself—it seemed like only a couple of minutes. "Why couldn't those other websites have been more like this one?"

Next, Michael types in the URL for a travel website. He is planning a vacation soon and hasn't yet decided on a location. He is presented with the home page. Just as he begins scanning the options—lodging, cruises, car/rail—a promotional ad window pops up for the second time that day and covers part of the screen. In the pop-up, he notices a photo of a floating bungalow in the South Seas Island of Bora Bora.

This time, he clicks the button to enlarge the pop-up window to get a better view of the inviting crystal clear, turquoise waters and the floating hut with the lush main island in the distance. He leans back in his chair, puts his hands behind his head, closes his eyes, and takes a long, slow deep breath. For a moment, he feels the sensation of the warm tropical sun and a light balmy ocean breeze caress him. After a minute, he brings himself back to reality, downloads the image onto his hard drive, and shuts down the computer for the night. "That's the place," he decides. He'll use the downloaded image as the backdrop to his computer monitor to remind him of the sensation and to book his travel on the website in the next few days.

The Online Shopper

Online shoppers have different needs and purposes as they visit websites. Three main reasons that shoppers go online are:

- To seek specific products
- To comparison-shop products
- To browse—for information for a future purchase or for entertainment

Generally, when people are seeking specific products, time is an issue. They have already decided what they want, and they simply want to get it. If they have not yet decided on a specific product, they will comparison-shop, still with time being an important factor.

Shopping process hierarchies depend on the purchase purpose, and the online store needs to address these purposes. Generally, for those shoppers who already know what they want to purchase, the process is simple and similar online to the retail process. The process normally features the following steps:

- The customer enters the store.
- The customer finds the right aisle, location, link, or code word.
- The customer searches for the actual product.
- The customer selects the product.
- The customer fills out the order or checks out.
- The customer leaves the store or logs off.
- The customer keeps the product or returns it to the store or through a return process.

The other two types of shoppers may shop randomly. The browsing third is enticed by a link, an ad, an end cap, or another promotional device. This shopper will move randomly around the store to see what is offered. The information shopper is more specific in searches and may look in catalogs, search at retail, or investigate on the web.

When Michael was seeking a specific product, he was not interested in the distraction of a pop-up advertisement. Yet, when he was looking for a vacation spot, the pop-up window did not bother him. In fact, he quite enjoyed it. He wasn't waiting for a client, and he had plenty of time before needing to book reservations for his vacation.

Most e-tail customers with specific products in mind want the same results as retail customers—to easily and quickly get in and out of the store. But the natural shopping patterns established at retail may not easily transfer online without adjusting the existing online structure and other e-store parts. Sometimes, customers shop just for fun. Shopping for "fun stuff" is very different than shopping for "have to" stuff.

The e-commerce website must play a hybrid role and be designed and balanced to serve both general and specific shoppers. Understanding the differences between these three situational needs is critical to enabling shopping success and affects overall satisfaction with the websites. It requires knowledge of customer shopping purposes and how customers interact with the different parts of the store while on different missions.

Types of Online Stores

There are many types of online stores in this hybrid marketplace. Auction websites have become popular places for people to buy and sell products. Internet Service Providers (ISPs)—and other portals to the Internet—have established shopping malls featuring links to different types of online stores. These portals also directly offer products and services to customers who log on to the ISP domain to check e-mail and browse the Internet. Pure-play public and multi-channel consumer websites were mentioned in Chapter 1.

In today's online environment, it's not uncommon to see a blending of these types of stores and a formation of alliances, mergers, and partnerships. Amazon.com, for example, blends new product sales with customers' personal auction products on the same product detail pages. They also offer links to other branded stores that offer an extension of product lines.

Regardless of the type of store, they have a few things in common. Two of the most important factors are (1) webpages—or shelves—filled with information and content and (2) the navigational models that connect them.

Six Functional Parts

Online stores use the following six basic component webpages in their store design:

- Home page
- Category pages
- Sub-category pages

- Product detail pages
- Informational content pages
- Checkout page

Integrating these web pages creates the basic structure of the online store as shown in Figure 5-1.

Each of these pages has specific purposes and inherited traits from traditional channels that must be balanced with the unique capabilities of the online stores. They function as standalone, independent entities, yet must ultimately be woven together seamlessly with intuitive navigation models.

Customer insight, rules, and tips for online store design and specific recommendations for improvement are provided in Chapter 7.

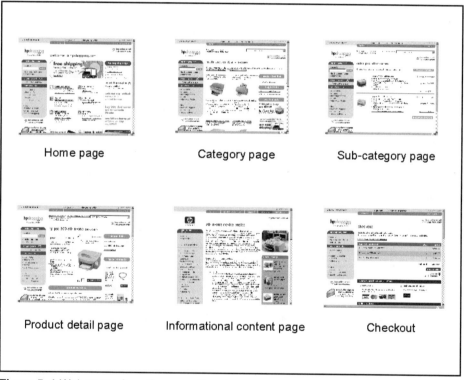

Figure 5–1 Web pages form the core site schema.

The Home Page

The home page is the main entrance and gateway into your store. It sets the tone and mood—the ambience. Online stores haven't yet achieved the relaxing feel of the piano music of Nordstrom's, but there are e-merchandising techniques described later in this chapter that you can apply using graphics, audio, font sizes, content, and graphical elements to reflect usability in a quality way.

Just like at retail, customers should clearly know the store's offering within the first 30-60 seconds upon coming into the store. This is rarely the case, however. Many home pages are jam-packed with too much information that interferes with the customer's purpose, which can be one of the three situations described earlier.

An example home page is shown in Figure 5-2.

The home page sets the shopper's expectations for the rest of the site and lays out the framework. The home page performs the following jobs:

- Provides the store framework
- Provides company information
- Identifies major product categories
- Provides special notices

Figure 5–2 A home page invites customers into the store.

The components vary in implementation from store to store, but all of them are essential to the home page.

Store Framework

The store framework—or page layout—sets the expectations for the customer for each subsequent page within the website. It usually consists of the top banner of the store, the left navigational bars, the primary content area (middle), and often has a third column on the right side used typically for advertisements. These areas are shown in Figure 5-2. The top banner and left navigational areas are usually consistent throughout the remainder of the store.

To help the customer remain oriented in the site, there are static elements that start on the home page and then remain constant. For example, the company logo and top of the page identification banner help ground the shopper in the store even though page content changes.

Company Information

The company name, logo, and positioning statement are important informational elements. In addition, a toll-free number provides another means to order or to ask questions and should be readily noticeable and available on the home page and all other pages of the store.

A link to a company information area will provide the company name, address, telephone number, parent company, and a key contact name. It may tell a little about the company itself, how long it has been in business, the types of markets it serves, and the range of products it produces. There may be a photo of the main office to establish credibility. This area can reinforce the value proposition and reassure customers that they will get the promised quality, service, or other attribute when they order.

Major Product Category Headings

The home page is the virtual retail store directory or catalog table of contents. Product categories on this page must clearly and quickly communicate the store product sets or service offerings. Most online stores carry a broader product assortment than traditional channels. They also carry specialty and hard-to-find products that create category-naming challenges. The shear number of products available for online sales also complicates product organization for the store developers.

Some top-level categories listed on home pages include the following: electronics, computers, toys, movies, books, beauty supplies, apparel, and shoes. Usually, online stores recombine traditional product assortments and create new category names that may not be intuitive to first-time shoppers to the store. If shopping occasions are infrequent, second-time shoppers may stumble again on unfamiliar names.

While each category name appears clear and logical to the merchant, the true test is to have real customers identify whether or not each is sufficiently intuitive. A category label—such as electronics—may no longer be as clear as it was in the past. For example, ask ten people what this category contains, and you will get ten different answers. Televisions, computers, printers, video recorders, and games may be offered in this category. It's important to define category designations to match your top customers' definitions.

Over the past couple of years, most online categories have grown and blended. For example, the paper category is one that has grown and now offers new choices and types. Five years ago, this online category had less than ten items. The paper category added specialty printing papers, and now there are hundreds of items. Organizing this category into a meaningful structure requires customer insight.

In our customer task analysis research—which is described in Chapter 6—the most preferred method for customer shopping navigation was to first review the category name links. When customers couldn't find an intuitive name, they resorted to using the search box to type their own choice.

Disruptive Elements

Product advertising on the home page should be limited. Over-promotion on the home page is like a retail sales representative offering customers special deals as they enter through the store's doors. Customers need a chance to become familiar with the store and aren't yet ready to make decisions on specials. The home page doesn't know a person's particular reason for coming to the online store.

People don't like to sift through choices on a home page that has been cluttered with irrelevant content, and it gives them a negative impression of the store. They may browse a little, but will opt out to another site that offers relevancy and less clutter. Customers on a mission aren't yet looking to purchase an irrelevant item when they walk in the virtual door. Yet, online stores sell this home page space, and it is part of their profitability mix.

Another disruptive element on some home pages is requiring people to register before they can browse. One customer in our research responded to the registration prompt with irritation:

> "Do I have to log in? Oh, do I have to? On some of these sites you have to give them information before you do stuff—I find that so annoying. At least let me browse before you ask me that—so I can at least see if you have it first."
>
> —*A Shopper's Lament*

This comment is representative of many others we heard when reviewing sites with this requirement. Some stores require customer information up front to check inventory levels at various retail stores. These stores assume the customer will want to pick up their order at retail. Other stores want to know the customer's location or zip code to change pricing to reflect regional differences.

Home Page Quality and Standards

Jakob Nielsen and Maria Tahir's book, *Home Page Usability: 50 Websites Deconstructed* (New Riders Publishing, 2002), takes an in-depth look at measuring the quality of home pages—usually the first impression for a customer. It provides recommendations and guidelines for managing home page "real estate" with a focus on page usability.

Standards for home page construction and evolution are emerging. If followed, they will help the customer's ability to leverage learning of website operation across many stores. While some stores attempt clever approaches to give the customer a "unique" trip to the e-store, most customers become annoyed or irate if the cleverness forces them to study the page or to learn something new.

Special Notices

This section of the home page should let shoppers know about any special terms of purchase. These could include available financing options, shipping options, or the types of credit cards accepted by the firm.

Category Pages—"The Aisles"

A main category link off the home page brings the shopper to a main category page or "aisle." These e-aisles collect similar products together—such as dresses, printers, or shoes. Category market structure and organization is discussed in Chapter 3.

Creating an aisle that is familiar to the customer minimizes confusion. Depending on the product assortment and mix, this page or pages will either list individual products within a category or become a directional page that "serves up" further choices to the shopper. In either case, it can contain product or multiple-product offers. Here again, care must be taken and the page evaluated to determine the appropriate balance of advertising and product information. Promoting products that a customer is not yet interested in creates shopping obstacles.

The online store consists of several category pages that require good downward navigation from the home page. They also require good horizontal navigation for shoppers crossing categories.

Like the home page, each category page must clearly communicate what that page or section has to offer in an intuitive manner and do it quickly. A category page example is shown in Figure 5-3.

In general, category page layout should give attention to each of the following prioritized elements:

- Sub-category name links (if needed to further break down choices)
- Product listings
- Relevant promotional offers
- Value-added content (information, examples, explanation, or demonstrations)
- Brand or boutique store links (mini-stores within the main store)

Most online stores carry thousands of products, and structures must take on a hierarchical nature, as discussed in Chapter 3. Having multiple category pages that further narrows the choice

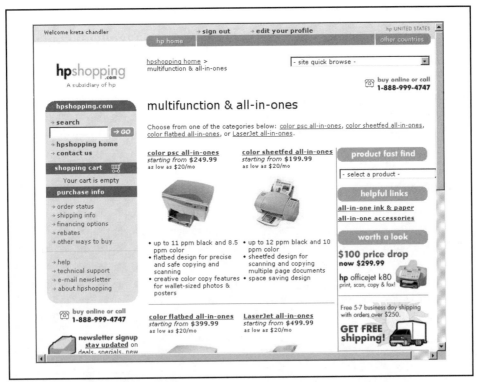

Figure 5–3 Category pages group together similar products or provide links to further narrow choices for the customer.

for the customer is acceptable as long as the customer does not have to stop and consider each link name. The customer must clearly understand what is in each of the further sub-category name refinements. Each element of doubt disrupts the purchase process. These listings break up long lists into smaller, manageable lists that don't appear as overwhelming to the shopper.

Clearly understood category links affect shoppers perceptions regarding ease of use with a website. Intuitiveness and simplicity of website design creates the illusion of fewer steps and clicks.

We tested a customer-centered design website prototype of a navigation model with actual customers. Customers said the navigation process took them only two or three clicks before they reached the destination product detail page, when, in fact, it took them five clicks. This phenomenon has a converse effect for non-intuitive names and models, however. Customers who are having difficulty selecting links on confusing websites believe they make more clicks than they actually do.

Product promotions on the category pages can be valuable to a customer as long as they have relevance. Usually, however, online stores sell this space to manufacturers to feature their products. These products may or may not be of interest to most customers at this point in the shopping process. Premier placement should be reserved for strategic and profitable products.

Also, consideration must be given to why most shoppers are there, which can be to seek a specific product or to comparison-shop.

Many people shop by brand for online products. Grouping products together by brand name makes these easier for customers to find. These are similar to special manufacturer sections in a traditional retail store. Fashion products are often shelved together by designer, while technical products are frequently grouped by brand. Online customers tend to be more brand-loyal to high-quality brands because they are perceived to be a "safer" buy on the Internet.

Providing additional shopping modes—such as grouping also by type and by price—can give customers additional choice and control.

Sub-category Pages—"The Shelf"

Because most online stores carry hundreds or thousands of products, it is important to break up the information into manageable chunks. Products are displayed on a shelf—whether it is physical shelving in a brick-and-mortar store, a catalog page, a TV infomercial, or an e-commerce website product page. The product shelf is any web page on which a product is merchandised and sold. It can be a category page featuring many products, or it can be a specific product page with a single product. An example of a sub-category page is shown in Figure 5-4.

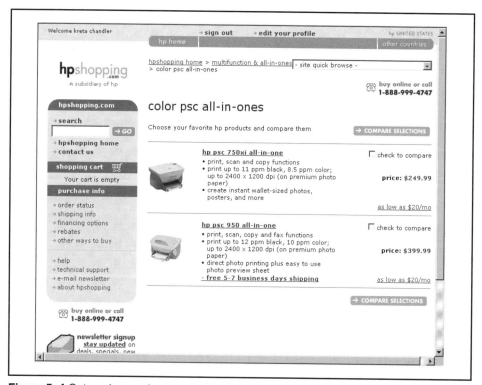

Figure 5–4 Categories can be grouped into more manageable and intuitive arrangements.

In this example, there are many varieties of all-in-one printers. The subcategory page helps to narrow down the offering. A thorough understanding of customer needs is necessary to structure these pages. Depending on product complexities, informational content can provide customers with "why to buy" information that helps them select the right product to meet their needs. Emerging online tools—such as the shopping wizard—can help narrow choices. This tool is discussed later in this chapter.

Product Detail Pages—"The Package or SKU"

Because customers can't pick up virtual merchandise and read labels, the product detail page represents the product or behaves like the product package. It must clearly communicate what the product is and what the customer will receive as a result of its purchase. Anytime a page offers a product for sale, it must provide the following information for each of the products offered:

- What it is—the description, picture, uses
- Relevant and complete compatibility, sizing, color, or other information
- What's contained in the package—what the customer will receive
- Other items needed for immediate operation (batteries, cables, assembly, UL specifications)
- Spare or complementary items (extra batteries, film, or a carrying case)
- "Care and feeding" of the product (special polish, cleaning instructions)
- The price and any hidden charges (extra shipping or handling)
- The manufacturer's or designer's name
- Sample content (for example, sample book pages)

The customer must know clearly what the product is and what it looks like. And for customers who know exactly what they are looking for, accurate descriptions and specific product numbers or models must be included so they may easily recognize the correct product, as shown in Figure 5-5. Our research across more than 25 major e-commerce websites identified incomplete or inadequate information. In many cases, the web stores did not provide complete compatibility information.

Shoppers will not purchase from a site that cannot confirm their choice or be specific about what the product is that they are purchasing.

"It doesn't tell me the size of the paper. I wish I had the box here. I bet the information would be on the package."
—*A Shopper's Comment*

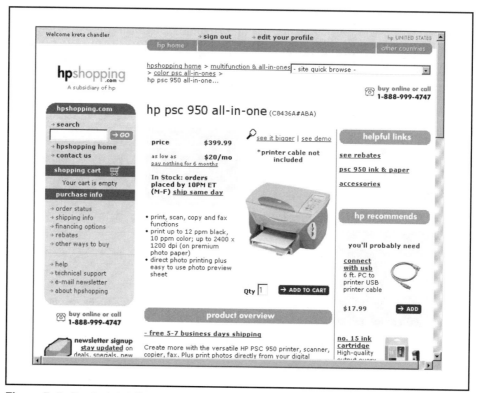

Figure 5–5 Product detail pages are a virtual representation of the product or the product package.

Product detail pages let customers know what they're getting and what else they may need or want. In this example, product features—the "speeds and feeds"—are listed. This includes products they may need to purchase in order to use the product. It also features other products the customer may want. Good clothing stores recommend coordinated accessories to give customers ideas to complete ensembles for a variety of social occasions.

The product detail page also needs to let people know how to buy the product. As simple as that sounds, customers who participated in website evaluation research had difficulty adding a product to the shopping cart. This function varies from website to website. Button labels can also vary. Some say "add to cart," "buy," or "add." The buttons also have different locations on these sites. Some are next to the products and some are far enough away to disassociate them from the product.

Also, some websites force customers to go to the shopping cart or checkout page every time they add an item to the shopping cart. This then forces them to start over or go back and forth if they are shopping for multiple items. It adds an unnecessary extra step.

> "I prefer to be able to click on items and not go directly to the shopping cart after each item. I don't like that…Where did I go? Oh, I'm back at the home page. Now I have to go back through all the layers again to get back where I was. I have to select every-thing all over again. If I were doing this for real, I would have defi-nitely given up. That was cumbersome, very cumbersome. I didn't like having to go back to the main page every time I added something to my cart."
>
> *—A Shopper's Comment*

Make it easy for the customer to know what they're getting and how to get it. Customers will leave tedious websites.

Content Pages—Adding Value to the Customer Experience with a Product

Trends in online store evolution go beyond pure product selling and promotion into product edu-cation. Education can provide customers with new ways to use products or explain how to oper-ate them. Additional pages may be required to provide information to help customers understand new categories or select products. These pages add decision-making depth to more complex products or categories.

Value-added content pages help narrow decision choices for customers. Page content con-sists of information that the customer needs and promotional information provided by the mer-chant. These pages usually include product and product category education, new uses for products, or selection information. An example of a selection content page is shown in Figure 5-6.

Value-added content pages can consist of simple compatibility charts or a sequence of pages refining selection choices. The information can be provided by static web pages, by pages that have been dynamically built, or by applications such as selection configurators—like the one discussed in Chapter 8.

Content is determined by general or specific shopper goals. Shoppers may just want to gather information for a later purchase—and not complete a purchase right then. Implementa-tion depends on content subject and value. Regardless of the goals, content must have perceived value and appear useful to the customer.

Manufacturer websites are heavily used to gather information. These sites allow customers to research products, have access to background data, or experiment with mock customized products. A car manufacturer, for instance, may show each model with a variety of interior col-ors and fabrics.

The new e-business landscape is more than just commerce. Online merchants recognize that price alone will not determine repeat visitation and are offering information and content to help build customer relationships. Websites must become more than electronic catalogs that merely sell products and feature only price, product features, and specifications.

These are perfect environments to develop the consumer community, if the site contains relevant content, so they get the most out of their purchased products. If the relevance is there, in

Figure 5–6 Selection content pages give additional information to help customers make purchasing decisions.

terms of operational support or expanded usage, customers will return to the site. For example, www.hp.com/create provides easy-to-use templates and project ideas with relevance to a home consumer and to a business professional. These ideas expand the capabilities of a current experience. An example of a content page website is shown in Figure 5-7.

With today's technologies and faster Internet connections becoming more prevalent in U.S. homes, there is increased capability to use emerging applications and file formats. New e-tools, such as videos and animations, will be discussed later in this chapter. Until broadband adoption becomes mainstream, however, consideration must be given to "real" customer shopping environments. Any new technology or application must still be tested on dial-up connections.

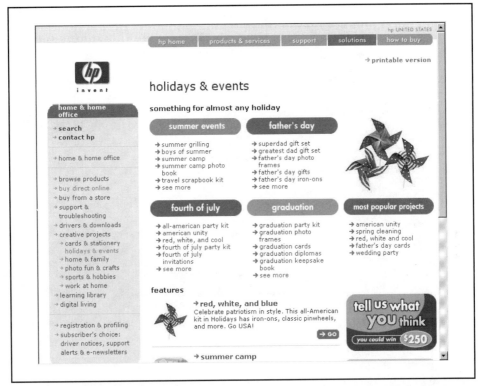

Figure 5–7 Content can increase customer satisfaction with a product and encourage return website visits.

Syndicating Managed Content

Managing thousands of products and their related content is resource intensive. It is a complex process to manage the database and the new data streams that keep it current. New content management models, such as syndicated content processes, can make the process more efficient from both a dollar and staffing perspective.

In this model, one content server source can provide a world-class electronic content database that is flexible, modular, extensible, and customizable to accommodate adding and deleting blocks of information and content. It provides for timely, simultaneous updates.

The value of this approach is in knowing what the customer needs and wants, knowing what the merchant needs and wants, providing the value, and then replicating it consistently throughout all of the websites through which it travels. An example of this model is shown in Figure 5-8.

Syndicated content models work equally as well for core product information and for educational content replication. An implementation of this model is described in Chapter 8.

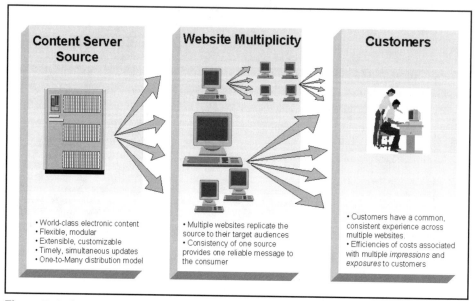

Figure 5–8 One reliable, consistent source is replicated and distributed to many.

The Checkout Counter

This page must clearly let a customer know cart contents, quantities, and prices. Checkout also provides an additional opportunity to recommend complementary products to your customers. Ensure, however, that these recommendations are relevant to the purchase, or you will lose credibility. For example, don't offer a wireless router that's on special when a customer has just added a children's book to her cart. You will waste space that could have been used to suggest a comparable age-related toy or additional book.

The Whole Is Greater than the Sum of the Individual Parts

Each web page has its own special merchant and customer needs. Products are merchandised and sold on the home page, category pages, product pages, value-added content pages, and in the shopping cart. Retail shelf product placement principles, catalog design page layout guidelines, and online-specific methods can be blended to maximize the virtual implementation. Taken individually, each page must stand alone and be carefully optimized for usability and profitability. Taken as an integrated web store "system," two critical online store considerations apply:

- How the webpages are linked together—the navigation model
- What's on each page when you get there—the content

The linkages between pages are based on customer insight and intuitiveness. What appears on each page is reflective of both customer needs and reseller business drivers.

Ten Essential E-merchandising Techniques

The following techniques incorporate the best practices from retail and catalog merchandising and blend them with technology innovations to create a profitable and satisfying online store. The online store provides its own best practices that are part of its technological inherent nature. It is this hybrid combination that creates new methodologies for merchandising.

Each online store is unique. The following techniques must be balanced against each other and applied to the store's needs:

1. Guiding the customer intuitively through the store (navigation)
2. Standardizing category names (the "aisles")
3. Placing products (where they justify themselves profitably)
4. Increasing items purchased (cross-merchandising and up-selling)
5. Increasing frequency of purchases (product purchase reminders)
6. Refreshing the e-shelf
7. Benefit selling
8. Valuing the e-shelf
9. Personalization
10. Enabling customers to communicate with you (chat rooms, etc.)

These e-merchandising techniques ensure the best possible product representation and the customer's ability to find and select them.

Guiding Customers through the Store (Navigation)

A challenge of the online store is managing navigation. Navigational models are like roads that connect the different parts of the store together and help flow customers from one city to another. Online navigation flows customer traffic through the "aisles" of the online store by way of sequential links, but it also provides for random access through keyword search. Each click is a chance to get lost.

E-planogramming and the resulting navigation model is the store's layout and customer traffic flow model. It is based primarily on how customers shop at retail. Instead of walking through the aisles, shoppers navigate by clicking links that take them from page to page and e-aisle to e-aisle. Once clicked, each destination page must deliver information that the customer would normally expect to see. For the customer, effective navigation is a process of elimination. Site structures must not only meet customer expectations, they also have to narrow choices logically.

The content of a page consists of the graphical elements and the information that a customer gleans from it. Both of these factors affect the shopper's ability to easily and simply identify critical information from that page. If needed, a navigation link can take them to additional pages.

Online traffic flow models are extremely critical to a store's success. Usability measurements are identified to help create, refine, and optimize these models for customers and are discussed in Chapter 6.

Entering the Online Store

This first impression sets the ambience and personality of the store. Each entry point must convey the personality and brand of the store in which the customer is invited to stay and shop. If it is an uneasy experience and the shopper can't feel comfortable, he will leave. There are now many more choices than ever.

An online store has unlimited entrances. Each entry point is a potential chance for the customer to be disoriented upon entering the store. Entrances to an online store include the following:

- Links embedded in emails
- Direct marketing campaigns with a unique URL listed
- Search engines and shopping "bots" (search websites that provide links to online stores)
- Shopping mall portals (ISP pages like AOL and Yahoo)
- Links from community websites
- Links from partner websites

Customers are not always delivered to the store's front door (home page). They can be dropped into an aisle or product detail page within the store, depending on the marketing activity and link.

"You Are Here" Signage

One navigational technique—breadcrumbing—is like having a "You Are Here" store directory in each aisle. It is a method taken from a children's story in which a child drops breadcrumbs on a path to follow on the return trip home to avoid getting lost. Used as part of a standard frame in the banner, each "crumb" has been modified for the virtual world and tells the site map path taken, as shown Figure 5-9.

This method keeps customers oriented and is valuable as a standard element in the store banner scheme and layout. It is most effective when used with other standards—like consistent leftside navigational bars—that keep customers oriented in store locations. Each "crumb" can be clicked so the customer can easily "beam" to where he was before he got lost. The first crumb in the string is the always the home page.

From store to store, configurations of webpage frames and content vary. Sometimes, key category links are displayed as tabs across the top or as text links listed down the left navigation bar. In any case, the e-merchandising techniques and concepts can be applied to fit specific page design layouts.

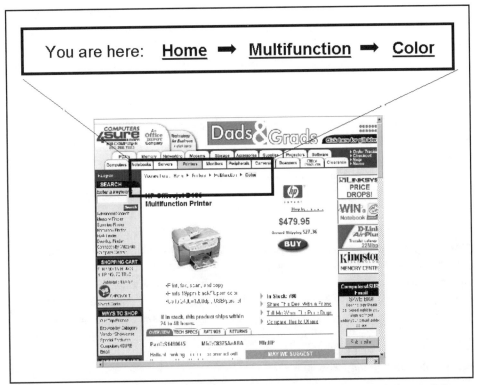

Figure 5–9 Breadcrumbing lets people know where they are within a website at all times.

Company Logo—All Roads Lead to Home

The store logo is another orientation navigational tool. Because the logo appears on every web page, it is now recognized as a standard link that people click to bring them directly to the home page. Besides being a navigational element, this standard fixture reinforces the brand and positioning of the store throughout the website. Establish a link on the company logo that delivers customers to the home page.

Standardizing Category Naming Conventions

The hybrid online environment combines retail category nomenclature with that of cataloging. Add the customer's preconceived naming familiarities and you get a mixed bag of confusion. While attempts have been made, there is no standardization in the industry.

For major categories, understand customer insight and set standards based on customer needs. Many online stores strive to set themselves apart by having a unique website, and they choose to develop their own category structures. This practice hinders the customer in achieving successful searches. Unfamiliar categories cause customers to contemplate unfamiliar names.

For strategic categories and products, conduct customer research that will help you design the names of categories and key products. This will help in populating the search functionality to return successful searches caused by incorrect text entries. It will also increase sales on the Internet overall as the searches become successful and frustration is minimized.

Redefining Market Structures

It may be necessary for you to define market structures for your website based on customer shopping preferences and predisposition. You can then reconstruct the store to meet customer and marketplace demands. Reconstruction allows you to relocate non-traditional "aisles" and virtually combine non-standard categories, if your customers prefer to shop that way. The first step is to understand how customers shop. Chapter 6 provides usability development and testing methods that you can apply to ensure success.

Improving usability of your website and providing intuitive customer naming conventions may be easier to implement than it sounds. You may discover that renaming or refining the name of a category listed on the home page resolves current frustrations. For example, research showed that each website that sold HP printing supplies was different, and often customers didn't even know where to begin. Because the supplies could be under "office products," "computer peripherals," "technology supplies," and a variety of other non-intuitive names, the category was difficult for the customer to find. A simple change on the home page renaming the category "printing supplies" increased sales immediately. Before the change, customers gave up because they didn't know how to begin.

Renewing Category Management in the Online Marketplace

Category management is a retail tool. Originally designed to manage efficiencies at the shelf, it has evolved to provide insight into customer shopping preferences. The data collected at the cash register is analyzed for sales by SKU and by outlet. The same practice can be conducted with more velocity and thoroughness online.

It usually takes a month to six weeks to obtain sales register data, clean it, and run it though predetermined algorithms. Managing your own data online should be a fairly instant process if you design your systems to capture appropriate information.

True category management provides insight into entire categories from a variety of online merchants. Unfortunately, the web is probably not conducive to this type of data sharing because so many e-merchants are smaller companies unlikely to share information. But you can certainly analyze your own information and determine which brands your customers select, how often they buy, which target customer group purchases the most, and the quantities they purchase at any given interval.

Other qualitative data may be available as well. If there are several versions of a garment, for instance, which color do most consumers prefer? Do customers purchase enough of an off-brand to continue to stock the product? You can create your own efficiencies through data analysis.

If your company is an e-commerce arm of a large retailer (click and mortar), try to integrate your retail category management program with your online program. If other retailers are willing to share information, the entire channel will benefit. Often retailers are very concerned with sharing data needlessly. While sales information is sensitive, most companies, if given competitive data, would not have systems in place to react to it anyway.

Whether or not your company is willing to share, analyze your internal data from e-commerce with the same data at retail. You may find consumers react to the same merchandise differently online. This may be because of inadequate explanations or customer confusion because a product may be presented in a different way on your website. The data comparisons will alert you to the issue, and you can then investigate.

Product Placements

Online stores lack the observable physical start and finish structure of a retail store. At retail, a customer can clearly see aisles and shelves filled with products and the checkout counters waiting to total their purchases. Online, there is a virtual space that is unseen and unclear as the customer "steps" through the store entrance and onto the home page. Once there, the shopper knows there are lots of products, yet he can't see how many. He also can't see the structure of the aisles or how products might appear on the shelf. And he can't tell the size or the depth of the store. This can be disorienting because the customer doesn't know if the store is a big operation or a small one—the tip of an iceberg or only an ice cube.

As the shopper starts clicking choices and wanders through the e-aisles, he can be confronted with virtual pallets full of random products (long line listings). Or he can be presented with structured, organized shelves filled logically with an assortment of products that are easy to select.

Some products are better suited for online sales than others. Multi-channel shoppers will choose to purchase products based on convenience and proximity to their businesses or homes. And this depends on the product itself. Many people shop online, regardless of where they actually purchase. They may research information for a higher priced or larger item online, but they make the purchase in person at retail. More routine, commodity, and low involvement products make ideal online purchases.

A strategic retail shelf-management technique determines product shelf placement. Typically, placement is determined by the number of turns—volume of product sold during a month—and value of the specific product. Unfortunately, key areas on web pages are sold for advertising space instead of reserving them for prime products. Also, dynamically generated product listings are often sorted by the database rules—such as alphabetically by product name or numerically by product number—and not by product value to the merchant.

Above the Pack and Above the Fold

Online products most frequently purchased or products that have other strategic value should be placed "above the fold." This is the viewable part of the web page as it renders in a conventional 600 x 800 resolution screen. It is analogous to placing the product on the retail shelf at eye-level. This placement makes it most convenient for people to find. Customers stop searching if they have to scroll too much or click to other pages, which is similar to putting products on the top or bottom shelf.

Considerations must be given to emerging technologies and adoption of Internet devices such as handheld PCs and net or web TV so that prime products are displayed first.

Limiting Choice with Conscious Intent

Even with the ability to offer a limitless product mix, there is a point where the law of diminishing returns comes into play. Unlike a retail store and catalog that have physical limitations, the online store has depth, limited only by the system storage space and servers running the website. The more products in the database, the harder it is to organize and merchandise them.

Limiting choice is a strategy employed to manage the structure to ease product selection and minimize warehousing and fulfillment transactional costs. Too much choice can actually be an inhibitor to purchasing and a reason for abandoned shopping carts. This occurs when the product comparison and selection tasks become too overwhelming. Even with the mistaken perception that online shelf space is limitless, customer considerations and business drivers must be taken into consideration.

Online shoppers look to their online merchants as experts in the products they sell. Many online resellers feel that providing customer choice equates with providing them every product that is available. This view forces shoppers to compare and make choices from long lists of possibilities with limited information. Shoppers often don't bother and shop somewhere else instead.

What better service to your customers can you provide than making recommendations to them? To start, this can be simply identifying products as "good, better, and best" for the shopper's need. These recommendations can be based on price and quality of the brand. These designated products can be placed above the fold for those shoppers who don't know where to begin to comparison-shop. Then, additional choices can be listed or featured for those customers who would like more choices and have more time to browse.

Product and category long-term value factors must be considered in developing the good, better, best model, however. Customers will develop trust for your store if their experience with the product matches your recommendations. They will continue to see you as the expert in the products you sell.

Increasing Cash Register Ring

Many techniques can influence the number of items purchased or the total value of the shopping cart. Three of these successful retailing techniques to leverage online are cross-selling, up-selling, and purchasing spares. In fact, there is more opportunity online through virtual messaging to attach these to products than in traditional retail or catalog phone orders.

Cross-selling products is a method by which the online store recommends complementary items for customer purchase. This technique drives incremental sales and is typically impulse related. These "add-on" products can also provide a fuller solution for the customer. Some example recommendations could be jewelry and shoes with dresses, cables with printers, batteries with electronic devices, or salsa with chips.

Relevant and complementary items work best for cross-selling. These items might belong to the same category or they might belong to a completely different category. Conduct a holistic evaluation on your website to put together recommendations for key products. Make it convenient and easy for the customer to add the item to the cart. Complementary products are good items to consider as bundles and "e-kits," a tool described later in this chapter.

Up-selling is a method by which a product within the same category with varying degrees of functionality is recommended that may better meet a customer's long-term needs. This method replaces a less-expensive product purchase with a more-expensive product purchase, while cross-selling adds additional products to the cart.

Another cross-selling technique is to recommend that the customer buy "spare" products. This technique is best for consumable, repeat purchases. It's never convenient to have to go to the retail store when you run out of a product. This can be an incentive to increase the number of products in the shopping cart, especially if your online store offers free shipping or other delivery options for a designated sale amount. This technique also keeps customers coming back as repeat purchasers making more frequent visits to your store. Many customers return to the original store for repeat purchases if their experience was positive.

Using valuable cross-sell merchandising space for non-relevant products doesn't work. Many online stores currently make the mistake of "down-selling," which happens when stores believe they are offering customers "choice." This practice can recommend a lower-quality product at a lower price, which may not be in the best interests of the customer. The store's perceived value of choice may conflict with the customer's perceived value of the recommendation. As one customer put it, "It's like going to a premium store, and being offered flea-market items."

Down-selling often occurs when webpage space is sold as manufacturer advertising or the product manufacturer offers "spiffs" (sales representative incentives) attached for the merchant. While seemingly harmless, this practice may cause you to lose credibility with customers due to the recommendations you make. As an online merchant, customers see you as an expert. If this is compromised by non-relevancy, customers may lose faith and trust in your judgment.

Customers look to online stores to recommend the right products, not to merely list products for sale. Used effectively, these techniques increase the total cash register ring and provide customers with complete and best solutions.

Increasing Frequency of Purchases

Increasing the frequency of purchases is an online technique that considers customers' purchasing behaviors. It is somewhat related to cross-selling when follow-up products are offered to customers at a designated time after an initial purchase is made. This is essentially a "postponed" cross-sell. For this technique, it is imperative to understand your specific target customers and have a thorough understanding of product-related categories and other categories as defined by retail customer segment clustering techniques described in Chapter 3.

Online sales data is analyzed for trends. For example, a trend might identify that customers who purchase a new desktop PC also purchase a new printer two months later. The store can provide printer information to the PC customer as a follow-up a month later.

Tracking customer purchases and integrating the information into your CRM database will allow you to customize messages to your customers when they enter your website. You can greet them personally and acknowledge past purchases. If the customer buys routine supplies from you at regular intervals, give the customer the option of placing a standard order. Even small companies take advantage of this technique. One pizza chain keeps records of each take-out pizza ordered linked to the customer's phone number. When the customer calls in an order, he is asked if he would like the same as his last order. The same concept applies online. But it must be non-intrusive and with the customer's permission.

Taking this a step further, the company can recommend, based on ordering history, what it thinks a particular customer might like to purchase in the future. This technique must be very customized to be on target and should be linked to a personal shopping service. Otherwise, it may be perceived as an annoyance.

Refreshing the E-shelf

At retail, refreshing the shelf includes activities such as replenishing products and removing torn or damaged products to ensure that the product is presented in the best light. New product introductions usually signal the need to refresh the shelf online. Most websites remain static until new products replace old ones or promotions or products *du jour* are featured. While the websites appear to undergo a refresh, they behave more like changing ads in a Sunday circular.

Refreshing the shelf is more complicated online because there are more things to refresh. A good site design ensures that customer usability is not compromised while at the same time ensuring that relevant information is updated. Taking a continual pulse to determine changes in customer online shopping preferences and behaviors will drive the need for shelf refresh, or in many cases, restructure.

Benefit Selling

Stores that are good at providing customer benefits are good at selling products. Online stores should take a lesson from TV broadcasting sales channels and infomercials. These excel at "showing the meal" and not just the ingredients.

Most online stores describe the products' basic specifications. It is difficult to convey customer benefits at retail, in catalogs, or online. However, there are advantages in online stores because they are not limited to the product's package or to a catalog printed description. New e-tools, such as video streaming and animation files, help present more information to the customer about how to use products. The right messaging can also convey product benefits.

A typical online scanner description would list dpi (dots per inch), USB connection, and other specifications for use in comparing scanners. Customers are more likely to be interested in the ability to preserve aging photos or to save time by not having to re-type text documents—the basic benefits of scanners.

Valuing the Shelf

The value of a product within a category determines how much space should be allocated to it to maximize sales. Also considered is the type of product. Is it a frequently purchased product in a "destination category"? In Chapter 3, we explained how SKU rationalization relates products to the retail shelf. Products are placed with the number of "facings" that justify the number of product "turns" and profitability.

Online, equal space is typically disproportionately given to two products with completely different values to the merchant. Would you give 50 percent of your shelf space equally to two products if one product represents 99 percent of the business of the two? It isn't sound business practice to do that at the retail shelf, but it happens frequently online. You can reinforce the value of a profitable, frequently purchased product online by ensuring that it is above the fold and has a premier presentation, such as a large image, compared to the other product.

Personalization

This e-merchandising technique leverages from customer relationship management knowledge and historical customer sales and registration data captured in prior visits. It also considers customers who return to purchase by applying redesigns and personalization capabilities to the web store. Returning customers should be able to easily log in and review their order history. If they purchase items on a regular basis, providing them with this history makes a difference to them, especially if they are loyal customers.

The IT group must know what information to capture from the customer and can collect this during shopping sessions. It must match up with the marketing department's needs to segment the data and send emails. Information collected can be analyzed based on geographic location, anticipatory and repeat consumable ordering, and identification of key product and complementary product purchases.

The website registration form must be intuitive and understandable to the customer and easy to use. But, as previously mentioned, it must be requested at a time that is appropriate and not annoying to the customer. Relationship building can happen in an order confirmation, which can be emailed after a product purchase.

As with any new and innovative e-merchandising techniques, be prepared to reconsider implementations if they stray too far from doing the job they intended. One early implementation greets customers by name and then recommends products. However, the products recommended to them have no relevancy to the returning customer and in some cases can be insensitive. It is difficult to anticipate why a customer purchased what he previously purchased or for whom. Making too many assumptions about a person's shopping behaviors is not always the best practice.

For example, Allison had purchased books from an online store. When she returned a month later to browse the store, she was greeted by name and offered items specially selected for her. From the store's recommendations, it would appear that she is a balding male favoring books on women's hormonal therapy and little blue bears and who likes to watch freaky night, scary DVD movies that were created for 17-year-olds. And to top off a rich evening of entertainment, she could also purchase a Harry Potter video and Lego set. If the store really knew Allison, they would understand that she is 25 years old and likes scuba diving. She has no children and loves classical music.

It's best to start off with a simple, known, and valued personalization capability. An example of an effective and relevant personalized model—My Printing Supplies Store—will be discussed as a case study of hpshopping.com in Chapter 8.

Communicating with Customers

The hard part of customer communication is making it easy for everyone given varying and preferred communication methods. Traditional toll-free numbers—real-time customer support—works in this channel as well as in direct marketing. Real-time chat rooms are an additional customer convenience for pre-sales and post-sales questions. QVC.com, for example, offers immediate online, real-time sales assistance should a customer have questions while placing an order.

Making it easy to talk to you is one of the most important customer relationship building techniques that you can employ.

E-tools of the Trade

There are many fixtures used at retail that call attention to specific products or aid customers in finding and selecting products. Here are a few essential e-fixtures leveraged from retail and redeveloped for online sales. Retail stores use fixtures such as peg hooks and shelves. Catalogs use copy and images to merchandise products. Online stores can take key merchandising components and create new electronic fixtures and tools, such as streaming videos and webpage layouts.

The following are some of the most effective e-tools:

- Virtual end caps
- Shopping carts
- Search boxes
- Online indexers
- Text, color schemes, images, and copy
- Virtual bundles (e-kits)
- Selection, configuration, and comparison tools
- Online product registration tools
- Online sampling and demonstrations

Virtual End Caps

An end cap at retail is a special shelf display positioned at the end of an aisle. This display collects together one or more products and designates them for special attention to distinguish the products from the "rest of the crowd." Online, virtual end caps are manifested as special promotional boxes highlighting products. Products can have a promotion attached or are featured at a special price. These promotional boxes—placed strategically on a category page—help to sell-through product, but only if they have relevance to the category.

Virtual end caps and solution selling are emerging in online store areas created to provide a full view of what a customer needs to do. This can be in a home office section, product "boutiques," brand stores, or solution-type product displays. The best use of these promotional online "end caps" relates specifically to the brand page, as shown in Figure 5-10.

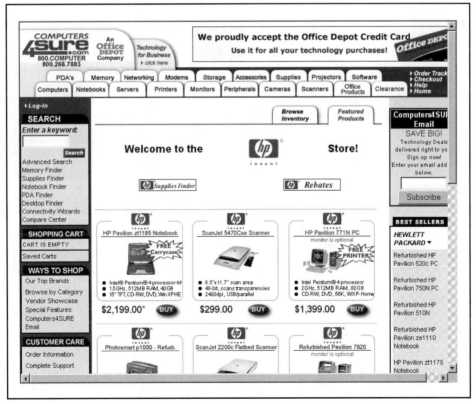

Figure 5–10 A brand store is an example of a "virtual" end cap.

Catalogs offer lessons as well. One large cataloger focused exclusively on its complete catalog until the company separated several specialty categories into smaller flyers. Websites can organize to accommodate the vertical, specialty markets they serve.

Shopping Cart

The online shopping cart collects products like a shopping cart at retail and also functions as the checkout counter and cash register. Unlike at retail, however, most online shopping cart contents are hidden until checkout. One of the contributing factors to abandoned shopping carts is the surprise totals and shipping charges of the purchase transaction. The customer typically sees these totals when she is ready to "check out." Also, on some websites, customers are often not sure if an item has been added to the cart, because the add-to-cart function behaves differently on each site.

"Sticky" shopping carts are becoming customer expectations. A sticky shopping cart, shown in Figure 5-11 keeps added items posted on each web page and travels with the shopper from page to page.

Chapter 8 features a case study on hpshopping.com, one of the first online stores to develop and implement this technology. Sticky carts today vary across e-commerce sites. Some are easily recognizable, but others blend in too much with the store's frames and colors. When adding this technology to your website, ensure that it is highly visible and not camouflaged by the other components on the page.

Figure 5–11 Sticky Shopping Cart.

Search Boxes

Most people use the text search box as a last resort when the page looks too difficult or the category names aren't intuitive in the list of choices. The search box can be an effective tool, however, when coupled with other selling vehicles. For example, direct marketers ensure website search by catalog number, which makes a good combination for those people who want to order online rather than call the toll-free number. It allows instant access to a known and desired product. Also, major search engines—such as yahoo.com, excite.com, or google.com—direct traffic to your site. Monitor these search engines so they are correct and kept current for your key product offerings.The search function may not be helpful, however, because there are many variations of how someone searches and types words into the box. People also misspell, add spaces where none are expected, and mistype. If the person does not type in exactly what is programmed into the search results, they receive a "sorry, no results" page even if the site has the product. In our online research throughout the years, we've identified the following considerations to include in the search engine development:

- If products have part numbers, consider the product numbering and three main combinations that people may type into the box.
- Capture common misspellings and attach appropriate products to the search results.
- Consider variations to text entry, (e.g., spellings, plural/singular cases, other common names for categories).
- Ensure advanced search is effective through task analysis testing; consider allowing advanced search in the regular text box.

Search box improvements and recommendations are further discussed in Chapter 7. A specific improvement in the functionality is used as a case study and is discussed in Chapter 8.

Online Indexers

An innovative new tool that is an alternative to the search box is an online indexer. This tool is leveraged from the software application program's index help function and from a catalog's index. Customers searching for products in a catalog typically go to the index and scan categories. They can tell quickly by process of elimination whether or not they are on the right track for finding a specific product or an area where it might be located.

Electronic versions of an index are common in software applications. They allow a searcher to type progressive keystrokes. The indexing tool narrows the choices while giving the searcher enough visible range in the indexed list to determine closeness to the destination.

This would help when a shopper has an idea but may not know the spelling or how it might be worded on the website. This model is similar to verifying spelling in a dictionary or searching through the Yellow Pages to get to some surrounding entries and then scan for specifics.

Text, Color Schemes, Images, and Copy

Chapter 3 described the effect that visual elements can have on people in a retail store. If people feel good, they typically purchase more. With the convenience of having multiple stores at a shopper's fingertips, an online store must be inviting and must ensure that the customer feels comfortable to stay and purchase. The web also has the potential of becoming more like catalogs and having a more recreational aspect versus a pure product hunt.

Effective online merchandising considers advertisement and newspaper techniques. They start with the most important attributes and put them in the headlines and sub-headlines. These same techniques must be applied online—with the most important customer benefits up top as the headline.

Some products are complex to describe, such as those with textures and other sensory attributes that would make the sale in retail. A silky, luxurious blouse in rich colors can be described with words and images, but subtle variations in the difference between sueded-silk and satin may not be easily described. Magnifying glass "close up" techniques can give a deeper view. This technique, coupled with appropriate copy writing and other imagery, can enhance product details and simulate the retail environment.   For expensive items, such as a large line of name-brand quality clothing, you may consider providing a swatch sample for your shoppers to order prior to purchasing.

Virtual Bundles—E-kits

Special product bundles have been a retail strategy to stimulate sales. Bundles consist of two or more products or a product with a special offer. At retail, physical bundles are created by putting two or more products into the same box or by strapping the products together to form a "hard" bundle. A new SKU number is created and assigned to the new "package" so it can be stocked, inventoried, and merchandised.

Online stores have an advantage over retail because they can create "virtual" bundles. Virtual bundles put the products or special offers together on the product detail page—the online "package." The virtual bundle is also assigned a new SKU number. Fulfillment can be notified to "pick and pack" those items that make up the bundle. Virtual bundles save on production costs and labor, because a physical hard-bundled product is not required. A hard bundle is created virtually through putting the separate items into the same shipping box.

These e-kits require special merchandising treatments, however, because they are not physically bundled items in one package. New photos may be required to show the bundle contents. All product categories are eligible for bundling. Dresses with handbags, crafts with tools, printers with cartridges, and dog food with dog toys are a few combinations. Bundles are limited only by the imagination and distribution capabilities. Bundles provide you a competitive advantage by providing "new" exclusive items for your target customers.

Selection, Configuration, and Comparison Tools

Another essential merchandising technique is to make recommendations to customers and to help them select products. To be relevant, this must be more than providing spec sheets that they study and compare. As mentioned previously, customers look to the merchants for recommendations. Online, products are promoted when they are new or if there are special promotions attached. Otherwise, they fall into the ranks of products within a category. Even with complex products, the onus is on the shopper to sift through all of the product information, which is usually extensive. But it may not help the customer choose.

For example, technology products, a leading sales category for online sales, often have detailed descriptions and specs attached to each of the thousands of products. Given the shear quantities and brands of cameras, for instance, comparing all available devices is a daunting task for a customer. Comparing by specs alone is comparing apples to oranges. Specs do not fully disclose product differences that may be important to a shopper, yet are unrevealed in the information. For example, new digital camera technology offers 35 mm. A disposable camera also offers 35 mm. So what's the difference besides the price? In the case of an HP digital camera, the lens is of the highest quality, and it's the lens that contributes to the quality of the photo. Patented technologies built into the HP cameras also differentiate them from other digital cameras, yet it is difficult to convey in a one-line description. This is often overlooked when comparing item to item and spec to spec. The customer doesn't often get all of the key information needed to make a purchasing decision.

If the online store understands the target customer, it can recommend products that are relevant and fit customer needs. This concept goes beyond product alone but recognizes the need to recommend products based on customer usage.

Shopping Wizards

A shopping wizard is like having a virtual sales assistant. It asks shoppers questions, and then uses the answers to recommend products or solutions to meet customer needs. They can be simple applications that can help customers select products, services, or solutions based on their tasks or usage. They ultimately guide customers to a finite selection of choices from which to make a purchase decision.

Configurators

Configurators are electronic interactive selection tools that provide choices or options about a product. They are used in build-to-order models, as in customizing PCs with the selected software programs, a CD or DVD writer, and the amount of RAM. Configurators—such as the one on Vehix.com—allows people to view different car colors or different wheel coverings on a model.

They are also used to narrow choices in complex selection models. For example, car parts are specific to automobile makes, models, and sometimes years. Most websites would line-list the oil filters by the oil filter product name. A selection tool—or configurator—would provide options from which a person could choose. The selection model is built from the customer's retail shopping selection process hierarchy. In this case, it would be best to start with the types of automobiles and select down to the specific model and year. Case studies in Chapter 8 examine processes and methodologies used to develop online selection tools. The complexity of product selection determines the tool.

Comparison Tools

Comparing products online is becoming easier with emerging tools that provide for side-by-side comparisons. An example of a comparison tool is in Chapter 8, and recommendations based on customer needs are in Chapter 7.

Online Product Registration Tools

When customers purchase products with extended warranties, merchants automatically capture the consumer's information. Similarly, e-merchants can ask customers to register certain purchases for a variety of services. New releases, add-ons, or service features can provide the customer with real value while giving the merchant data for a customer relationship management database.

Sampling and Demonstrations—"Demo Days Online"

You may have shopped in a grocery store and been given ice cream samples—a retail technique called sampling used to encourage incremental sales. Or, you may have seen an "infomercial"—an extended TV commercial that provides extensive information. The infomercial may be as long as 30 minutes or more, with the host describing the benefits in detail and giving hands-on demonstrations. TV shopping channels are very successful with this method. And at retail, staging special events—called "demo days"—is an effective promotional selling technique. The Victoria Secret online fashion show was a form of online demonstration coupled with entertainment and resulted in incremental sales.

Often, online customers are at a disadvantage over a retail store environment, where they can see, touch, feel, try on, operate, or "test drive" a product. Most online stores today minimally merchandise products with basic elements: images, product descriptions and specifications, sizes and measurements, and other information that comes from the manufacturer.

As shoppers scan pages, they may miss a key selling point that is hidden in copy or in the product specs. Providing product simulations online for strategic products or categories stimulates customers to purchase. Creating "demo days online" gives you a competitive advantage over line listing products. Educational, interactive, or downloadable content gives customers the information they need to make a purchasing decision.

Because of the expense of richer types of media applications—such as videos and animations—it's important to consider where the Internet is going and where you should be internationally. Reaching a global market must be considered, especially because the majority of Internet users are outside the U.S., with Asia growing at high rates. Even though online purchasing may not be commonplace in other countries, people still find information on Internet sites globally prior to purchasing in a local store or region.

For the more expensive technologies, such as animations or videos, consider using a separate sound track and creating voiceovers. This allows leverage of main content and minimal additional expense for localization. Also, animations are easier to localize than videos with people.

Operational Excellence

Perceived value starts when customers enter the online store and lasts until the time the product is delivered to their doorstep and the decision is made to keep the product. Operational excellence is achieved through working towards innovative future capabilities, such as build-to-order systems, virtual warehousing, and automated vendor-managed inventory.

Delivery to the Customer

Do you know what customers receive as a result of their online purchase? The customer experience with an online store does not end when they complete the checkout process. It continues until they receive the product at their home or office.

As part of our research on customer online shopping experiences described in online mystery shopping in Chapter 6, we evaluated website navigation models and completed purchase transactions. In some cases, the shipping cartons received were of a good, solid quality to withstand the rigors of transport. Packages received from QVC.com, for example, reflect the high-quality standards of their brand positioning. Boxes are sturdy and withstood transportation, still looking new. Quill.com also provides high-quality shipping boxes to their office products customers. They go beyond the basics, however, by sometimes including free product samples and a copy of their current catalog with a new customer's initial order.

Other online stores delivered products in different types of mailers. Sometimes, orders were split into different mailing vehicles. These "split orders" can be a result of a backordered item shipping at a later date or the item shipping from a different distribution center.

In these cases, the customer may receive different types of shipping boxes. In one example, we received a split order on four similar items originally ordered. One bubble envelope contained three of these items squeezed into the overstuffed envelope. The fourth item—of the same size as the other three items—was received on the same day, but packaged with peanut packing material in a large sturdy craft box that could have held 10 similar items. The envelope had been metered with postage and was crumpled, having been sent through the mail. The item pages were a bit squished, yet undamaged. The value on the three items was $100, yet the package received did not reflect their value.

Pay attention to detail—starting at your store's home page. Walk through the purchase process, order a product, and then see what your customers receive at their door. This attention results in increased perceived value and quality of your store brand.

Increasing Supply Chain Efficiencies

Hundreds of thousands of products flow through commerce annually. Some products are long lasting, while others are extremely perishable. Emerging information technology applications enable more accurate forecasting models, electronic data interchange (EDI) capabilities, and continuous replenishment programs that help move products through the system.

Build-to-Order Systems

Trends include manufacturer build-to-order (BTO) models that shrink inventory risk of perishable products, such as PCs. Because technology improvements and innovations move at lightning speed, PC components are outdated every few weeks, making them a perishable store item. For categories like this, space and time are enemies. The PC business is similar to the banana business: both are high demand, perishable products that must move quickly through the supply chain, all product touch points from manufacturer to the end customer.

PCs, cars, and other major items with multiple options are now part of a BTO system. This system allows people to select the options they desire and have the product built to their specifications. Customers are willing to wait longer for customized, high-ticket purchases, such as automobiles. This provides them with what they want and minimizes inventory risk of pre-configured products that may not "exactly" fit customer preferences.

Over time, technology improvements will shorten the length of the supply chain. Distributors and suppliers must determine cost versus benefit tradeoffs, because these infrastructures typically require large capital investments.

Virtual Warehousing

Another supply-side trend is virtual warehousing in which the manufacturer or distributor stocks product until receiving an end-user customer order from the online store. In this model, the role of the distributor or wholesaler has expanded. E-tailers can provide a broader product assortment and mix, even small or low-turning items, because the distributor or manufacturer holds inventory. This is a big advantage over retail stores and other inventoried businesses that must stock and shelve actual products and samples.

Some online stores use this model to sell refrigerators, barbecues, and other large, odd-shaped, or heavy items. This model shortens the supply chain in time and costs because merchants don't bring inventory into their warehouses.

Automated Managed Inventory

Vendor-automated managed inventory is possible due to e-commerce technologies and the ability to monitor real-time inventory levels on public websites. While traditional retail companies do attempt an automated process, it is difficult due to inconsistencies of sample usage and theft. Shrinkage, loss due to theft or inventory inconsistencies, is a continual problem in retailing. When high-value categories are sold online, shrinkage becomes a problem for the warehouse, which may affect inaccurate inventory level accounting.

With virtual warehouses and the demands on the manufacturer to drop ship directly to the consumer on behalf of the e-tailer, there is an alignment of technologies to accommodate automated managed inventory.

This process is set in motion when the customer purchases a product online. The quantity is immediately deducted from the inventory via a controlled level checker. When that amount reaches a designated level, a purchase order process starts. This can reach into the manufacturer's inventory systems. The manufacturer generates the purchase order, the online merchant commits and the product is built and then delivered to the distribution warehouses or cross-docks, which are intermediary re-distribution centers.

Integrating "Shelf" Merchandising Techniques

E-merchandising rules and techniques can be balanced by integrating merchandising and selling concepts from the other shelves to maintain the freshness of your site and avoid the rigidity of old rules. As new practices evolve, such as customer relationship management techniques, you can incorporate them easily when you have a consumer-centered focus. Shopping preferences evolve, manufacturers change systems, and technologies improve. Creating a flexible system to adapt quickly to these changes will help you stay ahead of your competition.

The prerequisites of e-merchandising are a thorough understanding of the following concepts that were detailed in previous chapters:

- Target the customer: Understand the first-time shopper and use customer-centered techniques to capture the sale and foster repeat visits to the store (see Chapter 2).
- Understand customer shopping patterns in retail, catalog, online, TV broadcast, or wherever your products or services are sold.
- Personalize the shopping experience for your key customers based on this knowledge.

Effective merchandising includes logical navigation models, e-fixturing tools, product placement logic, and other essential techniques created or leveraged from tried-and-true traditional techniques. All must be developed and implemented with the customer in mind to achieve true customer-centered design. Chapter 7 dives deeper into customer insights, rules and tips for winning websites, and actionable recommendations.

Getting More Bang for the Byte

The online store is a vehicle for an integrated marketing strategy. This strategy can incorporate other selling opportunities in the marketing mix. Promotions can be leveraged across all marketing vehicles or channels. These can be through e-mails, direct mail sent to a customer's home, or newspaper and magazine print ads. Integrated with the channels or selling vehicles, these can extend the power of your marketing dollars spent.

Structuring your store to accommodate these integrated activities provides a seamless shopping experience for the customer. For example, if you sell through different vehicles—such as a website and a direct mail catalog—having the same promotion across all sales motions extends the reach of an integrated marketing campaign, so at every point of contact, the customer has a chance to respond.

Combining store parts with intuitive navigation models gives customers a seamless shopping solution. Getting the customers to the store, helping them navigate, and making it easy to come back again is the goal.

Tools and Rules
for Winning
Websites

This section introduces usability engineering concepts to the business reader who may not be aware of the role this plays in the customer's experience.

The second part of this section is a process and new approach for benchmarking and measuring websites. It also provides a step-by-step process that you can use to evaluate your own website for effectiveness.

Chapter 6 guides you through designing an intuitive customer-shopping model.

Chapter 7 provides fundamental rules and guidelines to create usable websites.

Designing Intuitive Online Customer Shopping Models

One of the most important goals in website design is to ensure that customers can easily and intuitively navigate a website. The closer the experience is to being a "no brainer," the closer it is to a good, customer-centric design.

Operating a website is like operating a car. The controls of a car are its buttons, knobs, and switches that start the car, turn on windshield wipers, adjust seats for comfort, and play music. The controls of a website are graphical elements and text displayed as buttons and links. Just as each make of automobile may have different ways of operating the controls, websites do also. For example, in one car make and model, the windshield wiper control is on the turn signal shaft. In another make of car, it can be a knob on the dashboard.

Unfamiliar controls and control behavior—the action that is performed when the control is used—leads to customer confusion. Sometimes, feature creep and elegant, innovative development replaces common sense and prior learning methodologies. And because a customer shops several websites, the confusion compounds.

In Chapter 5, we identified the major components of a website: webpages, content on the pages, and the navigation that links them together. That chapter also provided recommendations on best practices for each of the parts. This chapter presents the methodologies and processes on how to use the parts of online stores to effectively create an intuitive customer online shopping model for key categories.

More on Navigation

You can never say enough on the importance of superior navigation. Navigating a website is like driving a car on highways and city streets. Highway road signs are pretty standard with shape and color. Highway exit signs are uniformly presented from state to state or from region to region and consistent within a country so that any driver knows what to expect and what the signs mean.

Some websites, however, are more like city driving. Each city makes its own street signage standards, which may help or hinder drivers and pedestrians. One city, for example, puts the name of the street only on one side of the street sign. This may be fine for those driving in the direction of the one-way street, but what if you pass it without being able to read it? You'd either have to go around the block or stop and get out of your car to ask directions.

Some street signs are small and barely readable, or they may be blocked by trees or shrubs. After they are put up, rarely does anyone go back to see what has changed in the environment. This is similar to websites that were designed based on early models, yet not refreshed based on the customer or environment dynamics.

Each time a customer comes to an unclear "road sign" or gets lost on a website, he must pause until he figures it out himself or asks for directions by calling a toll-free number. Having to stop and ask directions when you're lost is never convenient, either while driving or searching on a website. Don't forget to support the lost shopper.

In our quest to create the ultimate customer online shopping experience, we cannot ignore basic usability engineering methodologies. In addition, broadband and home networking adoption influences capabilities. It reinvigorates the need to assess how your customers are moving and keeping up with technology.

If you have an existing website, this means re-driving the paths of your customers to ensure that it meets today's needs. If you are creating a new website, it helps you build the roads and signage to help guide your customers successfully to their destinations.

Designing and Improving Customer Shopping Experiences

This chapter looks at two examples that apply knowledge presented in earlier chapters of this book and usability engineering principles and measurements. The first example shows the process used to design a new user interface for a vending machine that dispensed HP printing supplies. The second example shows the process used to measure the current customer usability of existing online stores and on an improved customer-shopping model.

Before moving into the examples, the next few sections highlight some of the usability engineering principles and measurements applied to the processes.

Usability Engineering Purpose

Usability is the effectiveness, efficiency, and satisfaction with which specified users can achieve their goals in their environment. Usability engineering and user-centered design focus on the user, the person who will be using or operating the product, for instance, a software program. In an online store, the user translates as "customer," and effective online store development takes on a new focus of customer-centered design. "User interface" and "customer interface" are used interchangeably throughout this book.

Just as software users are people who use a software product to achieve an end result, an online store customer uses the e-commerce website to accomplish a goal—whether it is to find information about a product or to purchase it. As a major, required component in successful software design, usability is engineered into the product through conscious intent.

This chapter highlights methodologies, principles, and processes applied to new user interface design. There are many good books that go into depth regarding specific graphical component web usability issues, such as Jakob Nielsen's *Designing Web Usability*.

Usability Measurements

Usability measurements provide the means to evaluate an online store at a point in time. They can be used to analyze existing e-commerce sites to identify areas needing improvement. They can also be used to influence the direction of a new website development.

For existing sites, evolution of the store is necessary for it to stay current with technology innovations, morphing marketplaces, and customer dynamics. Effective methods emphasize early definition of shopper requirements based on customer conversations and insight for new online stores. They provide valuable insight in any situation.

Measuring websites and reporting the findings is just the beginning of the improvement process, not the end. You must act on the findings. Usability measurements do not just identify problems. Like a trip to the doctor, they not only diagnose, but they also prescribe treatment.

A typical usability lifecycle includes defining requirements, designing, building, testing, and supporting. Methods to define requirements range from non-collaborative to collaborative methods with the customer. On one side, the greater the collaboration with customers, the greater the commitment and chance of being adopted by them. On the flip side, the less collaborative, the greater risk of missed opportunities and customer dissatisfaction.

There are two types of customer needs: what they say they need and what they reveal they need as identified through customer studies and actual observation. Some refer to this as the "say/do" split. What they do versus what they say is often quite different.

Customer studies may include influences on the customer, natural life or workflow patterns, product selection models and common shopping sequences, and the physical environment in which customers shop.

Influences can include friends who recommend shopping websites or stores they are required to use at work or those they enjoy at home. The shopping process is a subset of a larger work or life flow pattern. The shopping experience is typically integrated into day-to-day activities. It is not a one-time occurrence. Nor is it separate from every other experience. Work or life flow patterns can change frequently. Shopping patterns change with them, especially online.

Product selection models change from product to product, and shopping sequences for the same product can change from store to store. Knowing the most important tasks and sequences that are familiar to customers is a technique. How customers shop for products and how they "flow" through retail stores gives developers clues on how to accommodate the customer while designing or evolving a website. This must be factored in with business drivers such as category value or "destination" products that are shopped frequently.

The physical environment in which a person shops also dictates the quality of the experience. For example, people have many demands in a home environment: children, telephones, noise, and interruptions can affect the ability to complete any online shopping task. People who shop for products online for the workplace have constant interruptions as well.

Needs Assessment Process

There are five main steps in assessing online customer needs:

- Observing and listening to customers
- Reviewing market segmentation and customer profiling
- Analyzing current buying behaviors and online customer needs
- Defining user interface requirements
- Formulating value proposition and branding objectives

It is this collective knowledge that makes up the body of customer intelligence.

Listening for the "Important Stuff"

Putting together a good customer-needs picture includes understanding the influences, physical environment, sequences, and life flow patterns. From this, you can create customer modeling that represents the needs based on the customer's behavior. After you have identified your target customers, you need to build a thorough understanding of them.

Observing and talking to your customers identifies the following:

- *What* information they need
- *Why* they need it
- *How* they use it after they get it

Sometimes you have to ask "why?" several times to get to the rest of the motives. Though asking frequently may sound like a curious three-year-old, this is a key step.

The fundamental principles of information engineering minimize information complexity and optimize information delivery. This topic is extensive, but remember these two points:

- Identify and prioritize information for consumers.
- Evaluate information competencies and suggest a roadmap for continuous improvement.

Information engineering leads to helping customers make purchase decisions.

Segmenting Markets and Profiling Customers

Chapter 2 provides target customer profiling tools that help you describe your customers and the main markets in which they shop. For example, if your business is skateboard sales, you sell in the home market segment and your target customers are boys between the ages of 12-18.

This customer insight gives you design and content ideas to ensure your target audience preferences are met. Also, it helps to determine appropriate product mix and promote those products in your site that are most relevant to them. For this shopping audience, product promotions can include free music downloads. Or, you may want to plan to accommodate a streaming video that shows the skateboard in action.

Value-added information, such as skateboard tips that are refreshed monthly, is a way to keep customers coming back. It can also set your website apart from others.

Analyzing Current Buying Behaviors and Shopper Needs

Understand how the target customer shops for your profitable categories and products in retail. Know the key purchase decision factors that influence him. For example, is he likely to purchase a skateboard based on brand or because one features special art decals that create a personal identity? If he bases his decision on decals, he would need compelling product images on the web showing the intricate detail in the specialty decals. If he is likely to purchase based on stunt capability, compelling image shots or streaming video showing a skateboarder performing a variety of stunts and tricks would convey this capability.

Does he like to "test drive" the skateboard? Simulate a skateboard riding game on your website using the top-selling and profitable board—one that the shopper can virtually "hop on" and take for a ride.

Defining Customer Interface Requirements

There are three main areas for consideration when designing a customer-centric user interface:

1. **Function:** What customers want to do (tasks).
2. **Logic:** What steps customers must take to accomplish their tasks (organized sequences). This area must include signals and messages from memory. Look for natural mappings, like menus that provide choices.
3. **Look and Feel:** What customers see and how they intuitively operate the user interface. The look and feel evokes emotion, which is from memories of the customer that are applied to a current website.

After you've identified your key customers, you would analyze what their key shopping tasks are. As mentioned in previous chapters, online shoppers have three main tasks: find specific products, shop and compare products, and browse for information, education, or entertainment.

The next requirement is to understand the logic in their current shopping processes. This logic comes from their experiences shopping for products at retail, in catalogs, or from online stores.

The "look and feel" sets the ambiance and tone of the online store. The operational components and content required in the current shopping environments can be applied online. This can be achieved through usage of e-tools described in Chapter 5.

Key Steps in Defining a Customer Interface

There are four key steps in defining a user interface:

1. Prepare a web task workflow analysis (function).
2. Specify design features, standards, and performance (look and feel).
3. Define site navigation and information architecture (logic).
4. Identify customer interface data elements and relationships (logic).

Figure 6-1 shows the flow of the user interface development process.

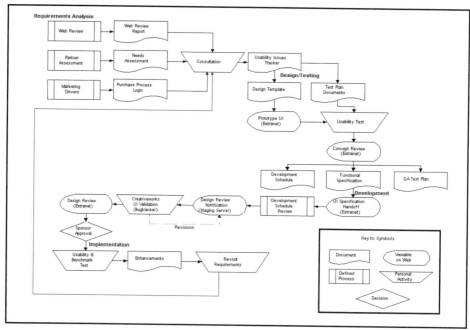

Figure 6–1 Developing a user interface requires a structured process.

While understanding the requirements and the process may seem intimidating, it actually is not. It just requires common sense and a rational mind.

Apply this information to a simple example. Say, for instance, one of your key product categories is jewelry, top-selling products are bracelets, and your key customers are women between the ages of 35 and 45.

The customer's task is to purchase a bracelet. The shopping logic is this: Look for a jewelry category, and then look for a bracelet sub-category. (Actual logic, however, is determined through analysis of current shopping habits.) The look and feel depends on your store's brand and positioning. If it is positioned on having only the finest jewelry, attributes are required that match customer expectations for it.

Customer requirements define the attributes and characteristics of the user interface. The interface reflects customer needs and expectations.

Formulating Value Proposition and Branding Objectives

The value proposition and brand of your store must be clearly discernable starting on the home page and on every page thereafter. It is reflected by your customer care center with each phone call. It is also reflected in the box that shows up at the customer's doorstep. You may not have control of all aspects of the customer experience, but knowing your company's value proposition and branding objectives helps you engineer these values into those parts that you can affect.

For example, if your value proposition is ease of use, you can reinforce this by making each major customer task easy to complete. For example, Apple is an ease-of-use player, so if the online Apple store were difficult to use, it would drain a great deal of value from the brand and the value proposition. Each page must reflect customer-focused category names and preferred navigational models.

Measuring for Success

Usability measurements are critical success factors to the design and evolution of an e-commerce website. There are common measures available for every phase to keep the website design and development on strategy to meet its objectives.

To measure e-commerce website usability, you must first define the shoppers or customers, their goals, and their online shopping environment at work or at home. There is a big difference between watching what people do and knowing why they do it. Merely tracking mouse clicks will not tell you why they got to a particular page in the first place, and it can't always be "operator error."

Some companies provide statistics on page views and clicks. Interpreted quantitatively, this presents an incomplete view as to why these people are clicking. In our online shopping testing, we discovered that most people used "trial-and-error" clicking methodologies. They clicked on a link and then backed up and started over until they found one that appeared to get them closer to their goal. Few selected the right path by conscious choice the first time.

Many research companies merely measure mechanics, such as site traffic:

- Click-throughs
- Lengths of visit
- Time of day
- Which browsers
- Most popular pages
- Most frequently asked questions

Mechanics do not explain the motivation behind a shopper's navigational choice. For example, with today's many interruptions, the lengths of visit can be lengthened further by going on a coffee break or by answering a phone call. While the time on a coffee break or phone call is not time spent shopping the site, it does get factored into the length of a session. Also, the most popular pages can be deceiving because you don't know how the shopper happened to get there—by trial and error or by intent.

Most frequently asked questions to your customer support call center can let you know what you need to fix first about your website. If they are questions relating to finding a popular product, then this merits reworking category names or ensuring that your search mechanism accommodates how customers shop for that product. After you satisfy the most frequently asked questions, new ones appear in the course of iterative improvement.

Tools focused on mechanics give you only one dimension to understand customer needs. There is a suite of common usability measurement tools from which you can choose to give you a more complete view. Use a variety and modify them to meet your needs. You can serve your customers better if you talk with them and listen to what they have to say. You can do this through formal and informal customer testing, customer call center analysis, online surveys, or reply bounce-back cards provided in the boxes with customer orders.

Usability Measurement Process

Usability measurement for web design is a means to ensure early, continuous, and systematic feedback from target customers during development or system architecture version rollout. This requires a development process that allows for iterative refinement of web design. It is not a one-time activity. Usability measurement is a process that factors in several components, such as methodologies, customers, and budgets.

Main steps in the process include setting objectives, defining measurement purposes, and identifying the right method and metric to use. They also include developing test plans and recording and analyzing test findings and results.

Usability goals should initially be stated in terms that reflect a known business need. For example, understanding the conversion rates of visitors to purchasers, or identifying customer success rates in specific tasks, understanding the intuitive navigation path and common link labels.

Measurements must be predictive of the desired goal. For example, one usability test may compare improvement of a remodeled website over its predecessor. Yet, it may fail to have improved much when compared or ranked with competitors' online stores. Therefore, refining the objective from improvement over itself to improvement in the competitive mix is necessary.

Other example objectives may include:

- Measuring customer satisfaction levels with an online store over time
- Improving task flow or customer shopping flow processes
- Measuring performance relative to previous website performance to ensure that usability is increasing across releases
- Tracking online store performance relative to competitive store performance
- Comparing ease of use with a competitor's website
- Providing product positioning, sales, and promotional information to influence purchase decisions
- Identifying the highest priority improvements for future website architecture or user interface rollouts

Defining the purpose is defining what you hope to achieve. There are two main purposes of measuring usability. The first provides information on what is wrong with an online store. This is called "diagnostic testing." To make improvements, it is important to have diagnostic data. These data identify *what* is wrong rather than simply stating that something is wrong.

The second evaluates whether or not an online store is meeting predetermined levels of customer usability. This type of usability measurement is called evaluative testing. Evaluative testing can include comparing an online store to a competitor's website. It can also provide measures on how well a website meets shopper expectations. Both diagnostic and evaluative testing should be conducted at ongoing intervals to ensure that the e-commerce website is keeping pace with customer requirements and marketplace changes.

Once the purpose is defined, you can choose the right method and metric. Match your requirements and constraints with the available methods for evaluating usability. Different types of websites have special characteristics—such as customer and market segments—associated with them. These characteristics make different usability methods and metrics more or less appropriate for them.

Usability consists of a number of different attributes. The attributes that are most commonly thought of as associated with usability are ease of learning, customer productivity, customer satisfaction, and website effectiveness. Different types of data are more relevant than others to understand these attributes.

A test plan is the key that unlocks the secrets to a more usable shopping model. It should include all steps for the test from start to finish.

Three Methods for Evaluating Usability

Different approaches to evaluating usability fall into three main categories. These methods are traditional ways of measuring software products. But they can be recombined and modified to apply to evaluating online store usability. The following are the three main categories:

- Inspection methods
- Lab testing methods
- Surveys and customer reporting methods

The purpose of usability measurement determines which measures are appropriate and when they need to occur. Selection of the appropriate methodology and integration of the results creates an in-depth view of the customer experience.

The first type of method—inspection—does not involve customers. Members of the design team, product category experts, quality and productivity and/or human factors engineers apply a formal review process of the online store to evaluate usability. These methods are usually quick and inexpensive to use. They also provide qualitative data used to derive some quantitative metrics. Because customers are not involved, however, it does not directly measure usability.

A few key inspection methods include heuristic evaluations, walk-throughs, and task analysis. Heuristic evaluations review an online store against an established set of common usability principles. The review is based on the expertise of the reviewers. Walk-throughs simulate a customer's experience with the website. The results of the simulation are compared with the goals, expectations, and knowledge that a first-time customer is expected to have with an online store. Task analysis defines a set of likely customer tasks and breaks it down into sub-tasks and steps, such as defining customer navigation for a specific product.

The second type of method—user lab testing—involves the testing of representative online shoppers. Objective data is collected on customers' actual responses. This method can be diagnostic or evaluative.

Three key user lab tests important to store usability are walk-throughs, formal tests, and benchmark tests. All tests ask customers to verbalize their thoughts and reactions to websites. All tests are also designed to be free of bias and to understand the customer's ability to operate the e-commerce website.

The third type of method is to survey customers about their experiences on the usability of websites. This method provides subjective data and is based on expressed feelings, attitudes, and perceptions of the website's usability and overall desirable qualities. Typically, this reporting method occurs in the design cycle when the product is almost complete. Just like with other surveys, the primary data are subjective opinions that are highly variable. As a result, they require large sample sizes to provide reliable data.

Developing Usable Online Shopping Models

The following two examples show how we combined and modified many of the traditional product usability engineering methodologies to meet specific needs of online customer-centered navigation models.

The first example shows the methods employed to develop a successful navigation model for the customer while selecting products from a vending machine. Because this type of selection is unaided and would be available at all hours, successful task completion is imperative.

The second example, leveraged from knowledge in the first, not only solved product selectability issues that were experienced at retail, but also increased sales for our online merchant partners when our recommendations were implemented in their e-commerce websites.

Both examples had the following goals:

- Create a superior customer shopping and navigation model based on ease of use and on successful task completion.
- Provide HP printing supplies customers with a common, consistent method of purchasing supplies in an interactive, virtual environment.
- Maximize product sales by making key products easy to find and cross-selling complementary products.

Example 1: HP Printing Supplies Vending Machine

The HP Printing Supplies Store was a vending machine developed to provide customers with convenient access to ink cartridges around the clock. Because it is never convenient to be out of ink, the vending machine was designed to be available to those people—such as students on college campuses or workers in office complexes—who needed ink or paper while printing projects in off-hours.

Each printer model requires a specific printer cartridge, and there are several different printer models among which to differentiate. The technology is such that each printer cartridge and its ink are designed to rigorous specifications for each printer model. While this ensures quality print-outs, it complicates accurate print cartridge selection. The ten different printer cartridges planned for the vending machine were compatible with more than 50 different printing devices from fax machines to HP DeskJet printers. Also, the black and color cartridges that teamed together to fit one printer model were often a different combination for another printer model. The vending machine is shown in Figure 6-2.

The standard-sized vending machine had a 15" touch-screen CRT on which the customer could make selections. Because the vending machine was a standalone "store," it had limitations. You could not "pick up the box" off the shelf to verify printer compatibility. Also, all transactions were unaided because no sales associate was available. Printing cartridge selection is a big challenge at retail, and this would transfer online, especially in an unaided environment such as at a kiosk in the middle of the night.

Figure 6–2 The HP Printing Supplies Store vending machine.

Our design and testing goals were to provide a customer-centered selection and navigation model with the following attributes:

- **Ease of learning:** Users must be able to walk up to the kiosk and immediately be productive without training.
- **Intuitiveness:** It must be immediately obvious what is in the kiosk, what can be done with it, and how to use it.
- **Navigation:** Users must be able to navigate from one screen to another and to "back out" if they have made an incorrect choice. They must have an understanding of the overall navigation and orientation paradigm.
- **Confidence:** Because consumers will have access to a range of products without being able to see them or pick them up, customers must be assured they are purchasing the correct product 100 percent of the time.
- **Integration:** Customers will need to interact with both software and the kiosk hardware. There should be seamless integration between mapping customer selections and dispensing.
- **Satisfaction and confidence:** The overall user experience must be enjoyable, comfortable, and without anxiety. The experience should reinforce brand image and reputation and encourage repeat business.

Because this was a global program, testing in other geographic locations was included in the plan.

The testing process was made up of four basic phases: preparation, profiling, testing, and analysis.

Preparation

To successfully evaluate the usability of the vending machine user interface, goals were first identified and a test process was created that would evaluate against those goals. The preparation stage included the following:

- Familiarization with the vending machine product
- Clarification of testing goals
- Identification of test subject profiles
- Preparation of test subject briefs and consent forms
- Preparation of test scenarios, tasks, questionnaires, and other materials
- Set-up of equipment

Preparation and planning is the most important phase of the testing process.

Profiling Representative Users for the Tests

It was important that the test subjects selected were representative of the real target customers of touch-screen kiosks, in terms of both domain knowledge and general computer knowledge. Where possible, users were drawn from a cross-section of the user population, reflecting a range of experience and demonstrating a range of usage.

Testing

A dry run was held the day before testing to identify any observable problems with the product equipment and test script. Actual testing was conducted with individuals and pairs of test subjects. It was run by an experienced facilitator and observed by the recorder, who documented observations onto logging sheets. Tests were videotaped for later review and transcription purposes.

Users were asked to perform tasks based on prepared scenarios that explored key aspects of the testing goals such as purchasing a print cartridge for their printer model. Each test session, including briefing, testing, and de-briefing, took approximately one hour. Time was allowed between sessions to discuss the results, make any necessary modifications to the test script, and prepare for subsequent tests.

Analysis

Interpreting the results included taking the collected information and the modifications to incorporate into later designs. As a result, the user interface was completed successfully, meeting the objectives originally set forth. The pilot launched on time with high levels of customer satisfaction and usability with the user interface.

Customers were able to successfully use the user interface to accurately find, select, and purchase printing supplies unaided.

Example 2: Designing a Customer Shopping Model for HP Printing Supplies

With the growth and adoption of the Internet, many online stores that sold printing supplies established their own selection and navigation models. These were typically based on lists of product SKUs provided by the wholesaler or distributor. Although they were comprehensive, they did not provide the customer with an intuitive model or confident selection.

With initial analysis, we discovered that online customers were having difficulty finding the correct printing supplies for their printing devices. Because we had great success in the model we developed for the vending machine, we used it as a foundation for future comparative testing.

In this next example of applying usability testing methods, we leveraged this HP supplies kiosk navigation selection model. This model was developed into a prototype for further testing with other kinds of electronic vehicles, such as the Internet or CD applications.

The current online customer shopping experience had to be understood before it could be improved upon. Also, the current state of an online store had to be benchmarked against a known standard before recommendations on how to increase sales or make other improvements could be made.

Because the Internet was a new form of software product, we took traditional usability methods and modified them to accommodate this emerging technology. Also, because the Internet is a marketplace as well, we modified methodology to create a measure of business drivers leveraged from traditional retailing techniques. Using inspection methods on e-commerce websites, we found that all websites were different, but a few key areas merited further focus and analysis:

- Intuitive navigation, offering the customer a logical and easy-to-use interface
- Good search, find, and select functionality
- Value-added content to stimulate demand and support the sales process
- Accuracy and completeness of product information
- Market basket leverage to support cross-selling of complementary products
- Conformance with best practices for web design

The hybrid usability measurement methods would allow us to quantify and qualify these attributes from which we could then make appropriate recommendations. First, we would conduct the tests. Next, we would interpret and blend together the findings from business and customer perspectives. Next, we would benchmark product sales data and re-measure after improvements were made to show improvement and the impact of change.

Two hybrid online testing methods that we created were the following:

- Online store benchmarking—from a business perspective, evaluating websites based on business drivers
- Customer online shopping task analysis—from a customer perspective, evaluating websites based on successful customer shopping task completion

The first analysis evaluated websites based on expert category knowledge such as product profitability. The second analysis used actual printing supplies customers. The ultimate goal would allow us to identify a customer-preferred shopping model that was intuitive and easy, but also profitable for the online merchant.

Online Store Benchmarking

This part of our web metrics program assessed and measured the current state of websites on which our products were sold. This initial assessment would then be compared to the same websites in the same measurement methods after improvement recommendations had been implemented.

This methodology uses parts from inspection methodology. Because it uses category experts as reviewers instead of actual customers, it does not measure usability. It does, however, measure how well a website is optimized for category and product profitability. This environmental scan is necessary to set the bar for improvement.

The strategy was to use an objective process to measure each site, provide recommendations and e-planograms to the online merchants based on what we learned, and then re-measure the effectiveness after the recommendations were implemented.

It was important that the results be reproducible, so back up copies of specific key findings were made in case the website changed. It was also critical to have a knowledgeable category expert conduct the evaluation because a nuance to one person could result in missed opportunities that would have gone overlooked. Benchmarking methodologies assess the current state of a website and how well it is optimized for sales.

Objectives

The online store benchmark program had four main objectives:

- Understand online store design and content in key areas that shape the user experience.
- Identify gaps and weaknesses in online store deployment and customer expectations.
- Define problem areas and issues related to performing key navigation and ordering tasks.
- Make recommendations for improved customer usability and chances for increased sales based on documented findings and conclusions.

The benchmarking must accommodate different types of store designs and configurations, because all online stores are different. The benchmarking must also accommodate the morphing online marketplace and have relevance to the online merchant.

Strategies

We defined the following strategies to accomplish our objectives:

- Establish objective evaluation criteria, and rate the store's effectiveness in selling key products.
- Quantify which important online sales features are present in key focus category areas.
- Develop search strategy and methodologies based on known customer expectations of the purchasing process.
- Recommend improvements of the site that will result in increased sales and enhance customer usability.
- Aggregate results, and relatively rank all stores evaluated.
- Track effectiveness of the store over time, and define ROI of this process based on the increased sales or consumer loyalty index ratings.

The benchmarking program was designed as an ongoing, iterative process instead of a one-time program. Because Internet selling was growing at a rapid rate, it was important to monitor this business. Also, online stores carry a broader product mix than traditional channels. The sites reflect changed navigation models and product profitability.

The Benchmarking Process

We developed and used the following process:

1. Establish search criteria.
2. Develop a metrics scorecard.
3. Conduct the evaluation.
4. Map out purchase process flow issues.
5. Purchase products.
6. Total the scores.
7. Recommend improvements.

There were many individual components that were developed separately, each with its own plan.

Establishing Search Criteria

Evaluation criteria and methodology must be objective and non-ambiguous. Therefore, we established a search criteria document that outlined the search strategy and methodology. The evaluation consisted of three areas that we wanted to measure and document to compare some of the challenges against the best practices of web usability and against our knowledge of customer shopping preferences for our products.

The search strategy consisted of detailing the specific search sequences for each of the areas to be measured. The strategy focused on two specific areas: the ability to find and select key, high-demand products, and identifying selection issues after the product was found.

Search evaluation methodology detailed for the evaluator exact steps to take and what areas to look at, score, or capture. Particular areas of interest were captured through printing the screen of the page being viewed and producing a screen capture that could be included in subsequent presentations that identified purchasing process flow issues.

- Perform defined navigation tasks related to identifying and purchasing products.
- Answer a series of questions (yes/no) that identify store effectiveness related to the user experience.
- Record webpage attributes while performing navigation tasks and reviewing content.
- Analyze and document results of online store review and consult with the project team.

The search methodology included starting from the home page, and looking at search text boxes or any other way you are testing once a person drops into a website. These search sequences are a system that matches up with retail shopping hierarchies for key products or categories.

For example, the search document instructed the evaluator to start with the home page, navigate to the category page, and then go to the product page—essentially all of normal paths you can take in the store schematic.

The Scorecard

The scorecard was designed to be used in conjunction with the evaluation criteria and search sequences. It was a checklist verifying the presence of important online sales features for key products.

The benchmarking rating form consisted of three main sections to measure. Within each section were lists of questions. Each question was answered with a "yes" or "no" response. The response was recorded as a checkmark in the appropriate column. Some sections provided write-in cells for the evaluator to document key points about each sales feature or to note areas of opportunity, interest, and/or concern. These notes were based on the reviewer's e-merchandising expertise and familiarity with key product values and known customer shopping preferences. A scorecard template is shown in Figure 6-3.

Benchmark Web Metrics Scorecard

Site URL: _____   Date: _____

Measurement Area	Yes or No	Reason for Rating
Can you search for this supply by both the printer platform/family and by printer model number?		
Can a keyword search be performed for both the product name and the product number that links directly to a product page for this supply?		
Is the product information provided for this supply accurate and complete, including both a current photo and complete compatibility?		
Is value-added content located on the product page for this supply to help customers use their printers better?		
Are other relevant complementary products promoted as a cross-sell item on the product page?		
Can you link to or purchase supplies from three different printer pages for this platform?		
Can you link to other relevant category products from the product page?		
Subtotal for section	**X of 7** **X%**	

Figure 6–3 A scorecard was developed to log search results.

A metrics rationale document was also created to assure that each question on the scorecard was relevant to the core business. A requirement for each question was that changing a "no" answer to a "yes" answer would increase product sales, improve website usability, or both. Questions that did not meet the criteria were discarded or reserved in another section for notable items that could be deemed relevant at a later time.

The scorecard had sections on overall presentation, cross-selling opportunities, and the purchase process. Each section's "yes" and "no" answers were tallied and percentage scores were applied. For example, in a section with nine evaluation questions, if there were five "yes" responses, the score was 56 percent (5 of 9).

The scorecard is a good method of measuring your website against a competitor's site. After initial benchmarking, periodic reviews (e.g., once every six months to a year) keep you alert to any changes in market or business behaviors.

Conducting the Evaluation

The reviewer conducted an evaluation following the instructions in the evaluation document and made appropriate entries on the scorecard. An example evaluation instruction is the following:

1. Begin by reviewing the home page to establish if there is a link to a printing supplies category. Note the results of your findings and use this information to help assess answers to the next three questions.
2. Search for the following product numbers and note search results.

These questions helped to identify any challenges that a customer could have in finding top-selling products in a website.

Mapping Purchasing Process Flow Issues

This benchmarking component builds the scorecard and is designed to visually present the purchasing process flow by shoppers in the store. We captured a sequence of screens to illustrate shoppers' progression to find and purchase important products. This documented the number of clicks and the successful path, once discovered.

Specific problems, issues, and opportunities related to site navigation, merchandising, content, labels, and usability design were highlighted on the appropriate screen captures in this map.

Purchasing Products—Online Mystery Shopping

Like the retail technique, we completed an online purchase and documented the number of days it took to receive the product in standard shipping. We documented the shopping cart process and identified any key issues. We also noted and photographed how the product was received, the condition of the box, for example, and whether or not there were any in-shipment pieces included. If multiple products were purchased at the same time, notes documented if they arrived in a split-shipment.

Because every point of contact with a customer reflects your brand, knowing how a customer receives product can reinforce online shopping confidence with your company.

Totaling the Scores

At the end of the review, individual sections were tallied and then compiled in an overall rating, as shown in Figure 6-4.

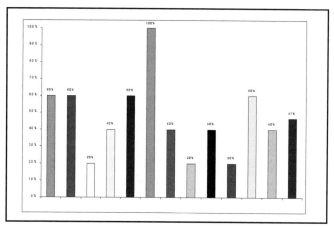

Figure 6–4 Aggregate benchmarking scores.

The scores of one online store were analyzed one by one and compared with scores of other online stores. Trends appeared as a result from which we could then develop recommendations for improvement.

Recommending Improvements

At the conclusion of the web metric rating process, the reviewer took a holistic view of the website and noted opportunities or areas of difficulties, such as the following:

- Cross-selling opportunities throughout the website
- Opportunities for promoting key initiatives
- Opportunities for promoting new and emerging categories
- Opportunities for incorporating value-added content throughout the website
- Issues regarding gross inaccuracies and confusing or incompleteness of product information
- Best practices used on the website
- Overall intuitiveness of category naming and navigation to key product areas

Recommendations were supported by annotated screen captures. Recommendations were detailed in an overall recommendations/assessment document that lists good and confusing aspects of navigation by area and category. It also noted best practices that reinforced what appeared to work well within the site.

A meeting was conducted with the online merchant to share key findings and deliver recommendations on online store improvement as it related to category profitability. Store executives, buyers, merchandisers, and members of the IT department attended the meeting, because all have an influence on the online store design.

Customer Online Shopping Task Analysis

This second part of the shopping model program leveraged from each of the methods of traditional user lab testing. Because it used real customers, it measured usability. Many companies study just the "store" and not how the customer interacts with it. This hybrid method encouraged customers to verbalize their thoughts as they went through the testing process.

While the benchmarking method measured the websites from a business perspective, this round of customer testing added the customer dimension and usability of the websites. The benchmarking and usability testing were designed to complement each other and to create a better purchasing sequence user interface shopping navigation model.

There were two primary goals of the customer online usability testing:

1. Establish user interface and navigational models specific to the process of purchasing HP printing supplies on existing online stores.
2. Profile and document online selection hierarchies and preferences of supplies purchasers—a preferred model.

Objectives

These objectives were similar to the benchmarking objectives. The main difference was viewpoint. Actual printing supplies customers would be recruited to conduct tests. The following were key objectives for this part of the program:

- Understand the current customer shopping experience with e-commerce websites.
- Identify customer expectations while performing common tasks.
- Define intuitiveness of category naming conventions and navigation models.
- Assess customers' preferences for current shopping models compared to the prototype developed from retail shopping hierarchies.

Online shopping was not mainstream. As an emerging channel, little was known about customer online shopping. The objectives were designed to provide insight into this new shopping medium and to assess how customers interact with this new kind of shelf.

We knew from the results of website evaluations by category experts that we could expect customer confusion and frustration with some stores because the experts did. It was highly likely that customers would have similar but worse experiences because they did not have the product knowledge that our experts needed to find products and make accurate selections. Online stores were in their embryonic stage of evolution with very basic capabilities of listing products. They had not yet developed the capability of designing for the customer. They were focused primarily on putting product on the shelf.

Strategies

The following strategies were developed to meet the objectives:

1. Establish a comparison test with targeted users, comparing existing websites against the customer-centered design website prototype.
2. Aggregate results and relatively rank the websites based on a common scale.
3. Establish overall user perception of purchasing experience.
4. Establish overall user feedback on user interface (design and content).
5. Compare with the prototype.

A key strategy was to develop the testing to provide customer insight on preferred shopping models and to refine an emerging prototype model. The first version of the model had been created based on internal expert knowledge. It lacked the customer insight that these tests would provide.

Customer Usability Testing Process

The following steps and tactics were developed:

1. Develop test plan with methodology and usability criteria.
2. Profile and recruit customers for the test.
3. Arrange facilities and logistics.
4. Create moderator's guide.
5. Develop the tasks.
6. Conduct a test session.
7. Record user responses.
8. Conduct a written survey.
9. Analyze data and prepare test results.

Like the benchmarking evaluations, these evaluation tactics required careful design to ensure that the results would meet the objectives.

Developing a Test Plan

Planning was the most critical element of the test. This step of the process included setting user test objectives and identifying the required components. What is acceptable or not acceptable? Expect to do as many rounds of testing as needed to ensure that you can make adjustments, but don't spend all of your test subjects on the first round, because this is an iterative approach.

Logistics were determined such as testing facilities, dates, and times for the tests. All documents were identified. Measures and expected final reports were identified and outlined.

Profiling and Recruiting Customers for the Test

Because six test participants are considered statistically significant in this kind of testing, care must be given to recruit the right six. These customers must be representative of the larger population of your key customers. Profiles are then used to develop the participant screener document and script that recruiters use to match test participants with customer profiles.

Customers for task analysis can fall into three main types: first-time e-commerce website purchasers (and technology novices), moderate Internet users and purchasers (intermediate), and experienced and technologically savvy online purchasers. Because most websites have a mixed audience and seek to attract new customers, it was important to test the range, yet not on the outward edges.

Other profiling considerations include the following:

- Market segment: e.g., home, small business, medium business, corporate
- Profession: e.g., florist, administrative assistant, school teacher
- Internet usage experience
- Product model testing
- Gender and age
- Purchased a similar product online
- Purchased a specific product online

In the testing, we identified specific products for the tasks and required customers to have purchased these products from at least retail stores. We also specified a balance of male to female and home and micro-business. Level of experience required knowledge beyond the basics of computer operation and required that they had completed an online purchase of any product.

The screening document was designed for use by participant recruiters. This document consisted of a list of questions asked by the recruiter, each question requiring a "yes" or "no" answer. A "no" response ended the screening interview politely. A "yes" response continued through to the end when the recruiter offered an invitation to participate in the web usability study. The questions were based on the profiling criteria, and they narrowed down the participants by a process of elimination to representatives of the specific target audience.

Arranging Facilities and Logistics—Behind the Scenes

There are different testing facilities available depending on the needs of the test. For example, the test room and facility we used required a one-way mirror for observation, an online computer, and a video camera to record the tests, as shown in Figure 6-5.

Figure 6–5 The research facility has one-way mirror and the subject is videotaped.
Photo by Kreta Chandler

This allowed recorders to sit in a room located behind the one-way mirror, observe the test subject, and record actions. A TV monitor was set up in this client-room to watch and track navigational choices made by the user, as shown in Figure 6-6.

Videotaping allowed customer shopping sequences and comments to be replayed at a later time for further analysis.

Figure 6–6 A TV monitor displayed user navigation and the customer.

Photo by Kreta Chandler

Creating the Moderator's Guide

The moderator's job is to give the initial instructions and make test participants feel comfortable in sharing their thoughts as they go through the tests, as there are no right or wrong answers. The moderator must also prompt them if they get stuck, gather feedback, keep them verbalizing, and note challenges. Our moderator's records were integrated with the videotapes and other testing documentation and records.

The moderator's guide included the task scripts. It also ensured consistency for user tasks and instructions. It clearly documented the instructions so they could be delivered to every user in the same manner. Delivery had to be unbiased and had to remain neutral throughout the test.

Depending on the kinds of tests, the moderator can play a more or less active role. Some researchers believe that it is better to have no moderator in the room and to provide audio help only when necessary. Moderating is a skill requiring a balance of knowing when to prompt and when not to prompt.

Developing the Tasks

Careful consideration was given to specific tasks, because results from success or failure can strongly influence redesign. Tasks selected should have relevance. In our example, we chose tasks that were common to our customers and involved top-selling products.

In testing the find, select, and purchase capability, the following were example tasks to be completed on a well-known e-commerce website and then on our prototype website based on the preferred customer shopping model:

1. Single product purchase

2. Multiple product purchase

Conducting the Tests

As a test protocol, each user was tested with a sequence of purchases for the printer that he or she owned. For each task, the user was given a scenario, asked to complete the task, and then left alone to do the task. Participants were asked to verbalize their thought processes as they went through the search—such as what they were looking for, what they were doing, or what they expected to find. The richness of customer testing in a neutral environment provides the ability to really say what's on their minds—and most don't hold back. Comments ranged from blaming themselves for not being able to figure out a website to being angry at the store for making it so hard to find what they needed. Some of these customer comments are highlighted in Chapter 7.

The user was given one task at a time, and the test stopped when the full set of tasks was completed. Each task was timed, videotaped, and recorded as successfully completed or aborted. Once the task was complete, the moderator asked the user to restate their experience. Users also were asked to quantify their experience on a scale of 1 to 10. The computer was reset, browser cleared, bookmarks cleared, and cache cleared for the next user. All tests were conducted using a standard PC with a dial-up Internet connection.

After reviewing the first website, users were asked to complete the same set of tasks on the prototype site. To avoid biases, the starting websites were alternated.

Recording Actions and Scores

The recorder's responsibility is to record significant comments, time each task, and record the ranking scores. What they are to record should reflect the following:

• What measurements are required to support the objectives of the test?

• What analysis formats (bar charts, pie charts, or other graphs) will be used?

• Who is the audience for the test results?

Knowing how you will present the findings determines what information needs to be recorded.

Conducting the Written Participant Survey

While we had the test participants in-house, we provided them with a survey of additional questions to gain insight into their current shopping habits. This was done as part of the debriefing after the test. We included modified questions like the following:

- How often do you purchase this product? (every month, three months, six months, year)
- How often do you purchase complementary products at the same time?
- How many of the products do you purchase at one time?
- Which of the following best describes why you typically buy this product?
- Where do you normally shop for these products?
- What is your household income (range for the home consumer)?
- What type of business do you have (type, size in annual revenue)?

Answers to questions like these can identify potential e-mail campaign timings, promotional e-bundles, or other comparison testing that may be required. The results are then included in the body of customer intelligence for a more complete view of the customer and current shopping habits.

Tabulating and Analyzing Usability Test Results

Synthesizing key findings is an important part of the test. Analysis determines possible implications and recommendations on how to move forward into the next phase of design or development.

Common customer challenges can be grouped and then prioritized into severity levels. Any rankings are tabulated and aggregated into charts showing comparisons or trends. The timing of tasks is also tabulated and entered into comparative charts. Key findings can then be put into a matrix of short-term or long-term fixes, levels of severity, and easy or hard fixes.

A summary document of common user actions, such as navigational paths taken in completing tasks or correct paths or those ending in "dead ends," is created. Summaries across all users on all websites are included in the key findings. Also documented is accuracy in completing the tasks. For example, did the user actually purchase the right product? In our testing, we found some users were so frustrated with the experience that when they found a product similar to the right one, they selected it just to be done with the task.

Observations noted that some customers completed tasks because they felt compelled to. Under real circumstances, users would not complete the task on the current frustrating website.

A New Method: Retail Task Analysis

We've invented a new method for usability measurement and added to the traditional tool set. It's imperative to measure against a retail dimension, particularly with e-commerce, because the customer experience online must be at least on par with or better than a customer's current shopping experience. This, in most cases, means the retail store.

While most task analysis compares an online store against improvements over itself or against a competing website, the customer's most proficient experience is with retail. Thus, the shopping comparisons are more logically made to physical shopping rather than to another virtual site.

This methodology applies the same principles to shopping and takes traditional mystery shopping to another level. In this model, we are comparing, start to finish, the tasks involved with a person's experience in the store and modeling that behavior online. The steps in this model are as follows:

1. Assign the same user tasks to the shopper to find and purchase a specific product.

2. Ask the shopper to verbalize while walking through the retail store her thought processes, expectations, and other verbalizations requested in usability testing.

3. Note and record observations in the same manner.

The retail experience can give understanding and clues about how better to structure the website and potentially overcome retail shopping inhibitors or challenges.

Sales Data and Other Relevant Measures

For existing websites, sales data and trends—such as units sold, category growth percentages, or market share of a product in a category—are data points to consider for benchmarking. These can tell you if an implementation is working or not. It's important to factor in seasonality or cyclical factors and other influences, such as the state of the economy, and then to be able to measure the success of the changes or recommendations.

Integrating Research Results

Stand-alone research results come from inspection methods or from user testing. Each gives you information, but it is the integration that will optimize your website for sales and customer experience. Convergence of research data gives you a comprehensive list of issues that you can prioritize for improvements or to make trade-offs. Properly interpreting testing sessions and scorecards will influence the next wave and versions because this is an iterative process.

Also, adding a retail shopping test version adds insight into the current customer experience that can be considered in the evolution of e-commerce websites. Because testing is iterative, other measures such as sales data can give instant feedback on whether or not implementations are working.

Key Findings and Related Actions

A summary list of the comprehensive set of issues can be charted. Key findings are issues to which an action can be assigned. Findings can be varied and can relate to customer navigation challenges, content on the website, or the shopping process. The following key findings are representative of common issues in our testing:

- Category and sub-category names and links were not intuitive to customers.
- Customers wanted to add multiple items to the shopping cart without having to go back and forth one product at a time.
- Product descriptions were incomplete; customers couldn't tell sizes and compatibility and couldn't differentiate between two like products.

For each key finding, you can assign a severity level and recommend a proposed action.

A common key finding in testing e-commerce sites is determining the challenges with category naming conventions. In our example, each of the ten online stores tested used different top-level category names and sub-categories for the same product. Users struggled to select the starting category listed on the home page and used "trial-and-error" methods to identify the beginning navigation.

Non-standardization of market structure and category naming conventions for key categories is the number one reason for unsuccessful navigation from home page to product searched. In a retail store, you can at least use visual cues to locate products. And a printed catalog has a complex index that helps you recognize similar entries and scan. Online, it is more difficult. You can type keywords into the search box, but in most cases, you need to be pretty accurate to have correct products returned.

Over time, changes in the marketplace, new technologies, and new products demand a fresh look at category and sub-category naming. Online shopping provides a chance to redefine and recombine traditional products into new categories or, at least, to cross-relate them.

Knowing When You're Done

You'll really never be done, but you know you're close when testers find only minor annoyances or rate the website as uneventful. Usability measurement does not stop when the website launches or the version rolls out. The Internet, products, marketplace, and customers all change over time at different rates and levels and in different directions. Usability measurement is your means to ensure that your website keeps up with the important evolutions. You also need to test to make sure that "uneventful" does not equate with boring.

In our research, we found that the customers of today are not necessarily the customers of tomorrow. For example, early online store research with customers showed the average age of an online purchaser higher than it is today. We've found that the online shopper and customer demographics have changed significantly from when we conducted our initial testing. Today—

five years later—purchasers are younger, more savvy, and more conscious about choices. Products in the marketplace are also very different.

Customers demand much more from online stores, and if they don't get what they want, they will make a different choice. Their patience is less than it used to be with the time constraints they face, and they won't hesitate to try another store if it is easier to operate.

The Art and Science of Online Shopping Model Design

Online shopping models are a hybrid of many factors. Good design requires the science of usability engineering and the art of merchandising to build a model that meets business needs and customer expectations.

This is a pioneering design technique that brings together customer retail behaviors and blends them with software product operation—the Internet. It then balances the mix with usability measurements to ensure that it works.

CHAPTER 7

Winning Webstores

What does it take to have a winning webstore? Customers can tell you. A customer's preferred shopping process is a one-to-one mapping to predetermined expectations. Customers tolerated poorly designed websites in the early years of Internet shopping, but now they've come to expect a base level of usability. Each day, as websites improve and provide new customer conveniences, the bar is raised.

What customers say, however, may be different from what they actually do. The key to these communications is in the interpretations. You must both listen and observe. You must also add other dimensions and opinions from Internet usability experts who've listened and watched thousands of Internet users, shoppers, browsers, customers, and surfers operate and vocalize their online behaviors.

In the opinion equation, however, don't overlook your own insights. As an influencer of web design or of an e-commerce business, you are also a consumer and no doubt have opinions of your own about what makes a winning website. Take a fresh look at your website through the eyes of the consumer instead of only through the eyes of the merchant to avoid a business bias. You may be surprised at what you see. It may be a humbling experience, or it may be a satisfactory one.

Ultimately, customers are judges who vote for winning webstores with their dollars. Analyzed information from customers—and from people who watch and listen to customers— becomes powerful, actionable customer intelligence. Applying this intelligence to web design creates websites from which people want to purchase.

Inalienable Expectations of Customers

Over the past several years, customers have clarified what they want and what they expect from the web. When customers find something that works well on one website, it becomes an expectation for others. While each online store is different, we've accumulated these common insights by listening to customers:

- Customers want control over their shopping experience, starting with the ability to select their preferred method of searching for the best product. In most cases, their search begins through intuitive text links. Most people use the search box when they can't find anything familiar to click on or they have an exact product number or catalog code.

- Repeat customers want the purchasing process personalized, offering them the freedom to shorten the task flow to get in and out of the store easily and quickly when they have specific products in mind. They want frequently purchased items to be remembered by the store and readily available on a return visit.

- Customers want to easily "walk" through the store without disruption. They become confused with unintuitive roadblocks, such as multiple drop-down menu boxes. These roadblocks slow them down.

- Customers want to compare products, but become overwhelmed if there are too many choices. They count on the online merchant to make qualified recommendations to them. They also want to compare products on the same screen rather than being forced to toggle between screens.

- Customers become frustrated when their text-box searches produce "no results."

- Customers want complete information to make a purchase decision. They want to know exactly what is included with the product, specifications such as size, weight, and color, and any accessories they will need to order. They also want shipping charges disclosed before they make a decision to purchase.

- Customers ignore or react negatively to web-based product information that they perceive as "marketing hype" or " sales-speak."

In recent surveys with customers conducted by Retail Forward, online customers identified other frustrations, as shown in Figure 7-1. Retail Forward is a globally focused management consulting, market research, and executive development firm specializing in retail intelligence and strategies.

Among common shopper frustrations, advertisement pop-up boxes and banners top the list, along with congested webpages that are packed with too many advertisements, images, and information to process.

Given the chance, customers will give recommendations on how to improve. Figure 7-2 shows customers' ratings of website improvements.

Figure 7–1 Customers share their online shopping frustrations.

Copyright 2001, Retail Forward, Inc.

The top five customer requests from this survey include the following:

1. Shopping cart running totals that include shipping and handling: Chapter 8 shows a case study of a shopping cart model that hpshopping.com developed and integrated.

2. Removal of advertisements: A noble request, but not likely to happen. The webpage is also an advertising medium. The challenge of the online store is to not let ads get in the customer's way. If overdone, ads are annoying in the same way as if someone were following the customer around a retail store hawking offers in each aisle, and irrelevant ones at that. Product promotions can look and feel like trusted advice if done well.

3. Improving site navigation: Designing navigation based on customer shopping preferences and logical choices creates an intuitive experience.

4. Better categorization of products into categories and sub-categories: Customers would like more meaningful and familiar category names.

5. Larger product images: People want to see what they are getting. New technologies allow for larger views and can provide 3-D imaging views of sides and backs of products.

Figure 7–2 Customers suggest online shopping improvements.

Copyright 2001, Retail Forward, Inc.

Customer recommendations give online stores clues to what's wrong and ideas on improvement. Improvement is an ongoing process. After you resolve the top issues, there are others that surface to replace them.

The 13 rules that follow are a compilation of the collaborative work we've done with Dr. Jakob Nielsen, a respected Internet authority referred to as "the world's leading expert on web usability" in *U.S. News & World Report*. Dr. Nielsen identified these top considerations in web-site design while recommending customer website improvements for online resellers.

The following pages also identify the success factors for online stores and provide a practical guide of do's and don'ts in web design and general recommendations on page layouts.

Thirteen Rules of Winning Websites by Jakob Nielsen

Customers will go where it's easiest to shop. Your strongest competitive advantage is to make the customer's shopping experience as easy and rewarding as possible. In real situations, online shoppers rarely provide feedback on site usability, but they often opt to purchase from another online store instead. Ease of navigation and simple, basic choices are fundamental. Dr. Nielsen provides the following 13 rules:

1. If customers can't find it, they can't buy it.
2. Make customers feel at home on the home page.
3. Create a smooth path to buying (navigation).
4. Help customers successfully search (search boxes).
5. Present good product pages.
6. Write for the web.
7. Cross-sell, don't over-promote.
8. Make it fast.
9. Optimize shopping carts.
10. Ensure a trustworthy design.
11. Provide e-mail contacts.
12. Test the experience.
13. Prepare for success.

To Dr. Nielsen's rules, we've integrated cumulative key findings and customer insight from our research. These rules, insight, and website design tips are elaborated upon in the following pages.

Straight from the Customer's Mouth

Some of the following sections contain actual customer comments recorded during hundreds of videotaped hours of website evaluation and testing sessions over the past few years. These customers verbalized their thoughts and experiences while searching for common products on over 25 different leading e-commerce websites. They were instructed to talk about what they liked, what they disliked, and what they expected when they clicked on links.

Customer segments represented were home consumers, small office, home office, and business shoppers. Besides capturing what they said, we observed their body language, which is also an important element. While it's good to hear what customers say as they work their way through a website, it's just as important to match that up with facial expressions and posture. These observations reflect the intensity of their experience. People are passionate about good and bad website experiences.

The following rules provide representative customer comments gleaned from videotapes. They also provide actionable recommendations for designing customer-centric websites and merchandising online stores.

Rule 1: If Customers Can't Find It, They Can't Buy It

Customers often have difficulty finding products. Metrics talk about abandoned shopping carts, yet customers often can't find products to start a cart in the first place. When shopping for multiple items, they'll start with the easiest item first. If they can't find it, they'll discontinue shopping the store.

Customer Insight

Customers looking for specific products had a difficult time finding them. The following comments are representative of unsuccessful tasks:

- "I'm done here. I'd go to a retail store."
- "I hate to admit defeat, and I would continue until I get frustrated. And that's where I'm at now."
- "Since I can't find it after clicking through, I guess I'll have to do a search or go to another site because the information is not readily available to me."
- "I felt a little bit stupid by not being able to find what I was looking for. I felt it was there somewhere, but I just couldn't find it."
- "They didn't have the product I needed."
- "I think it would be easier to go to the store, tell the guy what I need, and have him grab it off the shelf for me."
- "I'll go check one more time, but actually, I just want to stop."
- "I'm very frustrated at this point. I'm not a happy camper."
- "I'm done. I can't find it."
- "I guess I'm one of those that if I can't find what I want, I get out of the site."

Hunting for products on websites is either like a treasure hunt or a needle in a haystack. People were ecstatic if they were successful and very disappointed if they weren't. The process was arduous, and they came up empty-handed. When asked to describe their experiences, customers used the terms "frustrating," "horrible," "difficult," and "confusing." They often tempered their comments by saying that's what they expect from the web anyway.

All products that customers looked for were on all of the websites. They were top-selling products in their category. Customers tried a variety of methods, but they just couldn't find the products. Can you imagine what would happen if they tried to find a product that wasn't as important?

Recommendations

Help customers easily find what they're looking for by applying the following recommendations:

- Learn how your customers shop.
- Use familiar category names.
- Keep navigation simple, and structure the site according to the customer's understanding of products.
- Cross-reference links between categories if a product could belong to more than one.

- Provide a "breadcrumb" trail on top of the screen to show the customer's current location in the website.

People abandon shopping carts if they can't find products to put in them.

Rule 2: Make Customers Feel at Home on the Home Page

The home page serves as an entry point to the navigation scheme and user choices for the rest of the website. It also sets the tone for the customer's visit. It must be inviting and informative. It should answer the question, "What can I do with this website?"

Customer Insight

Customers verbally and physically reacted strongly to home pages. The following customer comments are representative of their reactions:

- "My first reaction when I see this screen is 'Wow!' There are lots of things to read. I want to find what I'm looking for and get it."
- "I hate it. Websites are supposed to make your life easier."
- "The home page had so much stuff on it, I didn't see the search box, so I didn't use it. I felt stupid trying to find it."
- "It's as busy as heck."
- "This has lots of advertising on it, and I find it kind of distracting. It takes me a while to figure out how I can get where I need to go."
- "Boy, there is lots to look at [laughs nervously]. It's a very busy website. I really hate looking at that much advertising."
- "They have too much information. When I'm looking for something specific, I want to find it easy and fast. If I go to a site and don't see it readily available, I don't stay on the site—I go somewhere else."

People had physical reactions to the home pages through body language, especially in their facial expressions. Some people became nervous or agitated just looking at busy websites, and they physically withdrew. They sat back in their chairs and folded their arms trying to avoid proceeding with the tasks.

Recommendations

Invite customers to shop and feel at home on the home page by applying the following recommendations:

- Inform the customer clearly what the website does, what she can do with it, and why she should care.

- Use simple and direct language to clearly state what your company does and why visitors should work with or purchase from your company.
- Structure the home page clearly.
- Detail any available resources on your site.
- Ensure that navigational areas are recognizable at first glance.
- Enable customers to link back to the home page from any interior page in one click (company logo, breadcrumbing).

Home pages should factor in clarity and accessibility for the customer.

Rule 3: Create a Smooth Path to Buying (Navigation)

The easier it is for customers to navigate through the site, the more successful the online store. Customers return to sites at which they have an easy time.

Customer Insight

Customers made the following representative comments about the challenging navigation of websites:

- "Kind of shuffled me around in more shopping than I wanted to do."
- "The first thing I'm trying to do is see if they have any major headings that try to point me in the right direction."
- "Nope, it's still not there. What did I miss? What's another definition of this?"
- "Since I can't find it after clicking through, I guess I'll have to do a search or go to another site because the information is not readily available to me."
- "Part of working with a new site is figuring out how to use it."
- "I'm just reading the descriptions because you never know what they put things under."
- "Predominately, my definition is not necessarily someone else's definition. Once I understand someone else's definition, it makes sense, but mine is not theirs. I'm now just looking under some items. It's not furniture, it's not accessory, it's not technology…"
- "I'm looking for another link since that one didn't give me what I was looking for."
- "That was a major pain in the butt."

People struggle to figure out new, unfamiliar terms, but only until they find a website that accommodates them. They clicked back and forth on links and browser buttons using the process of elimination. Frustrated customers didn't hold back their opinions. Although it may not be what we want to hear, it is important that it be heard to make appropriate changes.

Recommendations

Provide customers with a superior navigation model by applying the following recommendations:

- Make navigation instinctive, not complex.
- Minimize steps to complete a purchase.
- Don't require registration or passwords for first-time buyers.
- Don't complicate the checkout process with links or options that sidetrack users.
- Defer special offers to the confirmation page that is shown after the completed purchase.
- Use the mid-section of the page for text and supporting graphics that answer customer questions and are relevant to their needs.
- Do allow users to save their personal information to speed up the next purchase.
- Ensure that navigation sequences are predictable and repeatable.
- Provide visual feedback to acknowledge customer actions.
- Have an accelerated ordering process for returning users.

The mid-section of a webpage is the most important real estate on the page and should be used to help shoppers find products for which they are looking.

Many websites create barriers to purchasing by asking too much of customers too early in the shopping process. Customers are annoyed at having to respond to questions on zip codes, e-mail information, and registration information. Some sites make registration a requirement before a shopper can browse, which is a sure way to lose potential customers.

The web design also should provide a way to save information when a customer makes a mistake and uses the back or edit button to correct it. Customers should not have to start completely over if they make a small mistake.

Rule 4: Help Customers Successfully Search (Keyword Search)

Many users know exactly what they want and go straight for the search box. Unsuccessful searches equal missed sales, a diminished market basket, and eventual loss of the customer.

Customer Insight

The following are representative customer comments about their experiences with the keyword search text box and advance search mechanisms:

- "Keyword search didn't take me anywhere except where I've already been."
- "I didn't like the search. When I typed in my words, it really didn't find anything for me."
- "It would have been nice if it brought up what I searched for. But that's never been my experience."
- "I love search engines…when I type the words in right."

Some searches resulted in looping, where customers performed a search, received search results, selected an item from the list, and were brought back to the initial search box page. This occurred on several websites.

We also discovered that similar words typed in the search box brought back different results, which was also confusing to shoppers.

Recommendations

Users need to search when they are lost, and you don't know where they will be when they are lost. Help customers have successful searches by applying the following recommendations:

- Have a prominent search field on the home page.
- Keep the search feature available on all pages.
- Make it easy for customers to search by keyword, and allow for common errors.
- Allow search by SKU or product codes, but don't sort results by these numbers.
- Return search results that provide the necessary information for confirmation of the correct product.
- Provide logical sorting of search results—either by relevance, by group or category, or alphabetically.
- If searching for a product name, place that product page at the top of the search results.
- Ensure that search results lead to designated pages.
- Track the top 100 customer search words monthly.
- If searching for a brand, place the overview or compatibility page for that brand at the top of the search results rather than on random product listings.

Tracking the top 100 customer word searches on your website gives you insight into what customers are thinking or needing in the way of assistance. In some cases, you may find incremental sales opportunities if several customers search for a product that you don't currently offer. Or you'll gain insight into how shoppers look for products.

Failed searches lose potential customers. If you can turn that failed search into a hit, you have a new customer. Other search box recommendations were detailed in Chapter 5.

Rule 5: Present Good Product Pages

If people don't understand what they are getting, they won't purchase.

Customer Insight

The following comments were representative of customers who found products, but who were not presented with adequate information to confirm their choices:

- "There's not enough definition there to tell me that it's what I'm looking for."
- "Well, I think I got the right one, but I'm not positive."

- "So then I have to go back and take another course of action, which is aggravating. I think I found it, but I don't know for sure."
- "I found the product I need, I just can't buy it from them." [The add-to-cart button was too far from the product.]

Inadequate and inconsistent information was presented to customers often. Decision-making information was left out of most descriptions.

Recommendations

Make it easy for customers to understand and compare products by applying the following recommendations:

- Clearly state what the product is, how it operates, or describe its style. Include how it might be used, or list occasions for which it might be suitable.
- Include all available quantities or units (single, multiple) on the same page to simplify navigation.
- Clearly explain alternatives or variations of the product if it comes in different "flavors."
- Ensure that one product description can differentiate it from other products and that the customer has a good understanding of what he is about to purchase
- Include product photos, and use up-to-date images and graphics. Customers use photos to confirm their selection.
- Include SKU and product codes, but de-emphasize obscure numbers.

Sometimes information provided on comparable products is very similar, and it's hard for customers to distinguish differences in features or attributes. Routine reviews of products displayed in the category can let you see what your customers see. It's your job to help them know why they want one product over another. If information is unclear to you, it is unclear to your customers.

Online merchants must merchandise and refresh hundreds or thousands of products monthly. It is difficult to give attention to all products. It is critical, however, to ensure that your most profitable categories and top-selling products are presented appropriate to their values.

Rule 6: Write for the Web

The easier it is to read and understand, the more the page will be used. Writing for the web includes considerations for page design layouts.

Customer Insight

Many customers found pages that were packed with choices and small font sizes:

- "There's a lot of information and it's small."

- "The type is getting pretty small."
- "The writing is REALLY small. I guess that's why I haven't read it yet."

Recommendations

Writing for the web considers both content areas and dense text. Make the web page more readable by applying the following recommendations:

- Keep it short. People read 25 percent more slowly from computer screens. Users scan text, but they don't read long narratives.
- Use bulleted lists that are prioritized with key features and "why-to buy" information.
- Break up blocks of text with subheads.
- Ensure that pages are printable, and test printing on a variety of printer types.
- Use plain and straightforward language, especially in headlines.

People tend to print pages if they are too saturated with text. Printable pages should be a core design requirement, because many people print Internet documents for future reference. Use background colors, text colors, and fonts that print well on a variety of printer types.

Some colors, for example, do not show up when printed because of conflict with background and text colors. Avoid "white" text unless you're sure that it is visible when printed. It is also important to be careful that your printed page does not print a blank last page. The designer should print out pages on the site to make sure that actual information is on each page.

Rule 7: Cross-sell; Don't Over-promote

After the customer is in a product section or shopping cart, cross-selling helps to suggest options and accessories.

Customer Insight

Customers had the following to say about products cross-sold in advertisement promotional boxes:

- "Don't try to show me special deals that are going on rather than taking me to what I'm looking for. When I'm looking for something specific, I'd rather get right to it than look at a bunch of things."
- "If I'm looking for something specific, the ads aren't helpful."

These customers were presented with offers early in their product search process. People will not pay attention to them until they become relevant. Different types of cross-selling are discussed in Chapter 5.

Recommendations

Cross-selling does not mean complicating the customer's visit with ads or promotions for unrelated products and services.

- Ask questions. When the hamburger giant McDonald's cross-sells, the order clerks ask the customer if he would like fries with his order.
- Link to other products that would complement this product.
- Don't link to random promotions or unrelated products.
- Break up blocks of text with subheads. Promotions belong on the home page and category pages. Too many links cause users to ignore them (and you don't get to cross-sell the relevant products).

Online stores can redefine categories and cross-merchandise aisles that are physically impossible to combine in retail or in the catalog worlds. Incorporate a cross-selling selection matrix whenever possible to make it easy for the customer to spot and ensure that it stands out from advertising clutter.

Rule 8: Speed Rules

Internet users do not like to wait. The faster your webpages respond—and the easier it is for the buyer to understand the page and take the next step—the more successful the site.

Customer Insight

Customers made the following comments about website performance when they were asked to describe their experience with the website:

- "Horrible. It was kind of slow, and you had to go looking for things."
- "Pictures take too long to load, and I don't have time to wait."
- "Nothing happened. Oh, there it is. I'm just impatient."

Some websites performed slower than others, and customers became impatient. Some labels and buttons took too long to render. On one website, the add-to-cart buttons were so slow to appear that customers couldn't figure out how to add an item into the shopping cart, even though they had found the product.

Recommendations

The following are recommendations to improve website performance and speed:

- Keep response time to 10 seconds maximum. Less for high-speed connections.
- Utilize a fast server and a high-end Internet connection.

- Minimize download times. Too often, webpages load slowly, links are broken, and debugging messages pop-up on the site.
- Use few graphics, small graphics, and cached graphics
- Use task-sized product photos—people want to see what they are buying. Use a small photo on the initial page. Link to larger photos with more details, and include several shots from different angles.
- Don't use photos in long lists of products on category pages unless they help to clearly differentiate products.
- Provide visual feedback to the customer if a transaction is going to take more than a second or two.
- Test page downloads using Internet connection speeds representative of typical website visitors.

All pages accessed during navigation should download in less than 10 seconds. Download speeds can be affected by Internet usage cycles. Internet traffic and usage can be heavier on certain days, peak hours, and special seasons like holidays. Testing during different days of the week and at different times gives you a more complete snapshot of speeds and performance.

Even with high-speed Internet connections, many customers still access the web over telephone lines. If a first-time customer encounters extremely slow performance on the home page, she may transfer the perception to the rest of the site and may not continue.

Simple text loads much quicker than graphics. If performance trade-offs are being made, use simple text links instead of fancy font graphics on web pages.

Rule 9: Display Items in the Shopping Cart

The shopping cart is a simple visual confirmation and reinforcement of the shopper's purchase actions. It reassures the buyer and provides instant feedback.

Customer Insight

The following is a representative comment about the shopping cart and its surrounding process:

- "I prefer to go to be able to click on items and not go directly to the shopping cart after each item. And it took me a while to find the 'continue shopping' button."

Many customers purchase more than one item on a shopping visit and find starting the purchasing process over for each additional item tedious.

Recommendations

Help customers use the shopping cart by applying the following recommendations:

- A shopping cart is currently the best metaphor for buying online. You can take advantage of the customer's familiarity with retail shopping.

- Allow customers to see the number of items in their cart and a running total at all times.
- The shopping cart must have explicit features to (1) change the quantity for each item, (2) remove an item (don't ask the user to "buy 0 of this"), (3) continue shopping, check out, save the order, or e-mail it to somebody.
- Make the shopping cart clearly visible and easily accessible.
- Include important information such as the product name and price.
- Ensure that additional charges such as tax or shipping are clearly visible and understandable.
- Show the shopping cart icon on all pages; next to the icon, state the current number of items in the cart, even if "0."

By far, customers prefer a persistent "sticky cart" that remains posted on each web page so they clearly know what is in their carts at all times. This feature enables a more convenient method when purchasing multiple items. The persistent cart is discussed in the case study on hpshopping.com customer convenience improvements in Chapter 8.

Rule 10: Ensure a Trustworthy Design

No one wants surprises. Anticipating questions and having the answers on pricing, availability, and additional charges wins customers. Honesty wins in the end. Customers' experiences affect their trust in the online store.

Customer Insight

The following comment is representative of customers who had accidentally purchased incorrect products and were asked to describe their experience with the website.

- "Not pleasurable. In fact, detrimental to them. I'm one of their customers, and I had this experience with their website. I'm going to [a competitor's site] because I'm angry now."

People become angry when they feel the website deceives them. In several cases, customers chose incorrect items and would have had to return them in a real situation. Unclear or inaccurate descriptions are opportunities for selection errors and unhappy customers.

Recommendations

Provide information that the customer needs to know by applying the following recommendations:

- Disclose shipping and handling fees up front. Address delivery timing.
- List a price for everything.
- State whether the product is in stock or will be backordered before the customer orders.
- Provide complete company contact information: company name, addresses, toll-free phone numbers, and e-mail addresses.

- Ensure that all product claims are justified and substantiated.
- Help people easily distinguish products.
- Help customers know exactly what they're getting and when.
- Have a privacy policy, put it on the site, and follow it.

Real-time inventory checking provides availability information.

Rule 11: Provide E-mail Contacts

The response and confirmation process is reassuring. But don't use the customer's personal information to overload him with unwanted email.

Recommendations

Keep the customers informed about their order by applying the following recommendations:

- Send confirmation email immediately after receiving the order. Include the order number, a URL, and a phone number for customer support.
- Send a second confirmation when the order ships. Include a tracking number and URL for web tracking of the package.
- Ensure that all order-related forms are formatted and easily printable.
- Offer a newsletter and/or special offers for opt-in customers, those who choose to register and give permission to be contacted by the store.
- Generate special-purpose notification mailing lists for unique events such as long-awaited new products that are available for shipping.
- Never "spam," contacting customers without their permission with undesired e-mail advertisements.

Confirming e-mails give confidence to the customer that he completed the order transaction properly. They also provide a record of ordering information if follow-up is needed.

Rule 12: Test the Experience

You can gain valuable insights into your own design with in-house testing.

Recommendations

Apply the following recommendations to ensure that you're keeping track of the customer experience:

- Understand that no design is perfect the first time.
- Test your own site with real customers.
- Test your site against competitor websites.

- Use the web yourself for real tasks. Buy half of your gifts online for the next holiday season, and observe how other sites make it easy or difficult for you to buy from them.

Test early and test often. After you've tested, test again at planned intervals. Customer habits change, products change, and the marketplaces change. Routine testing should be built into the website schedules.

Rule 13: Prepare for Success

Preparedness leads to a successful site.

Recommendations

The following recommendations will help you meet the requirements and demands of a successful website.

- **Plan:** Always have the capacity for twice your current volume.
- **Realize:** Traffic can grow by several hundred percent after a big campaign.
- **Remember:** Anybody you turn away will not return.
- **Start Out Right:** Don't run a big campaign with a bad web design. Fix the site first.

The above rules are minimum standards, requirements, and current customer expectations. Periodic reviews and affirmations keep these rules in the forefront. Share these rules with others in the organization as business online basics.

The rules are fundamentals in guiding decisions or features of a website. Content on a page is a major contributor to the customer experience.

Page Design Tips and Considerations

Each element on the page should have relevancy. Provide information when it is helpful, but don't provide information just because it's available. This section contains tips on the following:

- Screen real estate usage
- Frame usage
- Page titles
- Copy scanability
- Text and background contrast
- Links
- Shopping for multiple items

Screen Real Estate Usage

Forward-looking navigation (links to other pages) and content accounts for at least 80 percent of page design. Deconstruct some of the pages in your website, and view them as blocks of similar kinds of page content:

- Print out the home page, a representative category page, and a product page.
- Highlight each type of content used with different colors.

For example, highlight ads in yellow, company information in blue, and customer navigation links in orange. You can then analyze the page for color dominance. The page is out of balance when yellow dominates the page and interferes with orange, the customer's task.

Frame Usage

Users do not like pages that require heavy scrolling and long product lists.

Customer Insight

Customers get tired of wading through long lists, and they don't take time to scroll for very long. In fact, many customers looked at the page, scrolled a bit, and then gave up. They appeared to be overwhelmed with too many choices on a page and did not want to continue.

- "What am I missing? Nope, it's not there."
- "It's like having to pick up every box to see if it's for me."
- "I guess I just have to pick one. I have no idea what any of these things are."
- "I don't have time to just browse and cruise. I need to get where I'm going."

The products that the customers were seeking were in the list. Line lists do not differentiate very well, and customers don't want to bother looking at each item.

Recommendations

The following recommendations will help you organize the webpages that contain lots of information:

- Avoid using long frames that require excessive scrolling.
- Add links at the top of the page to bring customers to various headings in a long list. This eases the work on the part of customers and lets them know key points in the hidden parts of the page.
- Repeat the links at the bottom of the page to help customers navigate after they have scrolled to the bottom of the screen.

People will scroll long lists of items. However, if the items are not clearly differentiated, they won't spend much time distinguishing between them. They may try one or two sample clicks on a "best guess," but they ultimately choose to abort the task.

Page Title Clarity

Page titles are like magazine article titles. They reflect what's on the page. They are used as search strings, in scanning, and in bookmarking, which is adding a page to the "favorites" list in the browser to enable direct return to an important website page. Use these recommendations to improve your page titles:

- Ensure that web pages have understandable titles that function in human (versus machine) readable form.
- Ensure that titles clearly represent the contents on the page.

Page titles are often used as keyword search strings to locate products. For example, a title could list a product name such as HP 51626A Black Print Cartridge. Also, people add important pages to their browser's "favorites" list. This list can become quite long and non-intuitive. A clear and representative title makes it easier to locate the desired page when scanning the favorites list.

Copy "Scanability"

People don't "read" websites; they scan. Provide easily digestible content by applying the following recommendations:

- Use short paragraphs for text copy.
- Use concise headings and subheadings.
- Use familiar, self-explanatory text labels.
- Use bulleted lists instead of paragraphs.

Page copy should be succinct and easy to scan using short paragraphs, subheadings, and bulleted lists. Text labels must be self-explanatory. Follow magazine or newspaper article principles, and put your major message in the headline, with supporting points visible and clearly understood. In the first few seconds on the page, shoppers must know what the product is and why they might need or want it.

Good visual design is a craft.

Text and Background Contrast

Provide a highly readable landscape by applying the following recommendations:

- Use high-contrast colors between the text and background by using plain color or subtle patterns for backgrounds.

• Avoid intense colors such as red.

Considerations for color-blindness should be taken into account.

Links

The all-important links required for navigating through the site should be visible without being touched by the customer's mouse and should appear above the fold. Make sure that the customer doesn't have to scroll to find what she came to the site for.

Apply the following recommendations when designing links:

• Use two different colors to differentiate between links used (e.g., blue) and those unused (e.g., black).
• Use a readable font size.
• Use roll-overs and other visual cues to let shoppers know that a graphic is an active link.

Changing the colors lets people know where they've been and paths taken. It's not always clear which objects are active links. People try clicking to see if they go somewhere. Also, many people in our research complained about font sizes that were too small.

Shopping for Multiple Items

Many websites have been designed for customers to purchase one item at a time. After a product is dropped into the shopping cart, the customer is brought to the checkout counter. Many websites use a "return to shopping" feature from their shopping cart after an item is placed into the cart. This feature often returned the customer to the home page, which is not typically what he expected. Return to shopping should go back to where the customer was last and not make him start over at the beginning.

The following comments are representative of customers' experiences:

• "And when I get to the screen that shows me my shopping cart, I prefer to be able to click on items and not go directly to the shopping cart after each item [after clicking the "continue shopping" button]. I don't like that...Where did I go? I now have to go back through all the layers again to get back where I was. I have to select everything all over again. If I were doing this for real, I would have definitely given up. This website is cumbersome, very cumbersome. I didn't like having to go back to the main page every time I added something to my cart."
• "I don't like that. I could have gone back and found another product instead of it taking me back to the home page. That doesn't help me any. What if I wanted to purchase more of the stuff?"

People made it clear that they preferred to add multiple items to their cart and not have to start over from the beginning each time.

Content That Adds Value

As explained in Chapter 5, people need different kinds of information presented to them depending on their goals. Content can be educational or solution-based. Besides product searches, content was tested with customers to determine interest and relevancy. Many customers said they would return to a website that had information that helped them use their products more effectively. The following insight was in response to value–added printing projects.

Customer Insight

Customers made the following comments when evaluating types of content they would find useful on websites:

- "Fun and creative projects for your home and family. That's interesting to me. I always like to look at things like that to see if there's anything fun to do with my kids."
- "Money saving business printing projects. Yeah, I'd like to see if there are ideas to reduce printing costs."
- "Certificates and forms. I'd definitely check them out. There are always business forms that you need. Rather than running out and buying a book or looking them up through a search engine, I'd check that out and probably bookmark it."

People will combine shopping and information. Value-added content is like a recipe to which you—as the online merchant—can provide the ingredients.

Recommendations

Provide the right information in the right manner at the right time to your customers by applying the following recommendations:

- Understand your categories and key customer needs.
- Provide relevant and usable content on your website.
- Make content easily accessible.
- Layer content to accommodate different shopper types.

Shoppers may need a little or a lot of information. Providing deeper layers of information accommodates those people without interfering with other shoppers' needs.

How Does Your Webstore Stack Up?

Regardless of the size of your online store or your organization, there are questions that you can ask of your site as a potential influencer of site design and customer experience. A website self-evaluation shows opportunities to improve site usability. Comparing your competitors' sites against the same criteria and analyzing the results reveals areas of focus to remain at a competitive advantage or to catch up.

Evaluating Your Website

Chapter 6 discussed methods available to measure the usability of your website. Here are some things you can do on your own to determine which in-depth methods to pursue, should you identify "show-stoppers":

- Step into the customer's shoes, and understand the shopping experience for top products in your assortment.
- Complete the simple 10-step checklist below, checking yes or no.
- Conduct the self-test on three of your competitors' websites.
- Rate how each of the sites did, and compare with your results.
- Repeat in six months. There is no room for complacency in the online marketplace. Products change, customer attitudes and behaviors change, and your competition can change.

Your evaluation will help you answer questions such as the following:

- Does your site help customers quickly and easily locate key products?
- Does it provide accurate product or other purchase decision information?
- Is it optimized to offer cross-selling suggestions and value-added ideas to improve customer experience with products purchased?
- Are all functions integrated such as sales and support?

Stepping Into the Customer's Shoes

First, it's important for you to step into the shoes of your target customer and perform a task analysis test on three key products in your website. Ask yourself the following questions: What do I want to accomplish? Can I get the information to decide whether or not to buy this product? How would buying from this seller be different from buying from someone else?

- Identify your most profitable and strategic product in a key category.
- Starting in a retail store that carries this product, enter the store and navigate through the aisles while noting the words you associate as you look for the product. These may

be the words that customers use on your website as they type into the search box or look for familiar names in of categories listed on your website.

- Conduct the same task on your website using the self-test below.

Viewing the home page, ask yourself whether the category names reflect the words that you noted as you looked for the product in retail. Compare with category names and try the search box to see what results you get. As you perform the task, time it and make a list of trouble spots.

The Self-Test and Ten-Question Checklist

The following checklist can give you a perspective on how you're doing. Have a stop-watch ready. This task starts on the home page on which you started shopping for your key product from the prior section.

1. Does it take you less than 30 seconds to know what you needed to click first?
2. Can you accurately assume which products would be found in each category link?
3. Type variations of the product name and/or model number into the search box. Is your product served up as a choice each time?
4. When you find the product page, does it clearly communicate what it is and why someone would want to buy it?
5. Does it have a photo and provide complete information, such as size, color, weight, usages, or what's in the box?
6. Does it offer complementary products and cross-sells?
7. Evaluating the website in general, can you make multiple purchases from a page?
8. Does a customer know at all times what's in the shopping cart, see totals, and have the ability to calculate shipping and taxes? Be sure to let the customer print out the order page.
9. Are you able to shop the site without needing to register or provide personal information?
10. Are a toll-free number, e-mail address, and other company contact information clearly presented on all pages?

At the end of the checklist, total up the yes's and no's. If you struggled with link names or paused to interpret them, your customers will too so give the question a no. The goal of this self-test is to give you a baseline for improvement. The scoring follows:

9-10 yes answers: Congratulations! It was great for that product. Now try the other top nine products on your website to see if results are consistent. Randomly take ten recent customer orders and walk through finding and purchasing those items in the same combination.

5-8 yes answers: Needs work. Further testing is warranted to understand major issues and obstacles.

0-4 yes answers: You've got problems. If you are experiencing challenges, you can be assured that your customers are also. Conduct deeper usability evaluations to understand key problems.

If you're having trouble shopping for your number one product, this likely reflects the overall shopping for all products. The goal is to turn no's into yes's over time. Reassess your website after you make modifications.

Improving your scores over time is important. However, while you're improving your site, your competitors are improving theirs—and may be including responses to new customer expectations that come to light through the natural evolution of the Internet.

Checking Out the Competitive Landscape

Knowing how you rate in comparison to your competitors is an indicator for your chance of success. It will also define how soon improvements must be made. To understand the competitive landscape, conduct the same task on three of your competitors' sites, using the checklist from above. Compare them as to the time it took for tasks, problem areas, and starts and stops along the way.

After the ratings, build a chart to show where you are in comparison overall, and then analyze a question at a time. Navigation from the home page and the ability to find and select products are crucial to acquiring new customers and retaining current ones.

You've probably discovered that each website is different and is a potential confusing or challenging experience. Although these simple tests may not predict the success of your store, performing the same task on a few sites gives you a glimpse into what it's like for your customers. Reviewing your own website from your customer's viewpoint identifies key areas that you may probe further using the usability methodologies in Chapter 6.

Conduct these tests every few months and after key site changes. After each test is performed, compare the results with the prior tests to gauge improvements. Also, continue to compare against the competitive landscape.

If a customer fails to accomplish a task on a website, it is because the site failed to provide the "right stuff" for the customer and follow through on the customer promise. Periodic testing will help you keep pace with customers, who change over time. Internet shoppers five years ago are not the same shoppers today. The age range of shoppers has broadened with the adoption of the Internet, and the sophistication and confidence of shoppers has grown. Customers are moving targets, and they become technically astute with time.

The Envelope Please

In the customer evaluations, there were a variety of reasons for shopper task failure. Even when shoppers were successful, the experience on most websites left them feeling frustrated.

At the end of each test, we asked customers to rate their overall satisfaction with the websites. We also asked them whether or not they would be inclined to purchase from the online store based on their experience.

In recent testing sessions, 33 percent of shoppers said they would purchase from the real online stores, while 100 percent said they would purchase from the customer-centered designed prototype store.

Knowing When It Works

Earlier in this chapter, we provided customer comments when things weren't working well for them while shopping websites. What does it sound like when things are working? Below are comments customers made about the prototype website that had been developed by applying customer-centered design rules and tips:

- "That was three clicks. Easy."
- "It looks simpler. It's easy on the eyes."
- "I like the picture because that is what I see on the shelf when I go to the store—so I know this is EXACTLY what I've purchased before, so I don't have to go into the store to get it."
- "It felt like it gave me choices that enabled me to make intelligent decisions."
- "Good navigation—I didn't have to use search"
- "I didn't have to do a search—I was there in two clicks."
- "It tells me what's in stock—that helps me."
- "Basically, everything was there that I needed, and that made it really simple and made it easier. It helped me to trust that site."
- "Cooool! I'm excited! It was easy. They had my stuff. It made me happy."
- "It was a satisfying experience. I got what I was looking for."
- "Getting there was fast, easy, efficient—Yeahhh—I'm accomplishing what I want, I found what I needed. And it was fast."

When compared, customer-centered models outperformed current, actual webstores. The operative word is "compared." When customers were provided a better, more intuitive method to find products, they were pleasantly surprised and delighted.

And the Winner Is....

Everyone wins with good web design. Customers are happy. Merchants are happy.

PART 4

Case Studies and The Future

T his section features a collection of case studies that describe the future of e-commerce.

Chapter 8 shares numerous case studies for actual application. These four case studies represent how various techniques in previous chapters have applied a customer-centric design and had a successful outcome.

Chapter 9 takes a look at the future consumer and the future of web shopping.

Case Studies

This chapter presents four case studies that demonstrate integration of knowledge from previous chapters. It gives examples of how combining customer insight, web usability engineering principles, and retailing and catalog techniques provided in earlier chapters dramatically improved the online experience for the customer and increased sales for the merchant. The principles, processes, and methodologies can be applied to your specific needs and include a broad spectrum of goals for improving the customer online store experience.

Each of the four case studies were projects that started with customer needs. They are the following:

1. HP and Computers4SURE.com (an Office Depot Company)—improving customer ability to find and select from complex product categories
2. HPshopping.com—engineering customer shopping conveniences
3. The Wine Gallery—helping customers find and select wines online
4. HP—improving information flow patterns for internal information "customers"

Each of these case studies uses the techniques in different ways to show how they can be combined and recombined to meet specific needs and goals.

Case Study 1: HP Printing Supplies Configurator

This case study shows how customer-centered design principles, processes, and methodologies were applied to an HP program to improve the customer's HP printing supplies online shopping experience and ease the complexities of product content management for the online merchant. One leading edge online reseller—Computers4SURE.com—was the first to integrate the printing supplies configurator (an online selection tool). Computers4SURE.com is a customer-focused online computer and technology reseller that operates as a subsidiary of Office Depot, Inc. Computers4SURE.com is one of the success stories in the online world. As president, Bruce Martin has used his vision and focus on the customer experience to earn this company numerous awards.

One part of the program resulted in improved success in customer product selection and increased total shopping cart transactions. Another part of the program improved product compatibility management and saved resources for the online store.

Situation Analysis

Over the course of several years, HP has launched over 300 different models of home and office printing devices, such as HP DeskJet and LaserJet printers and OfficeJet all-in-ones (printer/scanner/fax). All of these printing devices required printing supplies, such as inkjet or toner cartridges. Often, each new printer introduced required new printing supplies because each new supply is engineered specifically to meet exact printer design specifications.

There are several million printers in homes and offices around the world, with hundreds of different model numbers. There are also several hundred different printing supplies, each with its own unique part number. Some supplies fit several models, while others fit only a few. Managing the relationships of supply-to-printer model configuration is a complex task. New printers are often added to the growing installed base of printers, still used in homes and offices.

Over the past several years, we have conducted research across many e-commerce websites that sell the HP printing supplies. Almost all of the online stores listed print cartridges, giving only the supply product SKU number and a brief description, as shown in Figure 8-1. Shoppers were frustrated with long lists of products.

Many shoppers in our task analysis research studies aborted the task because they didn't want to click on each of the products in the list to look at compatibility details. Even when some participants did, the printer compatibility information was often not up to date.

Searching for products in long lists is tedious. One research participant started with the first cartridge in the list, clicked the link to the detail page, read the page to verify that it was not the right cartridge for his printer, and then clicked the back button on the browser. He selected the next four in the list going through the process with each one, and then aborting the task, visibly annoyed. He said that it was like having to pick up all 100 boxes on a retail shelf to read the package to see if it fit his printer. He also said that after a couple of minutes he would have tried another online store or got in his car and gone to pick one up at the store. In retail, customers can ask for sales assistance. Online, customers don't bother calling and remain frustrated with the experience.

To gain a deep understanding of the customer online shopping experience, we conducted an initial evaluation and benchmarking of the shopping process and customer experience on more than 20 online stores. Because online stores carry thousands of products that change often, it is difficult to manage relationships and compatibility of complex categories.

black inkjet cartridges	product #
hp black inkjet print cartridge for jetpaper	92261A
hp black inkjet print cartridge for plain paper	51604A
hp 34 black inkjet print cartridge (e-printer)	C6634AN
hp 14 black inkjet print cartridge	C5011AN
hp 33 black inkjet print cartridge	51633M
hp 26 black inkjet print cartridge	51626A
hp 15 black inkjet print cartridge	C6615DN
hp 45 black inkjet print cartridge	51645A
hp 20 black inkjet print cartridge	C6614DN
hp 29 black inkjet print cartridge	51629A
hp 40 black inkjet print cartridge	51640A
hp 19 black inkjet print cartridge	C6628AN

Figure 8–1 Finding the right cartridge for a specific printer model was difficult in early online stores.

As a result, we developed a program to improve the customer success in shopping online for printing supplies, and help the resellers update compatibility information.

Objectives/Strategies

The program had three main objectives:

1. Help customers easily, accurately, and confidently find and select HP printing supplies through a wide range of electronic catalogs and vehicles—Internet stores, vending machines, and kiosks.
2. Provide one, accurate, reliable, up-to-date printer supply compatibility online reference guide.

3. Help reseller partners manage the compatibility updates and complexities of the relationships between printer supplies and printer models.

The program's two main goals were to easily and intuitively lead people through the current confusing printing supplies selection process and to provide an automated process to manage complex product compatibility information. Online technologies offer creative ways of addressing the issues and enabling solutions. The implementation strategies in this program took a three-pronged approach:

1. Design and develop a customer-centric, find/select navigation model—a "configurator."
2. Design and develop a deployment process, and provide the configurator as a reference tool available through a link to online stores.
3. Design and develop a syndicated content model, update process, and customize for reseller website integration.

The design and development phase took over a year with initial roll-out of the reference guide tool spanning several months. The third approach was customized for resellers.

The HP Printing Supplies Selection Tool

The goal of the first part of this program was to design and develop a superior online printing supplies selection model, applying customer-centered design principles. The selection tool—a configurator—was an application with a user interface and a product relational database.

The configurator had the following design requirements:

• Flexible
• Extensible
• Modular
• Customizable
• Easy to use and integrate
• Innocuous to "look and feel"
• Cross-platform solution

The goal was to develop a robust, integrated electronic product catalog superset containing all printing devices, supplies, and established product relationships. The design allowed for customized subset modules that could be targeted to market niches or electronic vehicles. The flexible and extensible database allowed for easy customization, product updates, category expansion, and maintenance.

The entire configurator and its associated processes had to be easy to use, integrate, and maintain. It was essential that the user interface blend seamlessly with the reseller website's "look and feel," which created a transparent experience for the customer. Because there were varying system architectures in the e-commerce marketplace, the tool had to work flawlessly across major system platforms. An initial system technology assessment was made with the online stores to ensure that all popular architectures and platforms were considered in the development process.

The Process and Methodologies

There were several steps in the design and development process:

1. Identify customers' current shopping models and hierarchies.
2. Mock up a navigation model based on customer selection hierarchies.
3. Develop product catalog database structures, models, and hierarchies.
4. Create a rapid prototype.
5. Conduct customer testing.
6. Build the final product.
7. Deploy to online stores.

Identifying Customer Shopping Hierarchies

Current retail, catalog, and online store shopping behaviors were analyzed and defined. Surveys and research findings were added to the knowledge base. Customer shopping processes were synthesized from the research data, and a hierarchy was developed.

Almost all customers started the supply selection process the same way. The most common customer navigation processes and choices were identified and a preliminary hierarchy defined.

Creating a User Interface Storyboard

After the shopping process hierarchy was defined, a navigational storyboard—a written page mock-up of the steps in the process—was mapped. Variations were created and tested with a "next bench" method internally and refined. The storyboard turned the hierarchy process into sequential webpages.

Each page of the storyboard was then drawn out in detail showing elements such as category names and images. These pages would be used as the basis for developing the user interface templates required in the finished application.

Developing the Database Schema

After the final storyboard was determined, the information hierarchy model—or database schema—was proposed to accommodate the page sequences and category naming conventions in the storyboard model. A robust, extensible product catalog database was planned.

A subset of the database schema and information hierarchy is shown in Figure 8-2.

The information model showed linkages and relationships between the necessary elements.

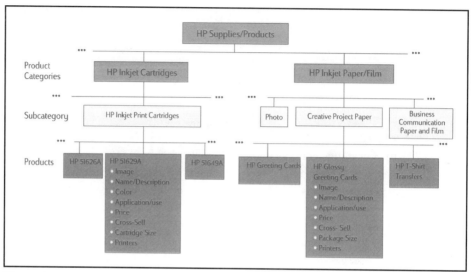

Figure 8–2 The database schema reflects the consumer shopping process.

Building a Prototype

The user interface and the database were brought together as an application and built into a prototype. For customer testing purposes, only a subset of the database was built. Major issues could be identified through testing that could require significant modifications to the schema. Therefore, only minimal investment was made in database development until customer testing could validate the models.

Testing with Real Customers

No matter how good you believe the first prototype is, customers are likely to find something wrong with it. Four rounds of customer testing were conducted throughout the development cycle. The prototype was modified after each test based on the results. The testing schedules were built into the development plan, with time between tests to modify the user interface.

The first round of testing was designed to establish navigational consumer preferences and validate the shopping process hierarchy. After the first test, we listed more than 30 items needing modification. We divided the list into three parts: critical, intermediate, and long-term. Critical findings were "show stoppers" and needed to be fixed before the next round of scheduled customer tests. These were severe trouble spots that affected the ability to complete a task. Intermediate items needed to be fixed prior to product release, but would not necessarily affect the next round of testing. Long-term items would be fixed as time permitted in the first release; if not, they were saved for the next version update.

We evolved and modified the prototype. Some of the changes made were to replace drop-down menus with page-viewable lists, to allow for printer platform search, to reorganize the paper category, to combine pages to shorten the process, and to add elements that better guided users.

The second round tested the refined prototype with the critical items addressed. From that test, there was a new list of critical, intermediate, and long-term items noted. However, because we had significantly improved the model after the first test, the list was much shorter. Only minor or cosmetic changes to the user interface were required after the third round.

The most enlightening test was the fourth round in which we altered the test plan to compare the prototype against actual online stores. The prior tests measured improvement over the previous version of the configurator. The prototype was mocked up into a fictitious e-store frame. Customers were asked to perform the same simple tasks on both websites, and then compare the two sites. This testing process was discussed in Chapter 6.

The results were encouraging. Customers were successful in completing the tasks on our prototype, while having to abort in many trials on the current online stores. Customers unanimously preferred the prototype model over existing sites because it was designed based on customer retail shopping hierarchies and was easy and intuitive to use.

Building the Final Product

The final product consisted of refinements to the user interface and proofing the database. The configurator also underwent a final quality assurance process. The user interface employed approximately 10 different page templates. Because of the relational product database, however, this resulted in more than 600 dynamically built pages—one for each printer model and one for each product SKU. Each link and page was proofed and tested to ensure that each dynamically generated webpage rendered quickly and accurately with images and text. This proofing also double-checked the database for accuracy of printing supply compatibility.

The product was "virtually" packaged on a server, ready for deployment. The program and launch plans were then created.

Deploying the Configurator

The configurator was designed with two deployment options:

- As a stand-alone online product compatibility reference guide
- As integrated "shelves" in an online store

The deployment options addressed short-term and long-term needs. The first option was an immediate "fix." Because of actual system integration, the second option required resource scheduling on the part of online stores and was a longer-term implementation.

The Configurator as a Compatibility Reference Model

The configurator is a selection tool and online compatibility guide on which shoppers can "look up" the supplies that fit their printers. This would be comparable to someone looking for an oil filter for a car. There are hanging compatibility charts available in retail aisles showing the makes, models, and years of cars, and the compatible oil filter that fits the car. The configurator is a virtual compatibility chart showing the models of the printers and the compatible supplies that fit the printer.

Resellers registered online and were granted immediate access to the configurator. During registration, the reseller was presented with useful linking ideas. After the link was established in the online store, it was available as a shopping aid. The customer shopping experience was as follows:

1. While shopping in the printing supplies category, a customer clicks a link to the selection guide.
2. A new window pops up displaying the home page.
3. The customer easily locates the correct supplies for her printer.
4. She writes down the cartridge SKU number, closes the window, and resumes shopping, searching for that cartridge SKU number.

While this method was not as seamless a method as full integration, it did provide a stop-gap solution while longer-term integration could be scheduled. Also, pop-up windows are often disliked by shoppers, because they disrupt what the customer is trying to accomplish and forces him to deal with two windows.

Full Integration of the Supplies Configurator

The goal with this deployment option was to achieve seamless integration of the configurator within an online store, Computers4SURE.com in a pilot program. Database integration allowed the configurator to run within the store's existing operating environment and platforms. The integrated result would be transparent to the customer. After the configurator was integrated into the website, the customer experience would be as follows:

1. While shopping for printing supplies for an HP printer in the supplies category, a customer selects a link that goes to the home page of the printing supplies guide. The guide is seamlessly integrated into the Computers4SURE.com frames.
2. The customer chooses his specific printer model, which returns a page showing the specific printer model and the supplies products that fit it, as shown in Figure 8-3.
3. He browses the list of compatible products, clicks the "add to cart" button next to each item, and—when finished shopping the site—continues to the checkout.

The fully integrated model allows for easy navigation and purchase in a fluid motion.

This page shows the recombined categories of ink cartridges and paper, a difficult organization for retail stores, but newly implemented online.

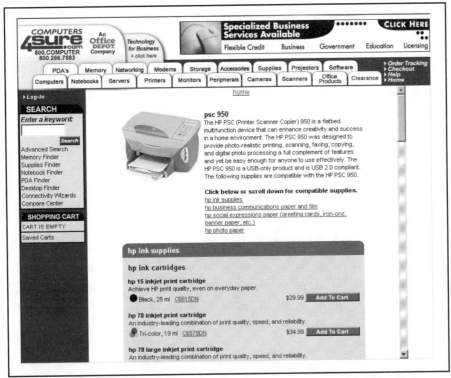

Figure 8–3 The supplies configurator improved the supplies customer shopping experience and made it easy.

Integrating the Configurator

For this option, the configurator web application was comprised of two key components:

1. End-user interface with which shoppers interact in the find-and-select process: This component is the configurator application consisting of the user interface and relational database.
2. Administrator's interface with which to customize the product catalog in the database: This interface has a set of administration tools that allows management of pricing and product mix. The tool can turn products "on" or "off," depending on product availability. It also acts as a staging area for new products waiting to be "turned on" at appropriate launch dates.

To accommodate reseller unique needs, schedules, and architectures, we provided two integration options:

1. We delivered the customer navigation model (user interface and database) to the reseller who could then integrate it into its own architectures.

2. We provided the configurator fully loaded onto servers to integrate into the Computer4SURE.com existing web farm.

Both options included an automated managed content and update process to save rework of product information. Cosmetic modifications to the user interface "look and feel" were considered, such as colors and fonts to match the rest of the online store.

Success Measurements

After the configurator was integrated, new customer task analyses were conducted, validating the improvement over the original benchmarks. Other metrics considered the following:

- Number of resellers registering for the reference guide
- Number of users launching the guide, most viewed pages, and repeat visits
- Improvement of customers performing the same tasks from benchmark testing
- Improved satisfaction by resellers on this new process
- Accuracy of product page compatibility information

Customer satisfaction on this new model earned the highest rating of all individual stores. On an aggregate basis, it earned an average of 8.04 (on a scale of 1-10, 10 being best) compared to the aggregate ratings of all other websites and customer ratings combined at 5.76.

Case Study 2: hpshopping.com—Improving Customer Convenience

hpshopping.com—a subsidiary of Hewlett-Packard Company—is an online retailer that offers the complete line of more than 500 Hewlett-Packard personal and home office products such as PCs, digital cameras, DeskJet and LaserJet printers, all-in-ones, and printing supplies and accessories. A primary customer value proposition for this online retailer is to provide a superior customer experience through personalized solutions. hpshopping.com also guarantees a safe online shopping environment with secure purchasing transactions and privacy policies for its customers. As a result of its customer-centered approach, it has been the recipient of four consecutive Web Awards and has been named "Computer Retailer Web Site of the Year" by the Web Marketing Association.

The Internet is a dynamic environment, and hpshopping.com includes continual customer convenience improvement as part of its routine processes. This case study describes four programs that demonstrate how hpshopping.com applied a customer-centric approach in its website design evolution to improve the customer experience.

The following four programs each improved the customer experience in a different and important way:

1. Establishing a persistent shopping cart.
2. Improving product comparison capabilities.
3. Improving the online purchasing experience for repeat customers.
4. Increasing success rates in text-entry searches.

Persistent Shopping Cart

The objectives of the persistent shopping cart were twofold: to enhance the customer experience and to increase cross-selling capabilities, thereby increasing average order dollar amount and revenues. hpshopping.com was one of the first online stores to implement this capability. The persistent shopping cart, also called a "sticky cart," was discussed in Chapter 5 and allows shoppers to view the items in their cart at all times and calculate taxes and shipping costs at any time. The sticky cart model simulates the retail experience with a viewable cart, but takes it a step further and provides the customer with a running total.

Situation Analysis

Research implied that customers abandon their shopping carts because of the surprise total or calculations of shipping and handling fees applied to an order at checkout. Also, the transaction process of adding an item to cart was frustrating for customers. Each time a customer clicked the "add-to-cart" button, she was brought to the "View Cart Details" page, which listed the items in the cart. If a shopper wanted to add another product, she had to go back and forth through this tedious process until shopping was complete.

This model works well for a single-item purchase. But, imagine what your retail shopping experience would be like having to go to the checkout counter each time you put an item into your shopping basket. It becomes tedious and time-consuming for multiple-item purchases online and discourages shoppers from further shopping.

With every order, hpshopping.com provides a "reply card" as a convenience for customers to mail back with comments, complaints, or opinions. Several customers used these reply cards to complain about this frustrating process.

Solution

hpshopping.com identified a solution to improve the add-to-cart process for customers. This functionality was added to the store's frame so a customer can always see the cart's contents and can calculate taxes and shipping charges, as shown in Figure 8-4. hpshopping.com remembers a returning shopper, and this implementation of the persistent cart keeps items in the shopper's cart for 30 days, also acting as a "wish list."

A persistent "sticky shopping cart" is an improved customer convenience. Online, each discovered improvement sets new customer expectations for other online stores. Other stores must also add this capability to stay in the running for a share of the customer's wallet.

Figure 8–4 The sticky shopping cart on hpshopping.com.

Success Measurements

Success was determined by the following four measurements:

- Decrease in the abandonment rate from the product detail page (PDP)
- Reduction in the number of complaints
- Shipping and taxes calculation feature usage rate
- Increase in the number of items per order (increase in the average dollar amount)

Adding the persistent cart functionality improved customer satisfaction with a multiple-product purchase. Also, the store received positive customer comments about the feature.

Enabling Comparison Shopping

The objective of this program was to help customers easily choose the right HP product from the complete category line-up.

Situation Analysis

Carrying a full line-up of printers provides customers with a broad range of products that can fit their specific needs. Having a large product assortment, however, can make it difficult for customers to clearly differentiate between products. Customers were sometimes frustrated by not being able to dynamically compare multiple products and understand in a quick snapshot the differences between them.

Customer call centers and reply cards conveyed customer frustrations with the lack of differentiation between similar product specs and descriptions, while price differences were wide.

Strategy/Solution

The goal was to allow customers to choose the products they want to compare and to structure the information in a way that highlights top features, but also clearly communicates the differences between them. Improving product descriptions also factored into this program.

Because content already resided in the hpshopping.com database, only light backend development was required, because the content could be pulled dynamically. Content improvement required the most work. Each feature was re-evaluated by the manufacturer's product category marketing groups for clear differentiation between similar products in a category line-up. Category and sub-category naming conventions were also re-evaluated and refined. A comparison tool was developed to display the products to compare selected by the customer, as shown in Figure 8-5.

This capability helps shoppers choose between seemingly similar products. It is designed to be part of an ongoing process for hpshopping.com, as products change within category line-ups.

Success Metrics

Success was determined by the following three measurements:

- Usage of features by users
- Conversion rates
- Customer satisfaction

While conversion rates are hard to measure and tie into the tool separately, customers did have a better process to narrow down choices and understand tradeoffs of product decisions. The site experiences a high usage rate for the comparison feature tool, and ongoing refinements are part of the store's process.

"My Printing Supplies Store" for Returning Customers

Some products are "routine or repeat purchases," meaning that customers shop for the same item more than once and often on a regular basis. The objective of the My Printing Supplies Store capability and program was to provide a more convenient shopping transaction model for returning customers shopping for HP printing supplies. This innovative approach creates a better-than-retail experience for printing supplies customers.

Situation Analysis

Printer owners purchase printing supplies products—such as inkjet and toner cartridges—routinely. When shopping at retail, a customer has to walk into the store, down the aisles, to the

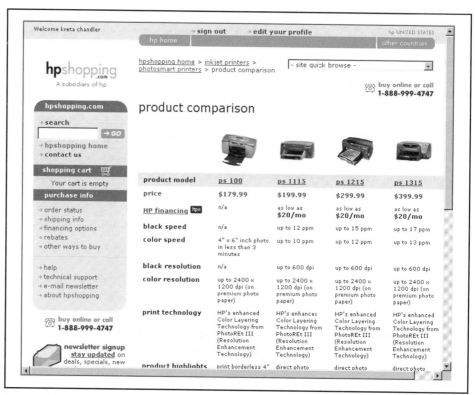

Figure 8–5 The comparison tool helps customers compare and choose the right product to meet their needs.

product, and then to the checkout counter. Online, the experience is similar. Each time customers purchased printing supplies on hpshopping.com, they started on the home page, navigated through the category aisles to the product page, went to "review cart" and then back to another product page (if ordering more than one supply, which is often the case), and then moved to the checkout. For customers shopping once a month for printing supplies, the process was tedious.

Solution

hpshopping.com recognized the need to improve customer convenience and used technology to design a new tool to shorten the purchase process for returning supplies customers. This new tool—My Printing Supplies Store, shown in Figure 8-6, allows quicker access to supplies products right from the home page for those customers who have previously registered for the tool. It personalizes a routine process for returning customers and enables faster checkouts.

Customers complete a simple and secure registration form to select up to 15 printer models for which they purchase supplies. When customers return at a later date to shop for more supplies, they click the "My Printing Supplies Store" button on the hpshopping.com home page and are delivered into a personalized store listing their printers.

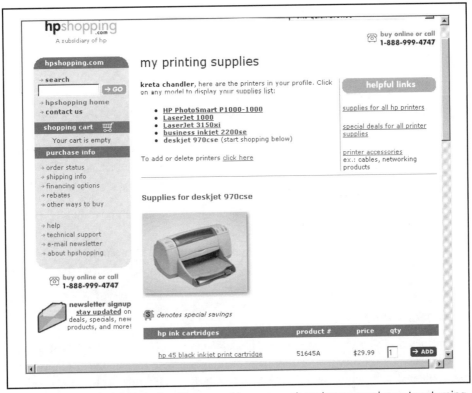

Figure 8–6 My Printing Supplies Store provides a new shopping convenience to returning printing supplies customers.

The customer then selects the printer needing supplies and sees all of the compatible supplies on the same page. In just one click, customers can add multiple supplies products for that printer to their cart. Because the store remembers payment details for registered customers, the customer confirms the security password and completes the transaction much faster than with the original method.

Success Metrics

Success was determined by the following two measurements:

- Customers registering with My Printing Supplies Store
- Return visits and usage of the store

hpshopping.com considered customer needs but also knowledge of the printing supplies category as one that is a "destination" category and one that is shopped frequently. Because of this, home page placement was given to this tool to allow quick and easy access.

Enhancing Search Capabilities

The objective of this program was to improve search results for customers entering text into the search box.

Situation Analysis

Most keyword search results are based on products or services for sale by an online retailer, but not necessarily designed to respond to how a customer shops.

hpshopping.com captures the top 100 search queries each week, which are then analyzed. Search metrics is a tool that hpshopping.com uses to improve customer satisfaction and increase sales. The review team found that many customers were entering search queries for obsolete printers and for "memory." After investigating, the group realized that shoppers were searching for obsolete product numbers and specific inquiries that returned either nothing or nearly 200 responses per query.

It was important to understand why customers might still need supplies for an obsolete printer and how they shopped for complex categories, such as memory. The search function needed to be updated and streamlined.

Strategy/Solution

For customers typing in obsolete printer models, the hpshopping.com team enabled successful search results by providing a landing page offering a link to the supplies page for that printer model queried. If the customer is looking for supplies, she clicks on the link and is delivered to a supplies page for that exact printer.

For customers typing in "memory," an interim landing page was created to provide customers with a basic categorization of the products. This landing page presented five links: memory for desktop computers, memory for notebook computers, memory for LaserJet printers, memory for handhelds/Jornadas, and memory for digital cameras.

Success Metrics

Success was determined by the following three measurements:

- Reduction in number of "no results" pages delivered in response to queries
- Increased printing supplies sales
- Increased customer satisfaction

These two simple solutions returned results pages to customers that were great improvements over the previous pages of "no results" and of "too many" results.

hpshopping.com continues analyzing the website for improvements to the customer experience.

Case Study 3: Designing a Website for a Wine Shop

Purchasing wine can be difficult. There are so many similar bottles to choose from—each about the same size and color—with only a label to tell them apart, as shown in Figure 8-7.

Figure 8–7 Selecting wine is difficult.

Photo by Kreta Chandler

This study takes you through the steps you might use to create a website for wine—short of the actual programming. The process is based on understanding the wine customer, determining the key attributes for the category, developing the hierarchy for selection, and identifying and integrating information services for the customer. This is the unique feature set that will be added to the basic structure of the website. These basics are addressed in Chapter 7.

The following actual case is based on a small wine shop in the U.S. The proprietor has a thriving retail business and wants to extend his reach through the Internet. His shop features a good variety of wines, an assortment of fine cheeses, and a selection of gift baskets.

His business has grown through personal connections with his clientele. He tries to learn each customer's preferences, offers them some wine education, and focuses on special orders.

The e-business challenge is to recreate this experience online. This example takes the knowledge of the business and designs an expert wine selection system.

Situation Analysis

The goal of this website is to extend the reach of an existing retail business. This is a typical application because each day new sites sprout up to support small businesses all over the world. This store will have special hurdles to overcome, however. The category it will sell is especially difficult—both from an educational and a selection perspective. In addition, the e-store will be limited to selling in certain geographical areas due to restrictive shipping regulations. The additional challenge will be to maintain the intimacy and close customer connections that the shop has built over the years.

Solution/Strategy

The solution develops a website that would create new services, build on educational capabilities, ease the selection process, and even improve it over the existing retail implementation. In order to accomplish these, we first had to understand the shop's current and potential customers, how they might shop on the web, and the roadblocks they might face when they select wine.

Understanding the Customer

Wine customers in the U.S. are a select group. Only an average of one bottle per month per capita is consumed—considerably less than other popular beverages. The consumption of wine in Western Europe is nearly twice that of the U.S.

This shop's typical wine consumer falls into two camps. The first is the astute buyer who purchases wine routinely and has some knowledge of this complex beverage. The second profile can be characterized as the novice. This is the customer who has a strong desire to learn about and enjoy wines, but who does not currently have the knowledge to select them independently without purchasing randomly.

Both groups value information and recommendations from the proprietor of the shop. Tutorials and basic education must be provided to the novice group, but both segments depend on the owner to sample a variety of wines and share his preferences. The two groups value personalized service equally, and the shop owner has invested in an individual buying process, developed a wine club, and invites his best customers to participate in wine tastings and other activities.

Obviously, he will have to forgo some of these personal promotions online. Those that require a physical presence, such as wine tasting, will have to be replaced by virtual activities. These may not be of equal value, but the site should compete well nonetheless with other wine dealers confronted with the same limitations.

Any replacement promotions will have to appeal to his customer demographic profile. This includes professionals, semi-professionals, educators, retirees, and business owners. His shop attracts an equal mix of men and women, but they tend to be over 35 years of age. While he has built relationships with his customers, he is not able to ask personal questions to determine further profiling, nor has he conducted any surveys.

Determining the Key Attributes for the Category

Wine is selected through a number of special attributes. Unless the customer is familiar with a particular label and vintage, he must either go through the selection process or seek a recommendation. The selection process is basically a process of elimination. It begins at the highest and broadest level to select among choices and narrows down the search through very specific criteria.

The selection choices for this wine shop include the following:

- Red, white, blush, sparkling, and fortified
- Variety (for example—cabernet sauvignon, merlot, zinfandel; chardonnay, sauvignon blanc; white zinfandel; champagne; port)
- The producer
- Foreign/domestic
- Region
- State/vintage/village (especially if it is a French wine)
- Sub-variety—Kosher, organic, dessert, vegetarian
- Price

While these are the basic attributes for selecting wine, there are other more subtle reasons for purchasing. Descriptions that help the customer understand more about the flavor of the wine help the decision process. In the wine category, these descriptions often have to be learned because they are somewhat dependent on jargon and imagination, but they still project images that help develop preference.

The e-tailer must depend on these descriptions even more than the traditional merchant. The customer may benefit by purchasing online because only about one in 20 or 30 bottles at the shelf may feature a printed description. The capability exists online for every bottle. Visualize the taste of this wine from the following description:

> Dark and rich, with intense flavors of blueberry, chocolate, mint, and black cherry. Firm tannins. Wonderful structure.

The wine merchant must guard against text, however, that may be a little too vivid for the average customer—especially the novice:

> Firm, with beef, spice, pepper, game, mineral, leather, and earth. Herbal dimensions linger on the finish.

The average buyer would not expect his beverage to taste of beef, pepper, leather, game, and earth. While the description serves to distinguish this bottle from the first, it still leaves the consumer wondering just what she might be purchasing. The wine connoisseur may know exactly what the critic is getting at, but the web is a vehicle accessed by all segments. Information shared on the Internet needs to be understood by a variety of customers. This site will benefit not only from a tutorial, but also from a list of standardized descriptors that provide simple, consistent terms.

The site can also share information about grape harvests for particular years and explain to the consumer why one year's wine may be preferable to another, given the climate conditions. A superior product may feature an award-winning vintage.

What else might the customer need to know about the product? Some wines are sold in splits or half bottles, while others are sold in a full bottle, so the purchaser should know the quantity of wine in the bottle. Some wine buyers also like to select by the label or the color or design of the bottle. A good, clear picture of the wine will help with the selection.

Developing the Hierarchy for Selection

The consumer now has quite a bit of information. Next, the e-tailer must organize that information with the most important data listed first. Products often have so many attributes that it's impossible to list them all. If that's the case, the hierarchy becomes even more critical because at some point, you must draw a line to eliminate less important material. That's why you must know the category as well as understand how the customer shops in that category.

Our wine website will be organized by the overall selection criteria but will be developed to allow more complex searches even as attributes are selected. For instance, if the consumer chooses to shop by selecting the producer, she will still want to pick the appropriate variety and vintage. The site must allow further selections to narrow the choice. This site will limit the first level of the hierarchy to four parameters.

Because the owner wants to feature U.S. wines, he will not need to set up a search by region or village. He has determined that the customer must be able to narrow the choice by the type of wine first (red, white, and so forth), then the producer, the variety, and finally the vintage. The second tier hierarchy will include the state of the producer/harvest, the price, and other variety types that are available (dessert, for instance).

If it is unclear how the consumer prefers to select products in a category, customer research is in order. Guessing their preferences may lead to confusion or customer dissatisfaction. But fully loading the website with all capabilities and then narrowing based on real-time customer input at the site is always an option. If the customer selects all wines, then the database should display all products. Shoppers should never receive messages that limit their choices or inform them that their selections were too broad and, therefore, could not be displayed.

Integrating Customer Services

There is an opportunity to serve your customer on the web in ways that are often difficult at retail. This wine site can offer menu suggestions and detail appropriate wine selections for certain meals. It can even present recipes and describe how to cook with wine. While some information may be distributed in a retail shop, it's much more difficult to find a central location for brochure placement that will be noticed by the customer. It's even more difficult to obtain personal attention, especially if the store is large.

We'll also include a newsletter on our site that features a "wine of the month." An invitation to a wine club sponsored by the shop will include special selections not normally offered at the store.

A section for frequently asked questions will be established to answer common queries about wine. Because the shop has been in business for a few years, the proprietor has collected questions to insert in this section. The buyer may also have questions unrelated to the product. A separate button will be provided to assist the customer with the order and other non-product issues.

Shipping regulations may create a major issue for the shop and for many consumers. Not all states allow the direct shipment of wine from the e-tailer to the consumer. The website needs to notify potential customers up front if their state prohibits shipments of wine. Some states also have interstate shipping and taxation requirements. For the most part, e-tail wine shops must work within a state that allows shipment of the wine in the state. A section for shipping information, including addressing concerns about legal requirements, costs, climate issues, fragility, and shipping instructions, will be designed to be interactive to accommodate specific customer needs.

Another feature on this website is a personalized and customized selection capability. The site will offer a questionnaire that asks about the customer's preferences. Then, based on the responses, it will help the shopper choose the appropriate wine based on the parameters selected. A memory function will store the preferences and selections for the next visit, if desired.

The ordering process will have interactive capabilities as well, and the store will hire someone to answer real-time questions online during business hours. Clicking on the wine selections will store the customer's order until ready for checkout. The total order is always available for review, but the customer will not have to enter the ordering process more than once.

After the process is completed, the e-store will offer the customer a variety of cheeses specially selected to accompany the chosen wines. The consumer will also have another opportunity to request additional information on any of the wines in the shop. After the shopper completes the order, the shipping and handling will be automatically added, relieving the customer of this chore. The site will confirm that all requested items are in stock, and the consumer will be assigned an order number along with an estimated delivery date.

Within two hours of order completion, a personalized "thank-you for your order" e-mail will confirm that the shop has received and processed the paperwork. When the order is sent, instructions for returning products or for claiming damage will be included in the box.

The home page should always have the name of the company, a contact name, the phone number (preferably a toll-free number), a street address, and an e-mail address. In this case, we will include a picture of the actual physical store to reassure the customer of the legitimacy of the business. Because the store is friendly and inviting, it also serves to personalize the transaction.

Now our shopkeeper is ready to conduct business online. He must remember to promote his site, or it will languish in the vastness of the Internet. Informing his current customers of his website will start the ball rolling. If he has the funding, he can purchase an ad on one of the other wine websites or in one of the popular wine journals.

Creating a specialized site is a process of asking questions to ensure that all possible opportunities are considered. By understanding the product category and the customer's needs, desires, and dislikes, you will be able to achieve the first step to integrating the customer into your sales process.

Success Metrics

- Provide the customer with the same products and service that he would receive if he had personally visited the store.
- Create an opportunity for the customer to receive expert advice and wine education to help the customer learn more about wines and to ultimately build potential customers.
- Develop sales on the web through honesty and trust.

Case Study 4—Back to Business Basics—Designing for Internal Information "Customers"

This case study describes the process and methodologies of developing an intranet website for internal "consumers" of information. The website's purpose was to improve timely distribution of core product information to worldwide marketing centers based on their needs and usage.

Situation Analysis

A global manufacturer launches many new products each year. Core tools and marketing information—data sheets, product photos, packaging specs, usage information, government regulatory information, etc.—are critical for worldwide marketing centers to launch new products and conduct day-to-day business with resellers and customers. The manufacturer's individual product lines created the information and delivered it to the marketing centers, who integrated the information into a product portfolio for the countries in their region.

Worldwide marketing centers received information from several product lines through multiple vehicles. The marketing centers, such as Europe and Latin America, used the core information to create an assortment of customer-focused and reseller-focused brochures, presentations, product advertisements, and other collateral that helped sell the products. The collateral—country- or region-specific—required translating into many local languages and required long lead times for development.

Core tools came from a wide range of internal and external sources. Different product lines created core information using different formats and product launch information sets. Some provided color and monochrome photos and other artwork, while others did not. Digital imaging was an emerging technology and not yet common. Each product line used its own document templates to create data sheets, resulting in missing, conflicting, inconsistent, or confusing information. Many creators of the original documents did not know how the information would be used in the regions.

Creation of core tools was a manual process and so was physical distribution. Once developed, these core tools were sent to various individuals in the marketing centers using a variety of methods: public mail, e-mail, telephone, fax, computer networks and shared drives, and CD-ROMs. There was no good way to easily replicate and make copies available to others. A great deal of duplication and replication was required to ensure that the regions had appropriate information.

After the regional marketing centers received the core tools, they needed to re-send the information to agencies to create language-specific marketing materials. Other departments also needed the information so they could begin communicating with the reseller accounts.

When the sales force did not have the "right" information, they tried proactively to track down individuals throughout the U.S. to seek answers to their questions. Sales reps were spending more than 30 percent of their time hunting for photos or other pieces of information for their reseller accounts. This means they were not selling 30 percent of the time.

Because of the inconsistent processes, the many product lines, and manual creation and distribution of physical documents, the marketing centers often received the core tools close to or even after a new product launch had taken place. When they did receive the materials, it would take a minimum of one to three months to translate and create country-specific marketing materials. These materials were then distributed to the resellers, who then often created their own ads and communications to promote the products to customers.

Searching for information takes time out from selling products in a region. It is critical for this core product information to be communicated, because it is the trigger for the channel readiness for all product launch activities. Delayed product images prevented new products from being in marketing materials and in reseller-developed catalogs that require several months of lead times.

The serial distribution of information was also an inhibitor. From the factory, the core tools went to the marketing centers, who applied resources and resent the information to agencies and others. Those materials were then sent to the resellers who also had to apply resources and develop ads and signage promoting the products. Finally, consumers would be recipients of this information, well after the product had launched. And sometimes, information and tools never made it down through all the layers.

Strategy/Solution

A program was developed with three primary goals:

- Create the infrastructure (system, vehicle, and processes) through which to deliver consistent brand messaging and timely, accurate marketing information simultaneously to a worldwide target audience.
- Provide critical, relevant content in a format that minimizes rework and attains global leverage.
- Reduce complexity and costs associated with creation, distribution, and maintenance of marketing information.

This "business basics" program sought to improve accessibility, consistency, reliability, and timeliness of product information consumed by internal business partners. Efficiency and specific process improvements were expected that would ultimately save resources in time, people, and dollars. A design goal was to allow direct and random access by all key customers simultaneously, thereby collapsing the traditional distribution layers.

The project was organized into three distinct phases:

- Assessment: Clear determination of the scope and nature of the customer needs that the design and implementation phase should address
- Design and implementation: Designing, implementing, and testing solutions that achieve the objectives set in the first phase
- Maintenance: Installing processes for day-to-day operation that maintain continuous improvements with respect to the accuracy, consistency, and timeliness of program goals

Two critical success factors were technology (system architectures and user interfaces) and information management (flow and content). The web was an emerging capability, and digital information was not yet widely adopted. Program success depended on how well the factors were understood and integrated.

The Contextual Inquiry

The assessment phase—the contextual inquiry—was to build a complete model of information customers: What information did they need, why did they need it, what form did they need it in, when did they need it, and what did they do with it when they did get it.

It also assessed processes and how information flowed to them and from them. This body of customer knowledge was captured and analyzed. Then a recommendation and plan for implementation were developed.

The contextual inquiry consisted of conducting customer visits and building customer and information flow models. Customer visits were conducted with worldwide marketing centers.

Interviews were conducted with key information consumers: country managers, marketing communication managers, product marketing managers, channel managers, and advertising agencies used by them. The purpose of the face-to-face visits was to gather, model, and understand customer needs for information. The interviews asked a consistent set of questions. Information was collected about the types of information used, how it got to them, and what they did with it. An understanding of the individual's role in the organization and how work flowed in general was gained.

Interview questions alone do not give sufficient information to understand what the "real" customer needs are. For example, when asked what his informational needs were, one product manager said his primary need was to have factory organization charts. After probing on what he did with the charts, he said he would have a list of people and contacts to call to get the data sheets and photos. Assessing this, his "real" need was not the organization charts, but the data sheets and photos.

Customers were also asked to "show" how they used a core tool and to provide the sequence of steps. For example, would they get the data sheet in their inbox, then pick it up and take it to the copy machine, and fax it to the reseller to ensure that they were providing timely information. In that case, the data sheet had an internal company project name and was not necessarily reseller-appropriate. The need that came out of that was the need to produce the materials up front in a reseller-appropriate format. This would minimize rework.

After the interviews, the customer data from all marketing centers was consolidated and modeled, as shown in Figure 8-8.

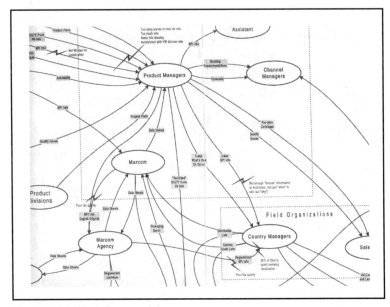

Figure 8–8 Work flow model.

The model showed needs, information flows, relationships, and sequences. The circles in the model were people, and the arrows and lines showed the direction of information flow. The lightning breaks in the lines were problem areas. Starting with the middle and working outward, the middle was the most important—those areas that had clusters of breaks were ones that needed fixing first. Customer model analysis mapped out information flow and content issues. As a result, an information engineering model and prototype for an intranet website and content were developed to resolve these issues.

Key findings and immediate needs were identified and an information engineering solution was recommended. Based on the customer information needs, these goals were set:

- Develop consistent product templates across all product lines that had the information required by the regions; ensure data integrity, and consider global needs.
- Migrate to electronic files for all materials, including photos and other artwork (print on demand).
- Develop a centralized information repository on which it is easy to find and retrieve files—enable "one-stop shopping" and "information-on-demand" 24/7.
- Develop, document, post, and maintain launch schedules.
- Develop notification processes to alert users of website changes.
- Provide for quick, simultaneous, and replicating update process.
- Maintain the website—add information, delete information.

The website was designed based on how the internal customers used the information. The long-term vision was to move beyond a one-size-fits-all repository model. The evolution aligned specific content to individual user tasks and jobs, optimized information delivery in form, timing, and content, and synchronized the worldwide system architectures. Worldwide marketing centers added localized content into the system.

Success Metrics

The following measurements determined program success:

- Usage metrics
- Improved information flow
- Reduced time to product launch implementation in regions
- Customer feedback

After the website launched, all marketing center team members used it as their number one source of reliable, consistent information. Usage grew as other content was phased in. Care was taken in the design to populate the intranet with only the files that were necessary. Too much information can get in the way of the customer's task.

The new model allowed for simultaneous distribution of electronic core information to all worldwide marketing centers and to their advertising agencies. This change shortened the marketing materials development cycle by one to three months, which led to a quicker engagement into the marketplace and produced earlier sales.

Many field sales reps commented on the time they could now devote to selling versus hunting. In one case, a sales rep met a tight deadline of getting the new information off the website and to the business customer and won a $100,000 deal. This was because the right information was in the right place at the right time.

A customer-centered design approach was applied throughout this program, which led to its continued success.

The above case studies are examples of how the information in this book was used to create a superior customer shopping experience. This book offers a menu of principles, methodologies, and proven techniques that can be applied or combined with others.

CHAPTER 9

The Future: The Not
So Final Frontier

With the plethora of changes in the marketplace in the past 10 years, what will the future hold? If you assume all revolutionary changes will be on the Internet only, you may be surprised.

It seems that retailing transformed slowly over the past 30 years, but it actually changed quite dramatically. The thought of selling TV sets or prepared foods in grocery stores would have raised eyebrows not that long ago. Electronic kiosks, self-scanners, and a variety of electronic product demonstrations in the store have not only changed the appearance of the store, but also the way it functions.

The fashion industry sports stores with waterfalls and live music for ambience, as well as changes in how the customer accesses merchandise. Many stores have removed fashion jewelry from protective glass counters and now allow customers to touch and feel the merchandise without the need for assistance. Similar changes to cosmetics counters are now underway.

Specialty "big-box" stores have proliferated the landscape. Everything from pet supplies to computer products and home-improvement goods are now sold in stores that focus on particular categories. These stores are usually large warehouse-type stores and are located outside mall settings. A phenomenon of the 1990s, these stores secured prime real estate throughout the U.S. Will the trend last or will one-stop shopping prevail?

Hypermarkets in Europe replaced small, individual stores. These retailers, in contrast to the big-box format, offer everything you need under one roof. They are usually anchored by a large retailer-grocery chain and flanked by individual service and product-related stores.

Grocery in the U.S. has consolidated and now features a wide array of restaurant-type facilities in addition to specialty coffee shops, gourmet bakeries, and wine cellars. Grocers have experimented with multi-media and entertainment formats as well.

Malls are anchored by amusement parks and skating rinks. It wasn't that long ago when the first covered mall made its debut. Now, multi-storied structures feature movie theaters, extensive food courts, and other entertainment delights. In one visit to the mall, you can have your eyes examined and purchase a pair of glasses, have your shoes repaired, select a pet, purchase your vitamins, buy your furniture, appliances, and clothing, and choose a diamond ring. There are exercise groups that conduct "mall walks," entertainment troupes that perform on makeshift stages, and auto and art displays.

Catalogs are not immune to the changes. Specialty catalogs have proliferated featuring a wide variety of high-end, quality merchandise. Items are so diverse that it appears there is a gadget, product, or solution for virtually every need. Some catalogs just specialize in wide shoes. Others sell nothing but uniforms. Whatever they sell, they are selling more of their products than ever before.

So what has happened to the Internet? Its boom was more about start-up companies than actually selling to its customers. Others misused the medium by taking advantage of unsuspecting customers who could neither see nor talk to the firms. Unfortunately, they couldn't check them out to make sure they were reputable either. But it has re-emerged to fill a variety of shopping voids.

The Re-emergence of E-commerce

Today, the web is re-establishing itself. Reliable retailers have jumped into the fray, and others have been forced to validate their reputations. While some customers are a bit gun-shy—especially due to security issues—most have renewed their interest, although somewhat selectively.

But what's the future? Although the changes at retail have been dramatic when compared with the past, they are no longer considered leading edge. What will the store of the future hold? And what part will the Internet play?

Seize the Future

Will you be prepared for the future? Before you can get ready, you'll need to anticipate what it will be like. We asked a few industry leaders and experts in their field to tell us what they thought the future would hold in five to ten years. How will it be different or how will it be more of the same? These leaders have come from different disciplines and have provided varying viewpoints relating to people, retailing, online selling, research, marketing, and distribution.

The following experts share their visions:

• Pradeep Jotwani is an executive of Hewlett-Packard Company. Since joining HP in 1982, Mr. Jotwani has held a series of positions in the U.S. and Europe with the printing and PC businesses. Most recently, he was a member of HP's executive council and president of HP's Consumer Business Organization, where he led worldwide strategic direction and overall operations.

- Jakob Nielsen, Ph.D., is a user advocate and principal of the Nielsen Norman Group, which he co-founded with Dr. Donald A. Norman (former VP of research at Apple Computer). Until 1998, he was a Sun Microsystems Distinguished Engineer. Dr. Nielsen is a noted international speaker and has been called "the guru of web page usability" by the *New York Times* and "the world's leading expert on Web usability" by *U.S. News & World Report*. Dr. Neilsen is the author of several top-selling international books on usability.

- Paco Underhill, is the founder and Managing Director of Envirosell, a behavioral market research and consulting company specializing in shopping behavior. Mr. Underhill is also the author of the international best-selling book, *Why We Buy: The Science of Shopping*, which has been published in 15 international editions. He is a frequent speaker for trade associations and professional groups around the world.

- Bruce Martin, President of 4sure.com—an Office Depot Company, is a pioneer and founder of one of the first e-commerce websites that services both business-to-consumer and business-to-business customers. A key strength of the company has been its focus on the customer and the customer's experience with every point of contact with the company. In 2001, 4sure.com became an Office Depot Company and is one of the Internet's e-commerce success stories.

- Susan Boyce is Chief Marketing Manager for hpshopping.com, Hewlett-Packard's award-winning consumer shopping site. She manages all sales and merchandising demand generation and customer experience activities for the website. In 2001, hpshopping.com was named "best computer retailer" by the Web Marketing Association, an honor attributed to its intense focus on building positive customer relationships.

- Judith Herman received her MBA from Columbia University and was a research associate at the Graduate Faculty, City University of New York. Her early career developed working under two pioneers in the field of market research, Bill Simmons, founder of Simmons Market Research Bureau, and Ernest Dichter, founder of the Institute for Motivational Research. She is the founder and owner of Information & Strategy, a marketing research company. Her years of experience with large consumer companies, including Oracle, IBM, Cirrus Logic, Levi Strauss, and General Foods, has provided her with a wide range of expertise in research design.

- Phil Lauria is CEO of Prism Retail Services, a pioneer of retail merchandising services. He held senior management positions at Kraft General Foods and founded LCA, a strategic retail sales and marketing consulting practice. He has worked with some of the world's leading consumer packaged goods and technology companies. He is active in several trade organizations and spends a significant amount of time in the field supporting Prism's clients in developing their retail marketing and sales strategy.

- Ron Wilbur is the founder and CEO of Luminor, a strategic brand marketing firm. He has lectured and conducted seminars on marketing metrics throughout the U.S. He was also an early adopter of electronic marketing, starting a Luminor consulting practice in online marketing in 1992, a web consulting practice in 1994, and developing one of the first communities on the web in 1995. He created a vertical portal for clients in one industry in 1996 that is still on the web and still profitable.

These viewpoints provide a diversity of direction and represent the limitless possibilities of the future of the Internet, the consumer, and online shopping.

The Connected Consumer—Pradeep Jotwani

We are entering a world where "convergence" has come to mean many things. Analog is converging with digital. Consumer IT and consumer electronics are converging. Technologies are converging—media and communications, imaging and audio, and wireless and so on.

At HP, we believe the trend is much larger than simply convergence of existing technologies. We believe there is a fundamental shift in computing architecture that will leave a lasting impact on consumers and how they use technology.

This new computing architecture is characterized by billions of consumer devices—everything from today's PCs and handhelds to future devices in our labs today—that are intelligent and connected.

They will be connected to one another and to an always-on, always available web via wired line or wireless broadband. And thus, these devices will be capable of accessing services, information, or rich media content over an always-on Internet infrastructure virtually anywhere, anytime.

With this transformation will enter the true mobility era—PDAs and instant messaging, always on, everywhere, end to end. People will be multi-tasking to the extreme, sending ideas to a partner halfway around the world while they eat dinner in an airport or wait at a stoplight.

We are beginning to see space itself be alive and wired—smart rooms, smart roads, smart elevators, smart chairs. High intelligence, or just enough intelligence to make life easier for us, will be dispersed into smart space.

In short, we will shift from being a computer-centric world to a web-centric world. This will be a world where the walls between the physical and digital worlds fall down, to enable delivery of what you need. . .based on where you are and what you want.

While the possibilities in this new world are mind-boggling, we do not believe this technological transformation will change what people do. Rather, it will transform how they do everyday things.

People will continue to do the things they do today—things like take photos, play games, manage their lives, watch TV and listen to music, and stay connected by communicating with family and friends. But, in a digitally enabled world, photography becomes digital. TV becomes interactive. Managing your life becomes electronic versus paper-based, and so on, giving consumers choice, control, and convenience.

This digital transformation will force companies of all sizes to take a fresh look at their existing businesses. At HP, for example, this transformation has prompted us to look at our mainstay printing business in a whole new way.

In a world where all devices are intelligent and connected, printers are no longer peripheral devices tethered to PCs. Printers become web-connected print stations, conveniently located at your local coffee shop or on the road at hotels and airports.

And, in a world where content is available virtually anywhere through wireless broadband, these web-connected print stations are capable of printing most any content, anytime.

We are working with Nokia on mobile printing solutions that will give you the power of printing most any documents from a cell phone. Using solutions based on industry standards, you will be able to send the URL of a document to a web-enabled HP printer. The printer then retrieves the file and prints it.

In this future world, technology will not be the challenge. Rather, the challenge will be how we connect technology to consumer desire. Consumers are squarely at the heart. They will no longer work the technology. Technology will need to work for them.

The fact is, even today, lots of technology products are being created in this new space simply because we can—not because they meet consumer needs. But just because we can make it doesn't mean that consumers will buy it.

For example, Internet and email stations that were merely repackaged PCs with less functionality but at the same price as PCs are gone for the most part. We've also seen odd combinations including digital cameras with an integrated MP3 player—perhaps interesting that you can converge these technologies into a single device, but it does not meet the litmus test of what consumers want and need.

We've also had our share of successes. PDAs have taken off, combining computing, communication, and entertainment capabilities into a single device that fits in your pocket. The convergence of printing, scanning, copying, and faxing into all-in-one devices also has been a proven winner among consumers. These devices have hit the sweet spot of consumer desire. Connectivity is shown in Figure 9-1.

This new world will transform how consumers think and how they live, how they imagine and how they relate, how they work and how they play, how they buy… and ultimately how we invent.

Our task, as an industry, is to understand that trends like these will drive our next wave of growth. Our industry, which traditionally has been centered on the PC, will be driven by new and different forces in the future. It will be driven by new applications and services that enable people to do everyday things in ways that are better, faster, and more enriching.

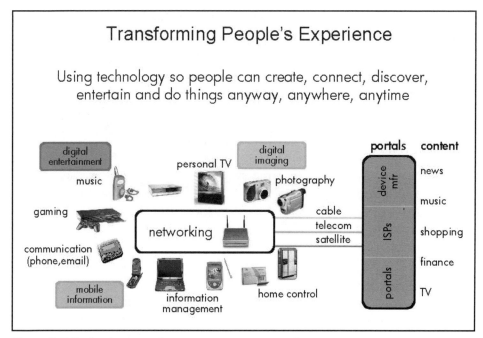

Figure 9–1 Technology—and consumers—are converging.

Bullish on the Future of E-commerce—Dr. Jakob Nielsen

E-commerce sites can do so much better than they do today if only they will design more for the special characteristics of the online medium. That's the main reason I am bullish on the future of e-commerce.

The potential of new technology is great. And the number of Internet users world-wide is expected to double from about half a billion in 2002 to a full billion in a fairly small number of years. Yes, both of these changes will happen, and they will both add substantially to e-commerce sales.

There is an incredibly strong trend on the web toward globalization. The majority of users are outside the U.S., with Asia growing at a fast rate. International usability is worse than in the U.S. We always find even greater usability problems when we study the effectiveness of North American designs in Asia, Latin America, and Southern Europe. Thus, sales in these regions could increase more if the sites sufficiently emphasized international usability.

I am a firm believer in the potential of e-commerce. Anything that can be sold by mail order can be sold better on the web, where you can provide much better information than is possible in a print catalog. Multimedia, if used correctly, can add a dimension that we will never get in print.

Assuming a decent product, e-commerce can work and be profitable if sites follow two basic principles: control expenses and improve usability so that fewer users are turned away.

The Urbanization of the Internet—Paco Underhill

The Internet is local not global. It's like water—it goes where it's needed. People in Kansas and New York have very different shopping needs and priorities. The Internet needs to perform more like Mom and Pop enterprises. They have different time equations and different delivery systems.

The future of the web— as with every other piece of technology—must include adoption by women. Women see it as a tool with an end. And shopping is inherently a female activity. There must be efficiency to it and a quality of life. As women's lives change, so does their relationship to shopping. Now with the same business responsibilities as their male counterparts, they find they must cram routine shopping between the job and the commute home. Women still enjoy shopping with friends and continue to shop as a social activity.

But women have increasing demands of the shopping environment—more than men. Men want to get what they need and leave quickly. If women don't feel comfortable, they won't stay and shop, no matter which type of store they're in. The Internet must fit the evolution of people's needs.

Retail, in all its forms, follows housing. We are on the edge of major cultural decisions regarding housing. We're also in the midst of a transition—especially with aging baby boomers—to determine our housing choices to spend the next one third of our lives. Again, it needs to be decided on a local basis—what we buy and how we buy it. London and Boise have very different housing choices. As people age, they will need convenience even more, and online shopping will increase in importance. And don't forget that the next group of seniors will be Internet-fluent—that will transform how retailers and manufacturers conduct business.

The future will continue to see consolidation. American entrepreneurial growth will be in businesses of less than 100 people. The science of shopping is a hybrid discipline, and it's transitory. It's part science and part art. Shopping behavior and even the store itself will continue to evolve. Shopping follows social change, and the shopkeeper must pay attention. Even a minor change can bring major improvements. The most successful stores will be the ones that best adapt to their environment.

Keeping Step with the Customer—Susan Boyce

Customer expectations and standards keep evolving and rising. New possibilities open up in a web-centric world for transforming daily life. Successful consumer companies understand that the only way to push the frontier is to continually refresh insight into what customers really want and need.

Connecting technology with customer desire requires substantial investment in customer and business intelligence. The stakes are high. It is very easy for customers to leave any given site and go to another. There are few switching costs or barriers. Comparative information across sites is often free and readily available. One of the key competitive advantages is how well you know your customer and how well you transform that understanding into a better customer experience for the customer. This means using information to create an environment and relationship with the customer that the customer wants to maintain. It means the basis for competition becomes much more focused on the total customer experience rather than products alone.

At hpshopping.com, we look for ways to open a two-way dialog with the customer and understand customer expectations at every interaction point throughout the lifecycle. Specific examples include usability studies, observational data tracking, click stream analysis, surveys at various points in the lifecycle, contact center activities and analysis, email and chat, etc. We close the loop with HP product teams by tracking and providing customer feedback on HP solutions to feed continuous improvement. We invest in systems to manage customer information and provide intelligence to drive real-time business decisions and relevancy for the customer. We establish goals and metrics for improving customer satisfaction and set the bar high.

Discussion about customer intelligence inevitably raises questions of privacy and security, areas not yet fully addressed through the adoption of common policies and safeguards in the online industry. It is not comfortable for many consumers to have information on their browsing behavior or past purchase behavior tracked and sometimes shared in co-marketing relationships, even if the benefit is more personalization of merchandising or promotional offers. At hpshopping.com, the customer defines the depth and nature of the marketing relationship. We disclose our policies and practices visibly on the site. Choice and control rests with the customer. It is a business imperative for hpshopping.com that customers know and trust that they are in a safe shopping environment.

The importance of customer intelligence and ongoing dialog is not a new concept. Catalog companies have typically been among the more successful companies as online resellers in part due to their understanding the power of customer retention, lifetime value, and customer knowledge management. Demands on customer intelligence will change as technology products and services continue to transform daily life, as lines between work and home blur, and as customer use evolves. More types of information across more touch points will need to be integrated and managed over time in order to deliver the intended customer experience.

Keeping up with the customer is not a one-time event. Today's issues become tomorrow's expectations and a new set of challenges forms. The key is ensuring an ongoing process for dialog to keep a strong pulse on the evolution of customer expectations. It is also driving that insight into business decisions.

The first wave of online selling was generally characterized by focus on scaleable systems, customer acquisition, and product selection. The holiday season of 2001 was centered on fulfillment execution and promotions. The future is about ensuring relevance and convenience to the customer throughout the lifecycle of their use of products and services.

The Duality of the Online Merchant—Bruce Martin

E-commerce on the web is entering toddler-hood. Many of the weaker and poorly built websites have gone away. More rationality has been built into business models because you actually have to make money at this. It will look so much different in five years. People will have more choices, and the online merchant must continue to play a dual role. He must meet customer needs and expectations and have a business model that keeps him in business.

The first most interesting dynamic that has emerged since the inception of online shopping is realizing that a customer buys in many different ways. The same customer might buy online, sometimes via catalog, sometimes in a store, and sometimes via phone. These unconscious shopping behaviors make them essentially multi-channel shoppers. Yet they don't necessarily think of themselves that way yet. They're just doing what they need to do, when they need to do it, and how they want to do it.

Where customers shop depends on what they need, what they need it for, and how soon they need it. It also depends on whether it is a planned purchase or an impulsive one. They might go to an Office Depot store on a Saturday afternoon and purchase file folders to complete a home filing project. Or they might browse catalogs on a Sunday morning and see something interesting. They can pick up the phone and call or go online and look a little deeper. In this new dynamic of merging online businesses and website integrations, we have to focus on integrating with the customers and where they want to shop.

Are online shoppers in the future going to shop in malls or in department stores? You can have a bunch of boutiques in a mall concept, or you can have one big store with general merchandise in a department store format. The boutique offers specialized products and knowledge. The department store model offers a broader product mix but more general knowledge. I would like the future to go in the direction where people shop in places that have the answers.

I recently bought online a set of custom-sized golf clubs for my seven-year-old daughter. I hadn't intended to purchase when I started researching them. Yet, the online experience was not only easy, it was also personalized to my daughter's specific needs. The store asked the child's height, weight, gender, and number of inches from the wrist to the ground. It then offered to build a golf club set that was perfectly sized to my daughter. The customer experience is the key to success. You earn customers when they find something that works.

The second most interesting dynamic is on the distribution side. The major challenges are with integrating all vendors—the manufacturers who provide products. It would be nice to think that the future will resolve all of these challenges, but the realities are that there are lots of them.

Just as important is integrating with services that fulfill the other half of customers' expectations. This is not as easy as it appears. There are hundreds of manufacturers supplying thousands of products in hundreds of different categories through several different suppliers. This complicates matters. There is not a common infrastructure that allows for integration of supply chain efficiencies.

There are two fulfillment pieces to the integration scheme. There are the systems, and there are different companies. This requires the independent online merchant to go to hundreds of different vendors to bring it all together. Whatever infrastructure exists, it must be transparent to the customer.

As a customer convenience, our company recently launched a voice solution for tracking orders. The customer can now call 24/7 on a toll-free number and have an interactive voice experience that helps them. It pulls digital information and converts it into an audio voice and verbally communicates the status of the package delivery to the customer. It picks up on all the files electronically from the UPS website and transfers it. It's actually a better experience than talking to a real person.

The online merchant of the future must continue to meet the needs of the customer while at the same time work in a multi-vendor environment with many manufacturers. The future will emphasize a tighter integration with all customers. Customers will do research and shop were it is most convenient to them, and our job is to anticipate their needs and make it easy. E-commerce must move in a direction that best suits the customer.

Research of the Future—Judith Herman

The future of research online is questionable. Research is dependent on what you're using it for and the quality of your list. Online focus groups are not really focus groups—which are small groups of people interacting with each other. In a true research setting, the participants often all talk at once, and they can hear each other. There are group dynamics. Online, the experience is very different. A researcher asks questions, and each participant replies separately. They are basically online questionnaires. A chat could be valuable, but a chat is still not a focus group.

Spam mailings are really poor research. You must wonder about the people who reply. Because most people don't like to be spammed, you're better off talking to people on the phone or sending a brief questionnaire to a qualified list.

In the future, voice capability for online research could be valuable. Unfortunately, the trend today is to make the consumer do all the work. Research conducted on the Internet today just requires respondents to fill out forms. But the future could provide the voice of the interviewer along with interactive video—so you can actually see her talking to you.

The Internet today is too complicated. If it is to grow, we have to figure out a way to get things sold to ordinary people and have a real shopping experience. There's a pleasure in shopping, and the Internet has to replicate that pleasure with a different kind of pleasure—audio, for example, or receiving a gift.

Take, for instance, a store like Macy's. If I clicked on "Macy's" and "blouses," someone would ask me what kind of blouse I wanted—and offer cotton or silk. First, they would show me a cotton blouse and how it looks on a model, then a flat 3-D shot so I could see the details. These would show up in very large displays—not just a tiny picture or banner ads. The last step in the process is the order. The store needs to make it easy for you to look and shop and not try to force you into the order process before you've had a chance to see the blouses without banner ads. Online shopping will grow if companies make it respondent friendly—not cheaper for the client so the respondent can do all the work.

Almost every focus group we conduct brings up the issue of service. We can hardly get to a discussion about the product because everyone wants to talk about service. Consumers seem to care less about new products than about service. Service is the most critical issue facing retailers today.

Future retailing needs to be more interesting and more fun. Providing everyday products at lower prices won't do it anymore. They must entertain—host a fashion show or a party and customers will buy while they're having fun. Shopping online can't be as much fun as shopping in person but it can be much more entertaining in the future. The entire environment needs to be more attractive.

The Dynamic Retail Future—Phil Lauria

The retail environment today is more dynamic than it's ever been. It's driven by store formats that emerged in the past 10 to 15 years but also by the consolidation of retailers. There has been a great deal of channel blurring. The differences among a club store, a grocery store, and a mass merchant are less clear in the mind of the consumer than ever before. There's a reasonable sense of overlap on a day-to-day basis because there is product overlap.

Initially, a club store like Costco had a limited number of SKUs. Today, there are lots of offerings including custom mattresses, diamond rings, high-end faucets, and an entire array of top-end merchandise. But they're slicing meat as well. They are playing a role today that they didn't envision when they first went to market.

The customer has to have a decision tree that starts back at home. They have to ask the question, "Where do I need to go to get what I want to get?" Store formats are becoming a challenge for the retailer to define. So they continue to generate interest in the store beyond the ability to service customers.

Because so many chains have consolidated, consumers see the same stores and formats when they go on vacation as they do at home. The stores are identical with the exception of some local additions. And across the parking lot is a competitor.

Consumers are defining where they are going to go and shop. People don't think of buying toothpaste in drug stores anymore. They purchase it wherever they do the rest of their shopping, whether that is at a mass merchant, a club store, or a grocery outlet. How they shop a particular store will be very different, depending on the products and needs set. Everyone is competing on every-day low price, and it's just not going to be enough anymore. There needs to be excitement in the store, but mostly there must be a buying experience.

People are less aware of new products now until they're actually in the store. It's incumbent on retailers to merchandise them well and provide seasonal needs. They need to make electronic information available so anyone can educate himself or herself on a particular category. Kiosks, samples, and demos will add to the interest in the store.

You'll also see the number of items in any particular category explode. Every category is segmenting. There's motor oil for cars that have more than 75,000 miles on them and senior pet food for animals over seven years old. The amount of SKUs that have to be merchandised is greater than ever. When people look for products, they need to be able to find them.

The web is an information tool. The category and price points will determine the amount of involvement. Some products require going back to retail to see and touch. In this case, the web will serve as an educational component. The consumer may even conduct shopping research online, go to the store to verify the color, and go back online to purchase.

Manufacturer websites really must provide up-to-date information to the home. The speed of connections, improved search engines, and common footprints are helping. Billboards are a problem. If you want to check out the boat category, for instance, you don't want to be inundated with ads for boat insurance, leak proof roofs, and sonar devices. You just want to find out about the boat.

Contrary to what people think, most people like going to stores. Parking lots are packed from Friday to Sunday. But if there's not enough inventory, no store associates are available to help, or the lines are too long, customers will leave and go home to turn on the computer. In 10 years, we won't recognize store formats. A 15-year-old today is influential, and future buyers— 13- to 17-year-olds—are already forming opinions about brands, services, and products they like and how they like to get them. They want stores that deliver high-end value with immediate gratification. Teens think that a grocery store is interesting only on the perimeter—that the center of the store is really boring. The peripheral area is where they're intrigued and are likely to spend their disposable dollars.

Today, people are less price-sensitive. They're unlikely to drive an extra two miles to save 19 cents on a cantaloupe. We're also moving to the European model—the boutique model—of shopping. Customers will shop more frequently for higher-quality products. They are also less likely to fill their carts to the brim on a weekly shopping trip. Young people certainly won't shop that way. They want stores to be cleaner and crisper with more valued added and information easily accessible from interactive kiosks.

To make all this work, it's essential that there's product in stock, there's value in the product offerings with differentiation, and the stores are well merchandised. Availability of the product and the need for real information are critical for the consumer in the store. And the virtual experience can be brought right to the store, establishing a virtual connection right at the shelf.

The online experience should be similar. The web designer should be able to reach into his own personal experience when he is in a store—whether buying a pound of grapes or a tire—and bring it back to the web and incorporate the experience in the design process so products feel as if you can pick them up and look at them from a 360-degree viewpoint. An audio track can explain two or three things about the product. You can take your virtual assistant with you when you shop and, with digital data processing, even translate information into a friendly voice. All the information and technologies are there, but someone needs to pull it together and bring it to the consumer.

Measuring the Future—Ron Wilbur

E-commerce had its siren call squelched a few years back. Now large and small e-businesses have entered an era that some are calling the revenge of the bean counters. This requires e-commerce models to be predicated on profit, not on market share. What's fascinating is that in the midst of this, one of the original promises of the web is finally being realized with micro-business models. The web is giving everyone access to global markets. These micro-businesses are companies of one or two people, using commercial storefront engines like Yahoo stores to set up their online store. What's even more fascinating is these stores are making more profit than the heavily capitalized, high-flying e-commerce concepts that became extinct during the 1999-2001 ice age.

Because these businesses are self-financed, without venture capitalist money, metrics are vital. When you've financed the business with a second mortgage on your house, you definitely want to quickly validate and evaluate how well you're performing.

There is an array of e-commerce metrics already in use. Some metrics are obvious, some are not. Cost of goods sold, gross sales, and net sales are all obvious. But most e-businesses also focus on additional indicators like sales per visitor (SPV), cost per visitor (CPV) and closing ratio of orders to site visits (CCR).

New metrics will spring up to help e-businesses measure the effectiveness of their differentiation, growth, and brand value. This is part of the reason for the rush to CRM—the hope of a true market of one, where you understand your customer so well you reflect that understanding in an increasingly personalized shopping or browsing experience. But what happens when customers long for the freedom of privacy, the beauty of anonymity, and the relief of not having "our latest recommendations for you" shoved under their noses? The answer starts with a measurement that identifies and quantifies that desire in a segment of your customers.

The heart of measuring e-commerce success stems from your objectives. That seems so basic, but good implementation requires vision. Sure your objectives must be stated in measurable terms, but they also have to stay consistent with the market. Otherwise you're measuring sales per visitor and not paying attention to sales per repeat customer. Or sales per strategic customer. Or retention of strategic customers. Or the factors for retaining strategic customers. To be successful in e-business today and tomorrow, you'll need to stop periodically and ask yourself, "If we were starting out today, what would we want as our measurable objectives?" And then set up the metrics to answer the question, "Relative to our competition, how are we doing?" In e-commerce, that's the most mysterious metric now. If you're not comparing your data relative to the market and relative to your competition, you're missing essential keys to your future.

There are still frightening statistics about the lack of adoption of metrics in e-marketing. A recent survey of 1,000 business managers reported that 82 percent expected their online marketing efforts would generate positive results. But only 34 percent had a method to measure success. Around 27 percent had less formal measures of payback—I guess that would be "hunch." And 25 percent of the companies surveyed stated they don't have the time or budget to measure ROI. But here's the frightening part—13 percent believed ROI didn't apply to them and 12 percent thought e-business was too strategic to measure!

Technologies come and go. The web affords a unique ability to track customers, understand their behaviors, and tie that unique information to the specific-individual level. Of those companies with a CRM program, 99 percent can't yet give you an ROI for their CRM investment. But the opportunity is to gain a lot more insight into your customer. The successful e-businesses of the future will get way beyond automated ways to deliver "personalized" information to their customers. And their metrics will tell them when their customers have changed behaviors.

Getting from Here to There

So, which is the right vision for the future? They all are. Integration and convergence of customers, marketplaces, technologies, and businesses are the trends to watch in the future. There is no "one" right answer. But "all" are needed. And there is much work to be done for e-commerce to grow and flourish.

The online store of the future will have cross-functional organizations that focus on the customer experience. It will have different malls that collect together services and other goods—similar to self-contained neighborhoods. These new communities provide everything a customer requires within a few blocks of his home: gas stations, dry cleaners, grocery stores, drug stores and other essentials. Everything is grouped together for the convenience of the people living there. Technology innovations also demand continual change in the online store.

The future of online shopping will depend on a few factors and we predict positive changes. E-commerce will focus more on the consumer and less on the medium itself. The form factor will be developed as a result of customers' changing needs.

E-merchants may not be able to solve today's fulfillment problems completely, but they will find what is acceptable to their customers and provide those services that deliver the best possible customer experience through research and prioritization. Today, many firms offer free delivery and easy return processes. As web shopping becomes more familiar and customer issues are identified, many e-stores will begin to cross this hurdle.

We predict security and privacy issues will be resolved through some innovative inventions. While the medium will never be completely secure, shopping can be as safe as ordering with a credit card over the telephone or writing a check in a retail store.

While the Internet itself often delivers thousands of hits per inquiry—a problem not easily resolved—e-merchants will be able to streamline their own sites, offer improved search capabilities, deliver product hierarchies based on customer priorities, and provide easy-to-use selection aids.

As e-commerce matures, online stores will use traditional retailing techniques to control inventory management, prevent out-of-stock product problems, and hold the customer's hand all the way through the ordering process.

Finally, the customer will be able to navigate a website intuitively once e-retailers focus on merchandising the online store as a priority. This evolution will not only enable consumers to find what they want quickly, it will also add pleasure to e-shopping through the use of animation and interactivity including enhanced use of audio and video. Web shopping will become exciting and add the fun that, up till now, has been the focus of physical retailing. And the personal connection the web offers through customization is unique.

How will these advances occur? Through using the principles of customer-centered design and placing the first priority on the consumer. Through careful consideration of customer needs, thoroughly understanding customer segmentation and demographics, and sincerely listening to the customer, positive results are unavoidable. Using these principles, spam will be history.

Customer expectations and needs don't remain static. Web shopping will evolve as it becomes more sophisticated and as customers become more familiar and comfortable with the shopping process. Of course, customers increasingly want more—more service and more quality. And in the past few years, many retailers have found the need to cut services and quality to maintain profitability. The key will be to find the balance. Profitability is based largely on keeping the customer satisfied. E-tailers must know customer priorities to determine to what extent any given service or attribute is valued. Sacrificing a low-priority service may have few consequences but cutting those with high-perceived value may be deadly. While providing a good variety of quality products is key, the most essential retailing attribute today is customer service. Unfortunately, not all companies have learned this lesson. Banks now charge some account holders a fee if they go inside the actual structure and ask a teller for assistance. Some insurance companies charge a $10 service fee just to mail out a billing statement. In the past, phone companies were happy to repair broken equipment without charge. Now, customers must purchase an "insurance policy" to keep from paying high repair fees.

But many retailers have learned to provide outstanding service—some above and beyond the call of duty. They have created customer loyalty that transcends the price tag. This is the framework—delivering on customer desires and needs—that will establish web retailing as a viable and profitable shopping environment.

Top Ten Internet Shopping Predictions

We believe there will be progressive and positive changes in the next 10 years that will generate substantial customer adoption and e-commerce growth. Here are some of those predictions accompanied by the elements we feel must evolve. The Internet is here to stay, with or without the positive influences that can shape it into what it needs to be.

1. Manufacturers will move from product centric-sites to segment-centric sites. There will be a website for kids, for instance, that shows them how to use products and explains simple projects. A seniors' site will cater to the needs of the older person—with content designed specifically for their interests. Everything will be simplified. Increased access for the disabled—those with impaired hearing or sight, for example—will be provided. Entire sites will be designed in large-type formats.

2. Customized sites will develop for special purchases and customers. Instead of getting the Sunday paper, going through the ads, and then going online to see all the properties

with URLs, a real-estate agent can create a site just for you. The personalized site will have tours of all the properties that match your particular specifications.

3. "Internet" money will create new ways to finance purchases that doesn't put consumers at risk.

4. Consumers will be able to search for any product by typing in a description in a general search box. The search function will then locate companies that offer the product, and a list will be returned to the customer. These lists will have all the relevant information including the exact location in the site. Online merchants providing customers with effective value propositions will get the sale.

5. Post-purchase support sites will be separated from their pre-purchase sales efforts. If you purchase a cell phone, for instance, a site will help you remember how to set up the memory or enable the messaging service. You will see your individual contract and plan, the number of minutes you have remaining at any given time, and any special services that are available to you. You'll no longer have to search through a huge site to find the service component.

6. The Internet will move from a URL-based medium to a descriptive medium. Consumers cannot remember URLs. E-commerce will be dependent on eliminating the obscure and technical from shopping.

7. Most products, unless routine commodities, will be featured in an entertainment production. This is analogous to the transition from old record albums to music videos. Each "show" will provide action—whether a person models clothing, there's a virtual enactment of an actual product demonstration, or a piece of furniture is displayed in your virtual own home setting.

8. Real people on the Internet will solve your problems. At any time of the day or night, you can log on and talk to a health-care provider who will immediately give you advice. While this service is available today on a limited basis, it will become the norm as busy schedules force us to re-evaluate how we access certain services. An investment consultant may work with you directly to help you select the right stocks. And a nutrition expert may help you plan healthy meals. Services and products will be sold equally in the future.

9. A live "operator" service will help you with overall Internet questions and problems. It will act as a referral service if you need further support and will serve as a high-level directory service.

10. A live technical-support service will take care of all your technical problems.

As you can see, simplicity and service will be the future drivers. It's all about using the Internet as a resource without having the limitations of the technology itself. Here's a future scenario that illustrates our point.

A Day in a Life in the Future

Dan decides he needs to purchase a new computer desk. He quickly takes his computer camera and scans his room. He calls his personal Internet referral service and tells them what he wants. They send him an instant connection to merchants with the desired product. He selects one and sends the video along with the room's measurements.

Within a few seconds, he receives a video back with the desk in place in his room. With a click of a button, Dan switches the desk with a variety of substitutes that the merchant provided. He settles on one and clicks again, and all the information about the desk appears on one page including cost, any promotions available, shipping information, and availability. Dan clicks again, and the purchase is automatically deducted from his Internet account when the desk ships.

Dan starts to get hungry and goes to the kitchen that is "always on." Food is routinely ordered to replenish the cupboards and monitor levels of usage. Linked directly to the Internet, Dan is set up to have staple items—like coffee and cereal—routinely ordered and delivered, sometimes along with his dry cleaning.

After getting a snack, Dan goes back to his computer to select from a variety of live concerts playing throughout the world. Without buying a ticket, he can see his favorite performers in concert and even "chat" with them later. He can order the concert t-shirts during intermission.

Looking Forward

The future of e-commerce will provide more than convenience. It will combine a variety of goods, services, education, and entertainment to seamlessly integrate shopping with every other facet of Internet capability.

In fact, the word "e-commerce" will probably go away with time. Shopping on the web will be integrated with every other function and service that the Internet will provide. Implementing customer-centered design today will set the stage for the Internet of the future.

The one primary component of shopping is, and will always be, the customer. Keeping your sights on how the customer shops, understanding customers' needs, and developing your website to meet customer preferences will create the building blocks for a true customer-centered environment.

GLOSSARY

B2B or B-to-B

Business-to-Business sales.

B2C or B-to-C

Business-to-Customer sales.

Brick and Mortar

Traditional retail stores.

Category Fact Book

A tool for managing the category that typically contains market, customer, channel, and other information.

Category Management

A system focusing on optimization of sales by managing the product portfolio as a group of brands in a category.

Channels

Channels of distribution and the supply chain through which product flows, such as wholesalers, distributors, and retailers.

Click and Mortar

Traditional retail stores offering sales through both the Internet and the physical store.

Competitive Intelligence

A process for gathering, analyzing, and managing information that may affect a company's decisions, plans and operations.

Contextual Inquiry

A structural field interviewing method typically based on understanding the context in which product is used and treating the user as a partner in the design process.

CPO

Chief Privacy Officer.

Cross-selling

The practice of recommending additional products with a purchase to leverage a customer's needs.

Customer Relationship Management (CRM)

A process that focuses on placing the customer at the center of a business. CRM requires a company to measure customer interactions at every stage to improve programs and services as a result of those interactions.

Customer Experience

The positive or negative experience of the customer during the product investigation, shopping, or sales process.

Customer-centered Design

Customer-centered design integrates and balances customer- shopping goals with store business goals and places emphasis on the customer shopping experience.

Customer Segmentation

A target marketing customer group with similar characteristics.

Demographics

The study of population statistics and trends.

Destination Categories

The product or products that brought the customer to the store for purchase. Also, any category that routinely brings a customer to the store.

Down-selling

Encouraging the customer to purchase a less expensive product than intended.

Electronic Shelf (E Shelf)

The virtual shelf or web page on which product is sold.

Focus Group

Type of qualitative research in which a trained moderator leads a small group of respondents through a group discussion of a selected topic via broad, open-ended questions.

Home Page

The beginning or main page in a website.

Human Computer Interaction (HCI)

A multi-disciplinary field pertaining to the application of computer science, ergonomics, psychology and other areas to facilitate design implementation and evaluation of information and communication systems. Also how people interact with the computer – operating the "controls" such as links and buttons.

Human Factors Engineering

The formal study of how people interact with their environment.

Integrated Shelf Management (ISM)

A holistic approach to providing one customer experience across a company's channels and shelves.

Internet Service Providers (ISPs)

Companies providing Internet connection and access.

Kiosks

Free-standing merchandising units, often electronic.

Lifetime Customer Value

The value of the customer over the lifecycle – typically defined as customer behavioral changes and potential purchases over time.

Line Listings

The rote listing of products accompanied by short descriptions, usually in a list.

Gross Margin

The difference between the purchase price of a product and the price paid by the retailer.

Merchandising

A technique using a broad range of products and services to help manufacturers and retailers gain profitable retail space, present, manage and organize products, and draw attention to products and the shelf through point-of-purchase fixtures and advertising.

Minimum Advertised Price (MAP)

The minimum price at which manufacturers allow retailers to advertise their products.

Multiple-channel Shopper

A shopper who purchases routinely through a variety of channels.

Mystery Shopping
Undercover shopping through any selling motion to evaluate the implementation of marketing programs and shelf presentation.

One-to-One Marketing Programs
Customer-relationship programs designed to reach an individual customer.

Planogram
The retail store map or layout.

Product Mix
The variety of products within a category.

Product Value Analysis
Evaluating the profitability of a product on the shelf (see SKU rationalization).

Psychographics
A discipline measuring consumers' beliefs, interests, and opinions.

Referral Marketing
Referring a friend to an online merchant in exchange for a reward.

Repeat Buyers
People who purchase an item more than once – most specifically from one store or brand.

Rooftop Targeting
Analysis of the physical trading area of a store's consumer base.

Schema
The web site map or layout.

Selectability
The ability of the customer to accurately select products from the shelf.

Selling Motions
Any means through which a merchant can sell or a customer can purchase a product.

Shelf
A retail term referring to the shelf on which product sits. Extrapolated to mean anywhere a product is located whether physical or virtual.

Shrinkage
Loss of product due to theft, both internal and external, damage, markdowns, and inaccurate inventories.

Single-channel Shopper
A customer who shops primarily in one sales channel.

Spiff
A small, immediate bonus for a sale/sales incentive. (Spiff is not an acronym).

Split Order
An order that is split and delivered to two different locations or at two different times.

Store Clustering
Analysis that assigns stores to clusters in order to provide the right mix of products in the store.

Syndicated Content Management (SCM)
A one-to-many model that replicates one source of content and distributes it to many websites.

SKU
Stockkeeping Unit. The individual product with a stockkeeping number.

SKU Rationalization
The process to evaluate which products will be placed on the shelf relative to their value to the company. Involves examination of cost and profit contributions of individual items.

Upselling
A technique to recommend a more expensive item to the customer. May be a "bait and switch" technique in which low- priced goods are offered to attract the customer before switching to higher margin products.

Usability Engineering

A systematic approach to measuring the ease or difficulty of use of a piece of software, such as a website.

Value Proposition

The unique selling proposition a reseller offers to a customer.

REFERENCES

Jakob Nielsenwww.nngroup.com

Home Page Usability: 50 Websites Deconstructed Jakob Nielsen & Marie Tahir, 2002, New Riders Publishing

Why We Buy Paco Underhill, 1999 Simon & Schuster

The Healing of America Marianne Williamson, 1997 Simon & Schuster

E-Retail intelligence Update Retail Forward, 2001

INDEX

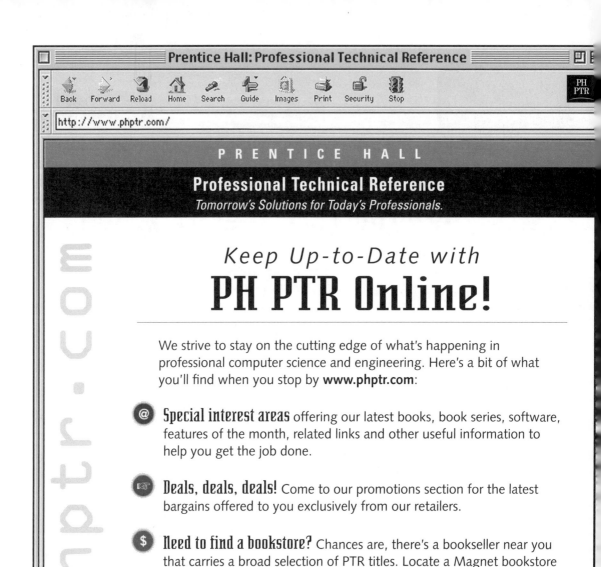

 **integrated** **hp education training** **it just works**

HP's world-class education and training offers hands on education solutions including:

- Linux
- HP-UX System and Network Administration
- Advanced HP-UX System Administration
- IT Service Management using advanced Internet technologies
- Microsoft Windows NT/2000
- Internet/Intranet
- MPE/iX
- Database Administration
- Software Development

HP's new IT Professional Certification program provides rigorous technical qualification for specific IT job roles including HP-UX System Administration, Network Management, Unix/NT Servers and Applications Management, and IT Service Management.

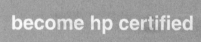
become hp certified

http://education.hp.com

fulfill your needs

Want to know about new products, services and solutions from Hewlett-Packard Company — as soon as they're invented?

Need information about new HP services to help you implement new or existing products?

Looking for HP's newest solution to a specific challenge in your business?

HP Computer News features the latest from HP!

4 easy ways to subscribe, and it's FREE:

- **fax** complete and fax the form below to (651) 430-3388, or

- **online** sign up online at www.hp.com/go/compnews, or

- **email** complete the information below and send to hporders@earthlink.net, or

- **mail** complete and mail the form below to:

Twin Cities Fulfillment Center
Hewlett-Packard Company
P.O. Box 408
Stillwater, MN 55082

invent

RECEIVED

OCT 2 3 2002

reply now to receive the first year FREE!

name	title
company	dept./mail stop
address	
city	state zip
email signature	date

please indicate your industry below:

- ☐ accounting
- ☐ education
- ☐ financial services
- ☐ government
- ☐ healthcare/medical
- ☐ legal
- ☐ manufacturing
- ☐ publishing/printing
- ☐ online services
- ☐ real estate
- ☐ retail/wholesale distrib
- ☐ technical
- ☐ telecommunications
- ☐ transport and travel
- ☐ utilities
- ☐ other: _____